TABLE

Roosevelt
(late 1640's)

(1658-1742)
(New York merchant)

Jacobus, or James (1692-1776)
(founded Hyde Park line)

Isaac (1726-1794)
(sugar refiner, Revolutionary patriot
— F.D.R. almost named for him)

James (1760-1847)
(left New York for Dutchess County)

Isaac (1790-1863)
(first doctor in family)

(1825-1905)　　Theodore (1831-1878)　　James (1828-1900)
(eccentric)　　(father of a President)　　(near millionaire,
　　　　　　　　　　　　　　　　　　country squire)

(1861-1933)　Elliott (1860-1893)　James Roosevelt (1855-1927)
　　　　　　　　　　　　　　　　　"Rosy" Roosevelt (half-
　　　　　　　　　　　　　　　　　brother of F.D.R.)

Eleanor (1884-1962)---Franklin Delano Roosevelt
　　　　　　　　　　　　　　　　　　　(1882-1945)

(1891-) Archie (1894-) Quentin (1897-1918)

Elliott (1910-) Franklin (1914-) John (1916-)

THE ROOSEVELTS

BOOKS BY ALLEN CHURCHILL

THE ROOSEVELTS: *American Aristocrats*

A PICTORIAL HISTORY OF AMERICAN CRIME

THE GREAT WHITE WAY

THEY NEVER CAME BACK

THE YEAR THE WORLD WENT MAD

THE IMPROPER BOHEMIANS

PARK ROW

THE INCREDIBLE IVAR KREUGER

THE ROOSEVELTS:

American Aristocrats

BY ALLEN CHURCHILL

HARPER & ROW, PUBLISHERS

NEW YORK, EVANSTON, AND LONDON

FIRST EDITION

LIBRARY OF CONGRESS CATALOG CARD NUMBER: 65-14649

D-P

CONTENTS

A section of illustrations follows page 120.

28520

THE ROOSEVELTS

1

ROSE FIELD TO NEW AMSTERDAM

ON A DAY IN THE MID-1640's A MAN WAS ROWED ASHORE FROM A
ship after a voyage of over fifty days from Holland. His name was
Claes Martenszen van Rosenvelt, which—rendered into English—
means Nicholas, son of Martin of the Rose Field, and he was the
first Roosevelt to set foot on the North American continent. Beside him as he did this was his wife, born Jannetje Samuels
Thomas and later described by a historian as "a young belle of the
New Netherlands, whose personal charms were rivaled by her skill
in spinning, weaving, cooking, and housekeeping." Presumably
these two were newlyweds, married just before embarking for the
New World. But of this no one can be sure.

On this dateless day in the 1640's Claes Martenszen and his
Jannetje were landing in New Amsterdam, a Dutch colony of
some eight hundred sturdy souls who lived surrounded by an un-
counted number of cows, pigs, dogs, and ducks. Approximately
eighty houses provided shelter for these citizens, all of them huddled at the tip of a narrow island which the Indians called Manhate, Manhadoes, Manhatte, or any of forty variations of an Indian

word for "small island," all of which to Dutch ears sounded like Manhattan.

New Amsterdam was the largest settlement in New Netherland, a giant circle of Dutch territory which embraced the land that eventually included Albany, Hartford, Long Island, and New Jersey, the last an unexplored region currently known as Pavonia. New Amsterdam was by far the most colorful community this brave New World had to offer. Though claimed and settled by the solid Dutch, it totally lacked the atmosphere of a quiet Flemish town. Rather, its intrepid settlers were a polyglot mixture of Dutch, English, Swedish, Danish, German, Italian, Huguenots and Portuguese. To the wild babel of tongues spoken by these assorted residents were added several dialects of the Manhate Indians which had been mastered by the more ambitious residents of the new colony.

Mystery shrouds the antecedents of Jannetje Samuels Thomas, who may well have been an English girl whose family had fled to Holland. Of Claes Martenszen it is known that he was a native of Tholen, an island-town in the Dutch province of Zeeland. Here he lived in a section called the Rose Field.

"Our very common ancestor," Theodore Roosevelt, twenty-sixth President of the United States, liked to call this pioneering Claes. Yet there is evidence that he was not so common, after all. His Dutch relatives must have been people of substance, for in the courthouse of Oud-Vossemer on Tholen hangs a sixteenth-century painting by Joseph Xavery. The subject is Justice, and decorating the frame are the coats of arms of Dutch families. One is the Roosevelt crest—a knight's silver shield with a trio of red roses growing symmetrically from a spot of well-tended greensward. Below this unfurls the motto *Qui Plantavit Curabit*—"He who has planted it shall care for it." Or, "He who sows shall reap." There also stands a gravestone in the Tholen churchyard which reads: "Marinus van Rosenvelt, in his life Burgomaster and inspector of dykes, died Jan. 29, 1710."

By name, Claes Martenszen van Rosenvelt appears to be thoroughly Dutch, but on the distaff side of his Tholen forebears some genealogists claim to have found a strain of rich Austrian blood. The Dutch inheritance of Claes Martenszen and subsequent Roosevelts, these authorities declare, brought him and his descendants a sturdy respectability. Simultaneously, the Austrian blood added a layer of energy and charm. This is so true of most Roosevelts that it becomes a theory easy to accept.

With this, knowledge of the background of Claes Martenszen van Rosenvelt ceases. Two of his descendants became Presidents of the United States, while a third was the niece of one of these Presidents who married the other. These three members of the Roosevelt family were probably the most photographed, talked about, and generally publicized individuals the world has ever known—a fact which brings a lacing of irony to the fact that so little is known of their not-so-common ancestor.

The most avid historian the family ever produced—far more so than Theodore—was Franklin Delano Roosevelt, thirty-second President of the United States. He dearly loved the subject of his American ancestors and as a young Harvard student chose the Roosevelt genealogy as the subject of his sophomore thesis. Franklin absorbed everything possible about the Roosevelts in print, and in addition had the unique benefit of intimate family reminiscence. Yet a lifetime of curiosity told him nothing new about Claes Martenszen and Jannetje. As President, he wrote in answer to an inquiry about his Dutch ancestors:

All I know about the origin of the Roosevelt family in this country is that all branches bearing the name are apparently descended from Claes Martenszen, who came from Holland sometime before 1648— even the year is uncertain. Where he came from in Holland I do not know, nor do I know who his parents were.

But if facts about Claes Martenszen are few, there are many questions swirling about his shadowy figure. What, for instance, did he look like?

It is odd to relate that the few references to Claes in New Amsterdam records are accompanied by the nickname "Kleytjen," or one of its many variations, including Klein Klassje, Cleyn Clas-sie, or Cleyn Claesjen. Kleytjen, in turn, has as many meanings as spellings. Among them are Little Fellow, Little One, and even a prosaic Shorty. "Claes, the Little Fellow," dim records say. This would indicate that Claes Martenszen was a man short of stature, but few researchers have been able to swallow this possibility. Nor are any Roosevelts likely to think of their ancestor as a short man.

In over three hundred years almost every Roosevelt male has been big, long-lived, vigorous. Only one or two have been short men, but even these were not conspicuously so. Thus it is hard to conceive of the progenitor of the American clan as small. It appears more likely that he was unusually large, with the nickname Kleytjen bestowed on him in ironic appreciation of his mighty size—this in the best tradition of heavy-handed Dutch humor.

Such, at least, is the explanation most historians—and, no doubt, all Roosevelts—choose to accept.

With this, other questions arise: Why did Claes and Jannetje depart their country to cross the Atlantic into the great unknown?

This is a provocative matter indeed. For at that moment in history Holland was the pleasantest place on earth in which to live. It was the era of Rembrandt, Franz Hals, Vermeer, Steen. Education stood at a high level, with Holland the only country that cared enough to teach girls as well as boys. Travelers also noted with amazement that the Dutch washed hands *before* meals as well as after. Such a thing was unheard of elsewhere.

The country itself was prosperous, not to say rich, for this was Holland's Golden Age, grandiose reward for heroic struggle against the forces of mighty Spain. After eighty years of intermittent warfare the tiny country had emerged amazingly victorious, dominant on the European continent. In defying Spain, Calvinist Holland had fought the imposition of Catholicism, in the process suffering the full horrors of the Inquisition. Yet from the horrors emerged one benefit. War with Spain called for ships to combat the Spanish fleet. Holland grew hardly a tree within its borders.

Yet by importing timber she built thousands of ships. With the 1600's came the Age of Discovery, and Holland stood ready. Ships and the spirit of adventure combined to turn the country into a world power, with Amsterdam the hub of a colonial empire reaching from Asia to the Americas. Holland's annual trade was $16,000,000, England's a mere $6,000,000.

This was Holland in her Golden Age. Still there were flaws. With prosperity, country folk had moved to the cities, creating a congestion unusual for the times. Bribery, fraud, and outright thievery flourished in this atmosphere of hothouse prosperity. Some families, impoverished by the long war, had been unable to recoup fortunes, while others lost roots in the long battle to survive the Inquisition.

Meanwhile, stories spread of the great wealth to be found in colonies overseas. Tales were told of fabulous treasure won by the conquering Spaniards on the Southern continent. If the Spaniards had found the south a magnificent treasure trove, why not the north? Many Europeans believed the soil of the New World was overlaid with gold, silver, and precious stones. All a man had to do was rake in his fortune.

Such was the mood of the Holland which Claes and Jannetje left behind for reasons that will never really be known. Possibly the good families of the Rose Field were among those dislocated by the Inquisition, unable to readjust to the new, booming Holland. Yet this is not likely if one family member was a "Burgomaster and inspector of dykes."

Rather, it may have been the bubbling optimism found in so many other Roosevelts that pushed Claes into bringing his bride to the New World. With this would go a love of adventure and a thirst for travel—all put into graphic words three hundred years in the future by Franklin Delano Roosevelt as he sat in a wheelchair before the American Congress. The President was reporting on Yalta, and even then the shadow of death lay across his face. But his voice rang strong as he said, "I am returning from this trip that took me so far refreshed and inspired. . . . Yes, I return from this trip refreshed and inspired. The Roosevelts are not, as you may suspect, averse to travel. We seem to thrive on it!"

It may, then, have been this same brave spirit that brought Claes Martenszen to America.

This provides another question: Had Claes been to the New World before?

According to one family legend, the Claes Martenszen van Rosenvelt who landed in New Amsterdam was an older man, a fellow who had been just a growing boy at the time of Henry Hudson's voyage in 1609. Four years later, in 1613—aged eighteen —he set out on foot for teeming Amsterdam Harbor, where he signed on a ship which planned to follow Hudson's pioneering course to New Amsterdam. In those days ships were small, carrying no more than twenty crewmen. Because of his large size, the legend says, Claes's shipmates gave him the ironic but affectionate nickname "Kleytjen."

Like all Dutch explorers, the captain of Kleytjen's ship had financial profit no less than exploration in mind. Reaching the Hudson, he sailed upriver in the direction of Albany, hoping to find better fur pelts there. One day, while the crew was ashore bargaining with the Indians, a log from the ship's galley rolled from the hearth and set the craft afire. This required laborious construction of a new ship from forest logs. During this time Kleytjen and two shipmates were either captured by Indians or voluntarily joined a tribe for adventure and exploration. Over the next two years the young Dutchmen roamed the wilderness. Champlain notes them in his diary, seeming to believe they were captives. When a Dutch ship commanded by Captain Adrien Block reached the mouth of the Delaware River, Indians ashore asked ransom for three paleface prisoners. Captain Block gave a handful of the trinkets and beads to the Indians and the prisoners were released. Apparently Kleytjen was recognized as leader of this intrepid trio, for Captain Block mentions him in the text accompanying his map of the territory: "According to what Kleytjen and his companions told me . . ." he writes.

It is a rousing tale and some Roosevelts show every sign of believing that explorer Kleytjen was indeed their rugged ancestor, Claes Martenszen. But under close scrutiny the story weakens. For one thing, if Claes had been eighteen in 1613, he would have been fifty when he arrived in New Amsterdam with Jannetje at his side. In the ten years following this, the couple begat five children. From this it would appear that they were young and recently wed, for it does not seem likely that a robust fellow like explorer Kleytjen would wait until his fifties to marry and raise a family.

Next, the matter of prominence. Kleytjen as an explorer had an impressive list of venturesome firsts to his name. He was a pioneer in penetrating the unknown continent, one of the first to live for any length of time with red Indians. The advice and counsel of such a man would be of tremendous worth to a colony menaced by these same Indians, its surrounding territory still unexplored. Yet in tight moments of New Amsterdam history the name of Claes Martenszen is missing from the councils of war. As one author has said, the only references to him are a few blots on contemporary records.

No, Claes was probably not explorer Kleytjen. No doubt he was a big fellow like the original Kleytjen. But he was no pioneer. The strongest knot tying Claes Martenszen and rugged Kleytjen together is the nickname, the Little Fellow. Yet the playful Dutch may easily have given the identical name to two different big men.

Claes Martenszen van Rosenvelt, stepping on unknown land, probably expected to find a settlement resembling his native Rose Field, with plump burgomasters puffing long clay pipes while debating the state of local affairs. In this he would receive a sharp surprise. New Amsterdam, a mere twenty years old as a settlement, was already a brawling spot, its small population stubbornly determined on lives of complete individualism. The settlement's most distinctive quality at the time, one writer has stated, was a crude boisterousness. The large number of English residents in the Dutch town marked New Amsterdam as a haven for dissidents and nonconformists, as well as those bent on adventure.

New Netherland, with its fifteen hundred over-all settlers, was a commercial enterprise run solely for profit by the Dutch West India Company. It had none of the religious zeal or pride in free-dom which inspired English and French colonies. In fact, it did not hold local elections, its laws being imposed by directors-general dispatched by the company in Old Amsterdam. New Eng-land, with twenty thousand residents, was dedicated to religious freedom, self-government, and free elections. Yet it is an odd fact that New Netherland offered greater freedom than New England. The Dutch colony never hanged a witch, and its stalwart citizens displayed a fine irreverence toward authority which was totally lacking in sobersided New England. In its way, New Amsterdam was demonstrating much of the lusty spirit later associated with the rugged American frontier.

The most visible manifestation of free spirit was the manner in which the rugged settlers consumed spirituous liquors. "They all drink here, from the moment they are able to lick a spoon," one Dutchman wrote home. Legend states that the first martini cock-tail known to the American continent was mixed in 1633 at a tavern run by Peter Koch (or Kocks) on the Broad Way. New Amsterdam males vastly enjoyed their guzzling and were aided in this colossal intake by the roistering sailors from ships anchored in the harbor. Beer and—when possible—rum and brandy stoked the spirits of New Amsterdamers to such a prodigious extent that the dominie of the Dutch Church complained to Holland that his flock was "very ignorant in religion and very much given to drink." What he neglected to mention was that his predecessor in the New World pulpit had delivered his finest sermons when in-toxicated.

Heavy drinking led inevitably to fisticuffs and the docket of the settlement's tiny court records many cases of simple assault. Disputes over boundaries of newly claimed land come next in number on the record. The good wives of New Amsterdam appeared plump, hard-working, and wholly dedicated to childbearing. Yet they had arguments with other wives and, in the white heat of altercation, the word "whore" rose easily to lips. This might result in charges of slander. Fornication constituted another criminal act, and there is listed a single case of sodomy. Yet sexual sin was well contained on the island of Manhattan, for the Indians saw nothing wrong in female promiscuity and freely bestowed wives and daughters on the white man. How the Dutch wives reacted to this largess does not appear on the books, but it kept carnal sin under a kind of control.

The first alien eyes to view Manhattan had belonged to Giovanni da Verrazano, a Florentine navigator serving the King of France. In 1524 he sailed into the harbor and anchored his ship *Dauphine* for two days. The Indians greeted him joyously, and in a report to his employer-king the gallant mariner described "a very agreeable situation located with two small prominent hills [the Narrows], in the midst of which flowed to the sea a very great river [the Hudson] which was deep within the mouth."

In 1609 Henry Hudson, an Englishman serving the Dutch, arrived in the *Half Moon,* an odd-looking craft with a stern higher than its bow and square sails on two masts. Hudson was romantically in search of a passage to India and, in hope of finding this, ventured up the river that today bears his name. Proceeding only by daylight, he reached the dead-end site of Albany in nine days. His dreams of India dashed, he gloomily turned back. The Indians were friendly but Hudson and his men viewed them with distrust. The commander himself called them "Wilde Menschen," a name retained by later settlers who shortened it to Wilden.

After Hudson came Captain Adrien Block, for whom Block Island is named. The captain and his crew spent a winter on the tip of Manhattan and mockingly gave the name New Amsterdam to their cluster of four crude huts—a name which also stuck. In 1621 the Dutch West India Company (as opposed to the East India Company) was chartered and dispatched eight men and one woman as settlers. Others followed, among them not only Dutch, but Germans, Danes, Norwegians, and Swedes. Soon the settlement was a few small houses around a mud fort. It was a full-fledged trading post organized to send furs, lumber, and wheat back to Holland to be sold at great profit by the Company.

Serious colonization began in 1626 with the arrival of Peter Minuit (or Minnewit), as governor-general appointed by the West India Company. It was Minuit who, on orders from the company, purchased Manhattan from the Indians for sixty guilders' worth of knives, beads, and trinkets. With this must have gone a few swallows of liquor, which the Indians quickly grew to cherish and christened "firewater." Minuit's island was forest land, swampy along the shores, rising into low inland hills crowned with oak and hickory. Where Canal Street lies today, marshes and ponds extended from river to river, covered at high tide by sea water. Minuit ordered a clearing of the forest at the tip of the island and built new houses, together with a general store and windmill.

Director-General Minuit went out of his way to win the closer friendship of the Indians and under this policy the colony flourished. Typical of his happy era was the ship *Arms of Amsterdam*, which sailed back to Old Amsterdam laden with 7,246 beaver pelts, 675 otter, 83 mink, 36 wildcat, and 34 ratskins, plus oak and hickory timber. In all, this cargo was valued at 45,000 guilders, or nearly $19,000.

Minuit also opened trade with the Plymouth Colony—Boston had not yet been founded. But in time he became overly pleased with himself and the potential of his colony. He decided to make the world rise up and take note of New Amsterdam by building on its shore one of the largest ships afloat. He and his men performed this near-miraculous feat, launching the *New Netherland,* a ship of 800 tons with thirty guns. However, the enterprise cost far more than anticipated, and as a result Minuit fell into disfavor with the money-minded West India Company.

In 1633 Wouter Van Twiller took over as governor-general, arriving aboard the same ship that brought New Amsterdam's first minister and first schoolteacher. It also carried 104 Dutch troops. Van Twiller was a gargantuan guzzler of beer and as one of his first official acts ordered the quick construction of a brewery. He next built a gibbet and a whipping post. Then he cast around and grabbed Governor's Island and other choice areas of land in his own name. This established him as a patroon, one of the fortunate lords of the New World who governed huge territories within the over-all territory of New Netherland. Having done this much, Van Twiller set about proving himself a thick-skulled burgher with no talent for governing. Of him and his friends it was said, "They know nothing but how to spend their time carousing."

To one historian, New Amsterdam was "a clever little town which went on increasing every day." It had to be clever, for with citizens imbibing, arguing, gossiping, and flouting authority, the settlement resembled a lurching ship on the brink of mutiny. A continuing problem was the nature of the governors-general. Van Twiller was followed shortly by one William Kieft, small, fiery, avaricious. Kieft immediately sought to improve his status with the company by levying a tax on Manhattan's independent-minded population. The outraged colonists protested to Old Amsterdam, but the company council did nothing. In New Amsterdam morale sagged. One account says: "The poor little colony, plaything of a foreign commercial corporation, drooped rapidly." However, Kieft was not all bad. He did straighten paths into something approximating streets and improved sanitary conditions.

Still his blunders were legion. He had been given the power to choose a council and set the number of councilmen. The crafty man fixed the number at one, then gave himself an automatic two votes to the councilman's one. He despised the Indians and made no secret of it. At the same time he lived in quaking terror of Indian attack. Finally, he ordered a night massacre which killed eighty or more redskins in across-the-river Pavonia. A second surprise attack in Connecticut murdered hundreds more. Friendly Indians rushed to New Amsterdam for safety and Kieft ordered them brutally slain. The colony's trade depended on amity with the Indians and Kieft was stirring them to hatred and fury. "The director acted like one bereft of his senses," says an early account.

Under William Kieft, New Amsterdam found its bottom point. Some disillusioned settlers returned to Holland or scattered to other New Netherland settlements. The remaining colonists petitioned Old Amsterdam, threatening open rebellion unless Kieft was recalled.

Such was the maelstrom of a colony into which Claes and his Jannetje stepped.

On the surface the little Dutch seaport looked deceptively quaint, with slant-roofed houses and a windmill or two bringing added color to the scene. Only the gallows and pillory before the stone Stadt Huys provided discordant notes. The burghers of the town smoked as well as drank, puffing out clouds of white smoke from long-stemmed clay pipes. Food was no problem to the residents of New Amsterdam. The good folk ate well on wild turkey, pigeon, partridge, goose, duck, and venison bought from Indians. In the waters around the tiny settlement lay shellfish in profusion. However, the colony suffered from a paucity of farmers to provide eggs and cheese, with much available farmland given over to rye, barley, and oats that might be turned into hard liquor or brewed into beer.

Wampum—tiny beads made from clamshells and perforated for stringing—had been adopted from the Indians as local currency. The one-room houses in which settlers lived were built of wood hewn from nearby forests. Most of them boasted Dutch half-doors, while inside sand carpeted the floors. The single-room interiors were used as parlor, bedroom, and kitchen, with the kitchen corner the most popular spot in fall and winter. Children slept on straw while their parents occupied the wooden bedstead. By night candles lit the domain. Chairs and tables were rough-hewn. Outside the air was beautifully fresh and, except for the shouts of roisterers, absolute silence reigned. Yet there were problems. One was the placement of privies and pigpens which some crass citizens had located in the center of the town's pathlike streets.

Exactly what Claes and Jannetje thought of their new home town is not known, but from the early behavior of the couple in the bright New World it is possible to draw conclusions about the first Roosevelts in America.

Robust New Amsterdam did have some citizens who sedately raised families, trapped furs above the protective wooden wall which became Wall Street, bartered with the Indians, cultivated gardens in summer, and reverently attended church on Sunday. With this God-fearing and well-behaved group, Claes Martenszen immediately allied himself. "He was a shrewd, strong, and sterling Hollander," a later record of him says, "who transferred to the New World the habits of thrift which had been developed by his race in the old." It seems to be true.

Soon after arriving in New Amsterdam Claes Martenszen bought a piece of land, and this tells more about his character. For one thing, he must have been a somewhat unusual Dutchman, since by heredity the Dutch were traders rather than natural tillers of the soil. Even when placed on a farm the average Hollander usually followed his true instincts and turned into a trader. Because of this the Dutch West India Company made particular efforts to encourage farming, offering as much free land as a man and his family could cultivate, "provided he paid after four years of cultivation one-tenth of the produce to the company."

However, Claes Martenszen's acquisition of land did not fall under this offer, and so another fact about him is exposed: he must have had money. For Claes bought a parcel of land which was far more than he and any family could ever cultivate. The good fellow purchased what was called a *bouwerie,* a word used by the

Dutch to denote large acreage. One of the saner acts of the wild-eyed Governor Kieft had been to create six large *bouweries* from the land above Wall Street. Claes bought one of these from Lambert van Valkenburgh. It was a farm which covered about forty-eight mid-Manhattan acres and included a small thatched farm house.

Two varying locations of Claes's acreage appear on the record. One is described as beginning at today's Twenty-ninth Street and Park Avenue South and extending eastward almost to the East River. The upper boundary is the region of the current Thirty-fourth Street. By a second description the farm began at the same spot, but extended west, approximately to Sixth Avenue. In later years this land would be worth untold millions, but even in Claes's time it was costly. Twenty years earlier Peter Minuit had bought all Manhattan for $26. But now a farm like Claes Martenszen's was valued at about 100 guilders, or some $50. Yet the truly important thing is that Claes Martenszen—unlike most other colonists—had that sum of money. He was not such a "common" ancestor, after all!

Purchase of the farm throws other light on its proud owner. If nothing else, Claes possessed good judgment, for his forty-eight acres represented one of the best farm regions in Manhattan. At the south end lay marshes, and at the north, the rocky slopes leading to Murray Hill. Between were fields, pastures, and thick woods, with a brook and pond close to the thatched farmhouse. The brook ran around a small elevation which Claes and Jannetje sentimentally called Rose Hill. Soon the entire farm was known by that name.

But if Claes Martenszen had the buoyant optimism of later Roosevelts, he lacked the cheery gregariousness displayed by the majority of them. By establishing himself on a farm he cut himself off from the activities of the turbulent settlement at the tip of Manhattan. Four rugged miles of wilderness, forest, marsh, and thick underbrush lay between him and the actual colony. It was hardly a journey a man would take frequently, and Claes may have made it no more than once a week to sell his farm produce at the market.

So Claes Martenszen van Rosenvelt was established in the New World. As one of the few farmers on Manhattan—and one of the biggest—he proved himself a man of industry and determination. He also had steady nerves, since life four miles from civilization was exceedingly dangerous. Wolves were a constant menace not only to Claes and Jannetje themselves but to their oxen, horses, hogs, chickens, and ducks. Bear and, by some accounts, panther also lurked in the murky woods. Hungry deer often trampled crops or ate corn and wheat. Indians were an ever-present hazard. Though the Wilde Menschen were friendly on the surface, they were capable of sudden murder by tomahawk or of setting a torch fire to a farmhouse by night.

All in all, it was a far cry from the Rose Field. But apparently Claes and Jannetje were satisfied.

2

A ROOSEVELT IS BORN

SO LITTLE IS KNOWN OF CLAES MARTENSZEN VAN ROOSEVELT THAT in his life small matters loom large.

Was he—one wonders—among the citizens of New Amsterdam who gathered on May 10, 1647, to greet Peter Stuyvesant when he arrived to take over from William Kieft as director-general? Or did Claes arrive at a later date? There is still another possibility: did he perhaps come in one of the two Dutch ships that arrived in convoy with Stuyvesant? If so, he and Jannetje had a rough voyage of nearly five months. For Stuyvesant's commission from the West India Company appointed him commander of all Dutch possessions in North America and the Caribbean. So, before taking over the seat of government in New Amsterdam, the new governor detoured to make a stop-off visit at Curaçao.

The entire population of New Amsterdam turned out to watch as Stuyvesant's vessel, the *Great Crow,* dropped anchor off the edge of Manhattan. Four brass cannons boomed salute and guns from the man-of-war fired back. Towering, stern, oak-solid, the Director-General stomped ashore on the wooden leg whose silver band had been given a high polish for the occasion. On his head

Stuyvesant wore a wide-brimmed hat with plume, beneath it a regimental coat with buttons from chin to waistband and breeches of brimstone hue revealed by a fashionable twist of the knee-length skirt of the coat. One hand guided his progress with a gold-headed cane, while the palm of the other rested on the hilt of a broadsword anchored by a wide sash.

Stuyvesant's first words were as grandiose as his attire. "I shall," he sonorously proclaimed, "be in my government as a father over his children, for the advantage of the Dutch West India Company, the burghers, and the country." The assembled populace received this declaration with loud cheers, some of which sounded suspiciously tipsy. At this precise moment the new governor discovered the temper of his subjects. As William Kieft stepped forward to welcome Stuyvesant, the cheers turned to howls of derision. Stuyvesant considered this a breach of official etiquette and raised a lordly hand for the howling to cease. The crowd paid no attention.

Stuyvesant took his oath of office a few days later, and on this occasion won few friends. A critical populace thought him haughty. "He kept the people standing, with their heads uncovered, for more than an hour, while he wore his chapeau as if he were the Czar of Muscovy," one witness complained. Following a preliminary tour of his new domain, the Director-General expressed himself as far from impressed. He scrutinized the fort which the colonists had allowed to tumble into ruin. "It is more of a molehill than a fortress," he grumbled. He found similar fault with the church begun five years before but never finished. He deplored the number of "Brandy shops, Tobacco, or Beer houses run to the neglect of more honorable Trades and occupations." After spending time closeted with church deacons, he emerged to declare, "The people are grown very wild and loose in their morals."

He took immediate steps to remedy this. First, he imposed a closing hour of nine o'clock on taprooms and set severe penalties on Sunday drinking. Then he placed a tax on imported wines and liquors. After a wider tour of the settlement he issued strict regulations for the location of pigpens and privies. Finally, he announced a master plan to force citizens to pay back any money borrowed from the coffers of the West India Company. Informed that this last would make him highly unpopular, he gave a majestic snort. "We derive our authority from the Dutch West India Company, not from the pleasure of a few ignorant subjects," he declared.

Stuyvesant let it be known that he wished to be called lord-general instead of director-general. He was, to be sure, absolute monarch in his little world, able to decree anything except the death penalty. Supposedly, a governor listened to the advice of a council he appointed, but he could always override any council objections.

Peter Stuyvesant had no self-doubts about his ability to govern, and he stood iron-firm in his insistence on total authority. Therein lay his strength and—as frequently—weakness. The Lord-General set about remaking the brawling colony in his own steadfast image. If the stubborn colonists did not choose to follow, they did derive much strength from his posture of implacable virtue. What the clever little colony had always needed was a firm guiding hand. Now it had one. Where Kieft and others caused confusion by greed and vacillation, Stuyvesant could be counted on to stand firm in his belief in God, the Dutch West India Company, and Peter Stuyvesant himself.

As company representative in New Netherland, Stuyvesant's chief responsibility was to make sure that enough furs, timber, and wheat got back to Holland to ensure a profit for company stockholders. But soon he had on his hands a rebellion which was inconceivable to his stern mind. For a group of young settlers, grown restive under the dominion of a company interested only in large profits for small outlay, now talked loudly of freedom to trade with anyone they wished and of adopting the New England pattern of electing a governor and council.

This was a healthy sign for the colony, since up to this point most men arriving from Europe had dreamed of making money and getting home with it as rapidly as possible. Now, at last, there were settlers who talked of remaining permanently in the New World. Yet Stuyvesant could not view the matter in this constructive light. Learning that the malcontents had drawn up a petition, he erupted into fury. "It excited in him a bitter and unconquerable hatred," a contemporary states.

Like most men with violent tempers, Stuyvesant tried hard to control his. However, at a council meeting devoted to the petition he exploded in a mighty rage. Clomping across the floor, the one-legged man grabbed the petition from the hands of the man reading it. After this, he slowly regained his vast dignity. But from this unhappy moment Peter Stuyvesant, rather than the avaricious mother company, became a villain to the restless community. The dissidents started a campaign to unseat Stuyvesant as director-general—and almost did. One group of opponents made the hazardous trip to Amsterdam to urge his removal. Stuyvesant partisans fought them. In 1653 the Lord-Governor's jubilant enemies were handed an order for his recall. Three weeks later the order was rescinded.

Next, the irritating matter of religious freedom arose to plague him. Stuyvesant, of course, was a strict Calvinist, convinced that God stood foursquare behind his every act. When his right leg had been torn loose by a cannon ball in Caracas, he attributed his recovery neither to robust health nor to the skill of a surgeon who operated successfully at a time when amputations usually meant death. Rather, God Almighty and the power of prayer got full credit. Stuyvesant believed in the Dutch Reformed Church and considered those of any other belief heretics. Allow the free exercise of their religion in their own houses, the West India Company had instructed him, but for once the Lord-General disobeyed an order. He banned Lutherans, Baptists, Quakers, and Catholics, all of whom were specified as dangerous dissenters. For years he hounded the Lutherans as they held clandestine services in private homes. Stuyvesant was especially confounded when twenty-three Jews arrived in flight from the Portuguese who had captured

Dutch Brazil. The Jews were greeted without enthusiasm and informed that they could never own property in New Amsterdam.

Meantime, Claes Martenszen quietly labored on his farm.

At this point one more of his acts shows him an astute man, perhaps an ambitious one, possibly a snob. The name Claes Martenszen van Rosenvelt was much too clumsy for the sensible New World. In the other colonies Old World names were being shortened, misspelled, and otherwise hammered into new and more convenient shapes. In Plymouth, for instance, the aristocratic French Huguenot name de la Noye had become Dellanoy or in some cases Delano. Faced with the problem of simplifying his name, Claes had two choices. He could become simply Claes Martenszen—Nicholas, son of Martin—or he could use the more aristocratic Claes van Rosenvelt—Nicholas of the Rose Field. He picked the latter.

In their first years in New Amsterdam Claes and Jannetje begat five children. The first, Christaen, died in infancy. Three girls followed, Elsje, Anna-Margaret, and Christina. In 1658, some ten years after the couple landed in Manhattan, a second son was born. He was christened Claes or Claes I—for Junior—in the Dutch tradition, the event being duly recorded in the book of the Dutch Reformed Church. This was a proud moment for father Claes, perhaps his last such in life. For shortly after Claes I was a year old his father died. At that unhappy moment Jannetje was pregnant with another child. Yet tragedy had not finished with the family. Shortly after giving birth to a baby girl, Jannetje herself died.

The problem of parents who died leaving offspring behind had already been faced in the growing colony, and the burghers had worked out efficient methods for coping with it. Usually parentless children were absorbed into other families, adopting new names and forever discarding the old. It is possible that little Claes and his four sisters escaped this fate because of the family property. Few in Manhattan—man or child—owned land and this set the

Roosevelt orphans apart. An Orphans Court record is testimony to the amount of attention given the van Rosenvelt brood:

Jannetje Thomas, widow of Cleyn Classie, commonly called so, has lately died, leaving besides some property five minor children, so that it has become necessary to appoint administrators of the estate, therefore the Orphanmasters herewith qualify as such administrators Tomas Hall and Pieter Stotenburgh, who are ordered to make an inventory of the estate, real and personal property, value and debts, due by others, to settle all and make a report to the board for future disposal.

After suitable deliberation, part of the Rose Hill farm was sold to make what might be called a trust fund for the five minor children. The executors then placed a Dutch family named Grevenraet in the farmhouse, paying Mistress Metje Grevenraet 200 guilders a year to take care of the children.

So life went on as before for Claes I and his sisters. Yet there was a great difference, for now the children had no real father or mother.

As young Claes grew, so did New Amsterdam. Peter Stuyvesant was operating advantageously on the home front. Five years after taking over, the doughty fellow persuaded the West India Company to change New Amsterdam from town to city status. So the lusty little settlement was no longer a mere trading post but the seat of a colony. With this came municipal rights and a charter patterned on that of Old Amsterdam. It permitted election of city officials, though not of the director-general.

At the same time the colony was slowly expanding and improving. In 1656, almost ten years after Stuyvesant's arrival, it had 120 houses and 1,000 people. "The increase of cattle and children, but mostly of children and pigs, proceeds merrily," a settler reported home. In 1660 the living was better, with 340 homes for 1,500 people. Two thirds of the population were women and children, an unfortunate percentage in case of attack. A second settlement of New Harlem had been established at the upper end of the island, and by 1660 thirty families dwelt there. Yet the polyglot nature of those who found a haven on Manhattan was again underlined by the fact that only seven New Harlem families were actually Dutch.

Streets and blocks were taking slow shape. A few streets were cobbled, with gutters in the middle. The dominant thoroughfare was Breede Weg or Broad Way, so named because of its width. It was hardly more than a wide lane over an old Indian trail, running north from the fort at the southern tip of the settlement to slightly beyond the protective wall at the north end. To the east was a narrower lane, cut in the center by a canal into which inhabitants had a deplorable habit of throwing refuse. Cows and hogs wandered loose, the hogs nuzzling the dirt of the walls of the fort and causing it to slide to the ground. One of Stuyvesant's innovations was the appointment of a village herdsman who each morning walked the streets blowing his horn. At this sound residents turned their cattle loose, creating a common herd which was driven north to the present City Hall Park, then known as the Flat. At night the herdsman drove the cattle back, leaving at each citizen's door his good milch cow.

Stuyvesant also established a covered marketplace where on certain days farmers brought produce to sell. Presumably Claes Martenszen van Rosenvelt was among them, joining his few fellow farmers from above-the-wall Manhattan, as well as those from the regions later known as Brooklyn, Queens, Staten Island, and New Jersey. Fire was a constant hazard in a town where chimneys were wooden. To guard against both fire and Indian attack, Stuyvesant organized an all-night watch. Four men stood on duty through the night, marking each hour by the reassuring bellow, "All's well!"

Along with such advances, the Lord-General also had failures. For one thing, he continued to treat his subjects like children. The people, in turn, reacted by greeting most of his ukases with hearty ridicule. One group of men enjoyed playing the "Goose Game," in which a live goose smeared with grease was tied by a

rope between two poles. Players tried to snare the slippery creature. Stuyvesant disapproved of such pointless pleasure and
banned the game. The men went on playing, at which the Lord-
General clapped them in jail. Manhattanites also sold firewater to
the Indians, though this, too, was forbidden.

A constant annoyance to Stuyvesant was the flouting of his cur-
few on drinking. New Amsterdam males still roistered through the
night and tippled lustily on Sunday. This caused the governor to
thunder: "Not only are the more honorable trades and occupations neglected and disregarded, but even the common people and
the company's servants seriously debauched; and what is still
worse, the Youth, seeing and following, as from their very childhood, this improper example of their Parents, are drawn from the
path of virtue into all sorts of irregularity." Yet drinking went on,
with the stern Lord-General particularly aggravated by the manner in which his male subjects celebrated Christmas. The holiday
itself and the three weeks thereafter were one long binge.

For all his rigid righteousness, Stuyvesant was an intelligent
man. Over him as he governed his boisterous colony hung the
fear—almost the knowledge—that the Dutch were doomed in
North America. England had always claimed the entire North
American coast by virtue of the 1497 discoveries of John and
Sebastian Cabot. Then, too, the Dutch had failed to lay official
claim to the new territory after Hudson returned from his voyage
in 1609. Added to this, the Dutch, always the colorful individualists, ended by working at odds with one another. Life in the New
England colonies might be drab in comparison, but the people
were at least struggling toward a common end. The Dutch in New
Netherland, living on land to which they held dubious claim,
could see the English colonies around them grow rich and more
powerful.

Stuyvesant, governing a colony of less than two thousand population, did his utmost to negotiate on even terms with the English
colonies of over twenty thousand. He demanded equal footing in
negotiations and dealt harshly with English settlers in New Neth-

erland who expressed the opinion that the territory was really British. He even became a conqueror, sailing with a fleet of three ships to New Sweden, a group of forts along the Delaware River which bolstered Sweden's claim to the region. From the deck of his flagship the Lord-General demanded New Sweden for the Netherlands. Without a shot, the forts capitulated.

In 1663 he made a final personal effort at persuading the Massachusetts and Connecticut colonies to agree to existing boundaries. The confident English treated him with an indifference infuriating to the proud-spirited man. He sent warnings to Old Amsterdam, expressing the fear that the English were in a mood to take over Dutch possessions in North America. The West India Company replied by accusing him of cowardice and refused to send help. New Amsterdam's money coffers were low, its manpower numerically weak. Stuyvesant imposed new taxes on the populace, and for once the community responded. The taxes were paid, while rocks were hauled and oak trees cut for fortifications.

In March, 1664, King Charles II of England gave his brother, the Duke of York, a most splendid gift. He presented him with the entire northeastern section of the New World, from rockbound Maine to Delaware Bay. Specific mention was made of the Hudson River, the territory of New Netherland, and "the ffort and cittie of New Amsterdam." The Duke of York was in a particularly happy position to accept this gift. He was England's Lord High Admiral, with immediate power to dispatch a fleet and lay claim to his rich prize. In charge of the fleet he placed Colonel Richard Nicolls, with orders to establish himself as deputy governor of the New Netherland territory.

Old Amsterdam placidly disregarded this new danger, telling Stuyvesant that Colonel Nicolls' four men-of-war were intended merely to tighten administration in New England. But the Dutch populace of Manhattan was not fooled. Amply assisted by liquor, a warlike spirit flared. Still, realistic souls pointed out that the city's supply of powder amounted to only six hundred pounds. "Were I to commence firing this morning," one gunner lamented,

"I would have used it up by noon." Nor were food supplies sufficient for a siege. Matters looked bleak on the hot morning of
August 26, 1664, when the first English ship anchored off the later
site of Coney Island. Four hundred soldiers debarked to march
through the woods of Brooklyn to the ferry landing across from
New Amsterdam. This indicated that the four warships held over
1,600 men. In addition, there was the possibility that foot soldiers
and cavalry might be marching from New England.

The English demanded unconditional surrender of New Netherland, at the same time guaranteeing that citizens would be allowed to live much as before. The turnover, Colonel Nicolls
promised, would take place at top level only, leaving life in the
colony undisturbed.

For all their Dutch truculence, citizens of New Amsterdam realized they were outnumbered and outmaneuvered. More, by
shedding blood for New Amsterdam they would be fighting for
the venal West India Company rather than for national honor.
Only Stuyvesant seemed unshaken in his determination to give all
for the company. City officials, objecting to his decision, asked to
see the English letter outlining terms of surrender. The choleric
man flew into a fury, tearing the letter to shreds. On learning this
the townsfolk converged on the Lord-General's quarters, where
representatives demanded to see the letter. Stuyvesant produced
the torn bits.

It was New Amsterdam's destiny to fall to the British, and the
doughty Lord-General could only delay the inevitable. By now
two English frigates had anchored off Governor's Island. As they
came within cannon range, Stuyvesant stood on the shore beside a
Dutch gunner who held a lighted taper in his hand. At a word
from the Lord-General, the gunner would fire his cannon—it
would be hard to miss so large a target at such close range! Stuyvesant cleared his throat, preparing to speak. From the crowd behind him stepped the town's two ministers. They pulled Stuyvesant back.

The angry Lord-General returned shortly to his post to order his few soldiers into positions of defense. New Amsterdam now lay directly under British guns, but through the night Stuyvesant resisted all arguments for surrender. In the morning he was handed a petition signed by ninety-three of the town's outstanding citizens. The second name on the list was that of his oldest son. This was one petition Peter Stuyvesant did not tear up. He put it down slowly, his fighting spirit gone.

Young Claes van Rosenvelt was only six years old when New Amsterdam became New York. Possibly he was already attending either the common school, established in the colony in 1638, or the more exclusive Latin school opened in 1652. How many days a year the growing boy, wearing moccasins bought from the Indians, hiked the four forest miles is a matter of question. Mrs. Schuyler Van Rensselaer, a colorful historian of the early city, states that Claes never attended school and in later years signed an X for his name. But Mrs. Van Rensselaer is wrong. On later documents Claes's signature can be found strong and sure, if not bold.

Claes probably grew up speaking Dutch and English, with Dutch his first language. For, as agreed, the English conquerors made little effort to change the life of the city. One of the governor's responsibilities was to appoint the mayor who, with aldermen and a sheriff, ran the local government. The mayor served a one-year term and was usually a leading merchant of the town. Since the successful merchants were Dutch, it is not surprising to find Dutch mayors serving under English governors. Yet final power always rested in the hands of the governor. Though few Dutchmen would be inclined to admit it, the colony was better off under English rule. As the historian Charles Burr Todd states in *The Story of the City of New York*:

Instead of being a mere trading post, the slave of a commercial monopoly, surrounded by enemy colonies, each superior to it in numbers and enterprise, New York became one of several provinces under the same central government, speaking the same general language, having the same general interests.

At the same time the conquering British showed surprisingly little initiative. Colonel Nicolls made a compassionate governor, but he got little support from overseas. The mud walls of the fort at the tip of the island were still loose and slipping from the probing snouts of hogs. It had been expected that the red-coated British soldiery would immediately mend the fort, but they did not. Nor did the English treat their soldiers well. British troops were quartered in the old barracks from which the Dutch had prudently removed all bedclothing, leaving only dirty straw. The English used this. And here matters remained, causing the well-intentioned Colonel Nicolls to complain in a letter home: "Such is our straits that not one soldier to this day, since I brought him out of England, has been in a pair of sheats."

Colonel Nicolls served four years as governor of New York. Then, patience worn thin by neglect from London, he asked to be recalled. His successor was Colonel Francis Lovelace, who, like most in the long line of English governors, expected to find Manhattan Island a graceless frontier outpost. Colonel Nicolls' last act of official diplomacy was to have Lovelace entertained at Rensselaerswyck, the great patroonship up the Hudson. This and the seemly deportment of senior citizens who greeted him in New York impressed the new governor. "I find some of the people have the breeding of the courts," he wrote home, "and I cannot imagine how it is acquired."

However, Colonel Lovelace governed under an unhappy star. He was in office when the Third Dutch War broke out between Britain and Holland. The conflict seemed so remote from North America that, early in August, 1673, he ventured a trip to Hartford, leaving his aide, a Captain Manning, in charge. On the morning of August 9 Manning awoke to stare in stupefaction at a sight before his eyes. There were nine strange men-of-war, along with ten other ships, in the harbor. It was a Dutch fleet, swelled by English prizes to make the largest aggregation of ships ever to gather there.

Captain Manning's position astoundingly paralleled that of

Peter Stuyvesant almost ten years before. The soldiery treated so carelessly by the British numbered less than one hundred. Fort and guns were in poor fighting order, with only six cannons capable of firing. What is more, English morale was low. In the harbor was a British merchantman with thirty-five guns. It did not even fire on the Dutch.

Indeed, the English citizens were more defeatist than the Dutch had been under Stuyvesant. Manning valiantly lighted beacons in the hope that English residents of New Jersey, Brooklyn, and Long Island would flock to his aid. Few did. The large Dutch population of the city was a problem comparable to the fifth columns of future years. One account calls the attitude of Dutch citizens "neuter," but it seems to have been belligerent. A crowd of Dutch men and boys—Claes van Rosenvelt, then aged fifteen, must have been among them—marched about, shouting defiance, adding immeasurably to the uproar in the little town.

The Dutch sent ashore an emissary who ringingly told Captain Manning, "We have come for our own, and our own we shall have!" The desperate English commander resorted to the time-honored tactic of getting the emissary drunk, which stalled matters for a time. But when the man finally lurched back aboard the Dutch flagship, the admiral angrily upended his half-hourglass, at the same time alerting a force of 600 men to put ashore behind Trinity Church to attack the city from the rear. In half an hour the Dutch fired a shot at the shore, and the English shot back. Two men, one on each side, fell dead in this exchange. Thereupon Captain Manning's warlike spirit evaporated. He waved a flag of surrender and that night Dutch soldiers pillaged English mansions.

Once again the Dutch governed the cocky little outpost, with the proud British reduced to second-class citizens. Instead of renaming the city New Amsterdam, though, the Dutch called it New Orange, in honor of William of Orange. Since there were two rank-conscious admirals in charge of the Dutch fleet, they agreed to govern the city on alternate days. Both were strict Calvinists who quickly issued decrees aimed at Sabbath drinking and games. Next, the dual governors banned "all vagabonds, bawdy houses, gaming houses, and such impurities." It was like the old days of Peter Stuyvesant, but Stuyvesant was not there to enjoy it. The doughty peg-leg had died a year before, after living out his life in contentment on a large east-side *bouwerie*.

For fifteen months to come the Dutch controlled New Orange. Then unhappy word reached the town. The Third Dutch War was over, and by the terms of peace the Dutch returned New York to the British. History books say the Dutch were outmaneuvered at the peace conference table. Yet it is possible they were not.

For over forty years the New World colony had been a headache to the Dutch government. At first the Dutch had wanted New Amsterdam harbor as a sally port and refuge for privateers and men-of-war scouring the Spanish Main in quest of treasure-laden galleons. But aside from this, all benefits from New Amsterdam had gone into the coffers of the Dutch West India Company, leaving the government only the onerous chore of protecting an unruly outpost. So there is reason to believe the Dutch were quite willing to let New Orange go.

For some time after this opéra-bouffe conquest of New York, no record mentions young Claes van Rosenvelt. Then, in 1682, he reappears on a momentous day. He has reached his twenty-fourth year, and in the records of the Dutch Reformed Church is an entry of his marriage to Heyltje Jans Kunst who, we are told, is the daughter of a carpenter, a girl more German than Dutch. So Claes, a Dutchman with a lacing of Austrian blood, who may have had an English mother, marries a German girl—a suitable beginning for an American line that would accumulate Dutch, German, English, Irish, French, Swedish, and other strains to become a clan with a wild admixture of bloods.

However, there is more to be said about young Heyltje Jans Kunst, called by one source "the mystery woman of the Roosevelt clan, perpetually wrongly identified." There is a good chance that

Heyltje was a granddaughter or grandniece of Annetje Jans, the first woman to make a strong impression on the New Amsterdam colony. Where the wives of most early settlers were content to be dutiful helpmates, Annetje Jans displayed a lively character. She was one of the first women to arrive in the new colony, and her sprightly remarks and independent spirit are mentioned in early records. Annetje became truly important when her husband died, bequeathing her a farm of sixty-two acres which included the future site of Trinity Church. In addition to being a flavorsome character, Widow Jans was the wealthiest lady in town. She remained so until 1638 when she married Dominie Evardus Bogardus, an outspoken foe of Director-General Kieft. After this, there are fewer references to the Widow Jans, who may have returned to Holland with her clergyman husband. But it is safe to say that anyone descended from such a pithy female would be lively and full of irreverent high spirits.

Claes apparently matched his bride in flavor. "He had more than a fair share of the family charm and all of the prancing Roosevelt energy," says one description. As with his father, it is possible to deduce a few things about him. Jottings by contemporaries indicate he was big and blond. He was also a realist. Burdened with the name Claes van Rosenvelt in an English colony, he began calling himself—or letting himself be called—Nicholas Rosenvelt, thus dropping the "van" so deeply cherished by some Dutch families.

Exactly how Rosenvelt became Roosevelt is a question. It may have been Nicholas' own doing, or his bad handwriting, or the bad handwriting of others. In his Harvard thesis, Franklin D. Roosevelt says of early records: "The name Roosevelt is spelled in almost a dozen different ways, due to the illiteracy not only of the members of the family but of the clerks of public offices." Among the curious spellings are Roosinffelt, Rosewelt, Rosewell, Raasvelt, and Rosvllt. In almost all, *Rosen*velt becomes *Roos*, usually pronounced "rose." Whether this was Nicholas' desire or a natural evolvement from poor penmanship is impossible to tell. But it makes Nicholas appear a straightforward type, a man anxious to spell and pronounce his name in the sanest possible way.

Nicholas Roosevelt, aged twenty-four, had been brought up in a farmhouse in the forests of Manhattan. Yet he made no effort to retain the family property or to regain the parts that had been sold. Instead, the bridegroom planned to leave New York. Just as Claes Martenszen had brought his bride to the New World, Nicholas now led Heyltje to Esopus, a settlement on the west side of the Hudson, site of the present town of Kingston. Like Albany and nearby Rensselaerswyck, Esopus possessed a colorful history. Settled shortly after New Amsterdam, it had been the scene of massacres of white settlers by Indians. In 1659 Stuyvesant had brought troops from New Amsterdam to quell the warlike Wilde Menschen.

Nicholas journeyed to Esopus in order to become a trapper and to barter with Indians for beaver, muskrat, and other furs. It is probable that he went with a group of settlers, for his name appears at the head of a petition requesting that Dominie Peter Taschemaker be permanently installed at Esopus. After that he began to live what has been called "the epitome of colonial life of his days, bristling with excitement and incredible happenings. Indian attacks might occur at any moment. Never was there any real security—or any dullness."

In Esopus, Nicholas is mentioned as a pioneer in treating Indians like human beings. He invited them to his cabin hearth and gave them gifts. If nothing else, this was an astute business move, for by Indian custom any present was acknowledged by a gift ten times greater in value. For any knickknacks given his Indian guests Nicholas received expensive furs and abundant friendship in return. A few accuse him of being purely mercenary in his friendship with the Indians, but his lifetime record shows him to be a genuinely tolerant, outgoing man who would have little difficulty in viewing the red men as friends. The affection the Indians

held for Nicholas gave him a unique function in Esopus. He became an arbiter of disputes between Indians and white men, and
between white settlers as well.

Altogether Nicholas Roosevelt held a prominent position in the
tiny community, at the same time amassing what must have been a
considerable sum of money. By 1690 he and Heyltje had two children, Nicholas I and Johannes. The family had been in Esopus for
eight years, and now Nicholas did a strange thing. As a boy, he had
been brought up in the forests of Manhattan; as a man, he had
voluntarily gone to live in the wilder frontier of Esopus. Now he
abandoned Esopus, returning with wife and children to the city of
New York. Nicholas was thirty-two and would live to be over
eighty years old. But from this point on he was a city dweller.
Never again, for any length of time, did Nicholas Roosevelt leave
the island of Manhattan.

3

NICHOLAS OF NEW YORK

THE NEW YORK TO WHICH NICHOLAS ROOSEVELT RETURNED IN 1690 already had assumed many of the characteristics that would mark its turbulent future.

The city was, of course, larger. New houses were built of brick and stone rather than of the wood logs of the past. Lawns, trees, and flower gardens, bright in spring and summer, surrounded a few homes. The rich had mansions staffed with servants, in which living was almost as elegant and graceful as in England. The good wives of the town had approached Mayor De Peyster, appointed by the English governor, to complain bitterly about the garbage and other refuse dumped into the street by careless citizens. After pondering the problem, the mayor decreed that each householder must be responsible for the cleanliness of the path or street outside his domicile.

In front of City Hall stood a cage, pillory, and whipping post as warning to all those who might be tempted to break the law. At the same time the town had relaxed, with religious freedom a half step forward. The once beleaguered Quakers had a meetinghouse, and the Jews had begun to agitate for a synagogue. Life below the

Wall Street wall was not quite so rugged, but it still offered hardships. Water was poor, for one thing, with better springs beyond the wall. Water vendors carried large leather buckets up to these springs, then lugged them back to town to be sold.

New York's harbor had always been the major factor in the city's growth, and a teeming local industry was the building of ships in the docks running east from the end of the island. The finished ships were sailed to England to be sold at high profit. Men who went down to the sea in ships comprised a large part of the city's population, with sailors from the sidewalks of New York manning mighty vessels bound for Asia, Africa, and Europe. Other ships traded along the rivers and the east coast of North America. By far the greatest activity in the New York harbor came at times when England was at war, for then plundering of enemy shipping was allowed.

The population was increasing, coming close to 3,500 citizens, in the same perverse ratio of nationalities as before. In days of Dutch rule the Dutch seemed to be a minority group in their own city. Now the same was true of the English, who lagged behind other nationalities in contributing to the population increase. One governor lamented this in a letter home, saying, "Our chiefest unhappyness here is too great a mixture of Nations, & English ye least part." New York retained the look of a Dutch town, with respectable burghers and their wives predominant. However, it continued such a polyglot place that even the French were represented in local government. Germans, Scots, Irish, Swedes, all had a foothold, while one sixth of the population was made up of Negro slaves.

The city had exchanged rule by an impersonal company for government by the Duke of York, and in the process had gained a greater voice in its own affairs. In 1681 the populace drew up a monster petition to be sent to the Duke. Particularly, this requested an elected assembly to manage city finances and taxation. In London the Duke angrily perused the lengthy document. Meeting with William Penn, he complained of the many irritations connected with running a colony by remote control. Warming to the subject, he threatened to sell New York together with his other American possessions. Penn, who had devised a wise and liberal government for his own American colony, tried simple psychology as a means of winning the same for New York. "Sell it!" he exclaimed in mock horror. "Don't think of it. Just give it self-government and there will be no trouble."

By self-government the canny Penn meant granting the concessions New York asked. The idea of agreeing to the petition had not occurred to the Duke, but now he consented. An English governor still ruled the colony, and under him was an appointed mayor. But aldermen, common council members, freemen, assessors, and constables were elected by popular vote.

In 1690, the year of Nicholas Roosevelt's return, the city had been plunged into turmoil over the matter of a governor—or lack of one. King James II of England, a Catholic, had been forced to abdicate in favor of his daughter Mary and her Protestant consort, William of Orange. When this news reached the New World, Sir Edmund Andros, the Governor appointed by the King, was promptly clapped into jail, leaving New York and New England without a guiding hand. In New York no one knew what to do. Some thought the officials appointed by King James should continue until the wishes of the new monarchs became known. Others believed James's rule ended with his abdication and that the people were free to appoint interim officials. This was quickly done in New England, but in New York both mayor and citizens hesitated over so bold a step.

The city militia was already on the alert, for the hostile French in Canada had reputedly incited Indians to the warpath. One fiery band of local militia was led by German-born Jacob Leisler, a New York citizen of some thirty years' standing. Uneducated but vigorous, Leisler was a successful merchant, a deacon in the Dutch Reformed Church, and a fanatical anti-Catholic. He had always believed that a colony like New York should govern itself, and at this moment he was prominent among those who wanted the citizens to grab power. When no one else did this, Leisler nominated himself. Using his popularity with the militia as backing, he strode center stage and declared himself New York's interim governor.

So begins a peculiar and nearly forgotten episode in history. According to most authorities, Leisler was the first American man of the people, the first true democrat to rise with the support of the common man. "The Spirit of 1776 was foreshadowed in 1690." writes one. But to the wealthy aristocrats and elderly New Yorkers of his time Leisler presented a different picture. He was that most terrifying of figures—the man of the people who rises to disturb a pleasant status quo.

In opposition to Leisler and his so-called People's party, there quickly arose an Aristocrat party, led by Frederick Philipse, Stephanus Van Cortlandt, and Nicholas Bayard. Philipse was the richest man in the city; Bayard, a nephew of old Peter Stuyvesant. The attitude of the Aristocrats toward Leisler was a combination of burning hatred and terror. Leisler hated right back, and one night ordered Bayard pulled from the silken bedsheets of his mansion and carried to the common jail. He was placed in a filthy cell, his leg chained to a wall, and there he languished for the next thirteen months.

Leisler's arrogance antagonized some of his partisans and he was once attacked in the street by a disgruntled group of onetime followers. Added controversy followed the marriage of his lovely young daughter to one of his middle-aged henchmen. Enemies said Leisler forced the girl into the match to keep the man's loyalty. Friends called it true love. Despite the uproar surrounding him, Leisler continued a hero to the average New Yorker even though families split asunder because of him. "There was little sociability or amusement in New York during this period of suspense," the record says.

Members of the Aristocrat party could do nothing but pray nightly for the appearance of a governor appointed by William and Mary. Finally, on March 19, 1692, the boom of a cannon down the bay proclaimed the arrival of the frigate *Archangel* bearing Governor Henry Sloughter. Leisler reacted by locking himself inside the fort and refusing to order the customary welcoming salute. Leaders of the Aristocrat party clambered into small craft and raced down the bay to pour the story of Leisler's infamy into the new governor's ear.

All day Governor Sloughter listened. At midnight he landed, greeted only by a few stay-up-lates who looked at him with hostility. He immediately ordered Nicholas Bayard released; the unhappy man emerged, aged and emaciated beyond recognition. Leisler was arrested and placed in the cell Bayard had just vacated, chained to the wall by the identical leg iron. Soon he was brought to court and, in an eight-day trial, found guilty of treason. His middle-aged son-in-law was condemned with him.

Having done so much, Governor Sloughter dallied. He not only seemed to have sympathy for Leisler but appeared to sense that some members of the English Parliament would feel the same way. The Aristocrats, impatient for blood, were dismayed when Sloughter spoke of sending the traitor back to England for proper punishment. By now the Governor had exposed himself as a prodigious tosspot. Members of the Aristocrat party remained patiently at his side through one epic drinking bout, and at its finish shoved Leisler's death warrant at the unsteady Governor, who agreeably signed. Before the Governor could sober up, Leisler and his son-in-law had been hanged at the edge of Beekman Swamp. The bodies were buried at the foot of the gallows—a fate then called "the grave of dishonor." Only one segment of the story has a happy ending. Leisler's beautiful daughter, widowed so young, married Milbourne Gouverneur, to become matriarch of a notable family.

In this bitter dispute, Nicholas Roosevelt sided with Leisler and the People's party.

With his Esopus money Nicholas had set up a small wheatgrinding mill near the waterfront. Old records call him a "bolter" or miller. So the farmer's son who had made money as a fur trader and trapper became a city-dwelling miller or merchant. In this, Nicholas demonstrated what became a Roosevelt family trait. In the future male members of the clan showed a neat instinct for involving themselves in the main currents of the era in which they lived. As times changed, so did Roosevelts change businesses.

By siding with Leisler and his People's party, Nicholas also began another noble family tradition and showed that even in those early days a Roosevelt could be a political paradox. By 1690 his family might already be called an old one in America. Nicholas, the man of strong personality, had an abundance of charm and energy. "A burgher of the major right," city archives call him. In other words, a man of property and position. As such a figure he was free to choose either political party, though the Aristocrats would seem to have the stronger claim on him. Yet Nicholas sided with Leisler and the people.

In fact, Nicholas not only expressed political sympathies but acted on them as well. The liberal spirit of the Leisler party survived the death of its leader, and soon Nicholas was running for the office of freeman as a People's party candidate. He won in a manner that points up the robust informality of the times. Nicholas ran against Aristocrat Brandt Schuyler, who actually received a vote or two more. Still the contest was so close that the mayor was called upon to pick the winner. He chose Nicholas, who thus won an election he really lost. The mayor's decision brought no ill feeling, for one of Nicholas' daughters grew up to marry Schuyler's son.

Yet more important than the election victory is the family pattern Nicholas inaugurated by running for office. Of all the old New York families, the Roosevelts eventually established the most exceptional record of public and political service. *Qui Plantavit Curabit*—"He who has planted it shall care for it." Where most mottoes are empty phrases often violently incompatible with family behavior, the Roosevelts cheerfully accepted theirs as an inherent obligation. In each generation family members worked hard for personal gain. But hand in hand with this ambition went the conviction that, after taking from a community, something must be given back. Unlike most American dynasties, the Roosevelts appear to have operated with one eye on the welfare of the locality in which they lived. This pattern of kinship with the community was both established and continued by Nicholas, who did not cease public service with one election as freeman. He later went on to become alderman.

Nicholas Roosevelt was obviously a popular man, capable of winning votes from his fellow citizens. He also possessed an enviable objectivity, together with a sense of humor. By now his wife Heyltje had added more children to the two born in Esopus. Still a lively young matron, she one day showed her Jans blood by wearing a flamboyant petticoat and letting it be seen as she crossed a muddy New York street, thereby exposing her ankles "in unseemly fashion, to the scandal of the community." For this she was brought to court on a charge of "wearing and shewing luxurious petticoats."

Another husband might have been outraged by this busybody smirch on the family honor, but Nicholas Roosevelt only seemed amused. He sat beside his wife in court and even rose to argue her case. After clearing her of the charge, he filed countersuit for slander against her accuser. Having done this, he led his good wife to the nearest drygoods store where he bought her another brocade petticoat of even more colorful hue.

Altogether, Nicholas and Heyltje had nine children, three of whom died in infancy. Presumably the close-knit family lived in or near the waterfront mill, which allowed the three boys and three girls to grow up surrounded by all the color of New York's most picturesque era. For this was the city's Romantic Age, a time when New York boasted an almost Oriental magnificence. Shops along Broad and Cherry Streets showed rare fabrics from Teheran and Samarkand, while Arabian gold was accepted as common currency. Wealthy women donned robes woven for queens of the East, and in homes of the rich Persian rugs covered floors.

Never has there been another era like this in New York and the reason for it was the swashbuckling privateers and pirates who called the city their home port. Between privateer and pirate the line was thin. Supposedly the privateer was a respectable marauder, the private owner of a skiff or merchant vessel which in wartime was commissioned to proceed against the enemy. But if a privateer succumbed to temptation, turning guns on the ship of a nation not in his commission, he became a pirate. Many did this and in the process supposedly became enemies of all mankind. Broadminded New York, however, attached no stigma to piracy. By law, a pirate who set foot in the city was subject to arrest and hanging. This simply never happened.

"Pirates are so cherished by the inhabitants that not one of them is ever taken in," an Englishman wrote home. It was true. To the docks of New York came pirate vessels with such rakish names as *Charming Peggy, Sturdy Beggar, Dolphin, Black Hawk, Speedwell, Sea Flower, Dreadnaught, Horne, Tyger, Decoy, Wheel of Fortune, Irish Gimlet, Lovely Martha, Spitfire, Game Cock,* and *Favorite Betsey.* Swaggering pirate captains were a frequent sight on city streets, together with members of outlaw crews, wearing brass earrings and cutlasses, drinking and brawling in taverns. People spoke with special awe of Captain Thomas Tew, slight and swarthy, who wore a blue jacket bordered with gold lace and embellished with large pearl buttons. The dashing captain used louis d'or for small change and the hilt of his dagger was studded with diamonds.

While pirates swaggered through the streets the governors sent from London rode in the only carriage so far known to the city. For the most part these English governors were a strange group. Reprobates, the historian Mrs. Van Rensselaer calls most of them, and the lady is not far wrong. Over the years Britain dispatched to New York some twenty royal governors, who served under eight kings and queens. A few performed the job well, but others arrived boiling with indignation at being plucked from the gaming rooms of London to serve in so dismal an outpost. Some were impoverished noblemen who had sought the post in the hope of accumulating a quick fortune. And if the governors were unhappy at being sent so far from glamorous London, their wives and daughters were more so.

By far the oddest of these English governors was Edward Hyde, Viscount Cornbury, chosen "regardless of his enormous debts, his profligate character, and his total disqualification for such a delicate and onerous position." He was a relative of Queen Anne, who had ruled England since the death of her brother-in-law, William of Orange. Cornbury was one of the Queen's embarrassing brood of poor relations, and she had hopes that his tenure in New York would improve his fortunes.

Lord Cornbury was accompanied to New York by his wife, a person of low station and little education. When asked why he had married her, Cornbury replied airily, "I fell in love with her beautiful ears." At a dinner of welcome tendered him in New York, Cornbury was given a gift of £2,000 to defray the expenses of the trip from England. In reply, he delivered a eulogy of Lady Cornbury's shell-like ears, calling them the most beautiful in Christendom. He then required every gentleman present to stand in line and march past her Ladyship, to feel for himself the texture of the lovely ears.

This curious pair nursed the notion that they themselves were royalty and tried to set up a local court in emulation of Queen Anne. Lady Cornbury informed the local aristocracy of this and invited daughters of the city's wealthy families to live in the Governor's Mansion as ladies in waiting. The girls leaped at the chance, but soon found themselves performing the work of common servants. If the housework was not done to Lady Cornbury's exact satisfaction, the young ladies were soundly slapped. Nor would the Cornburys allow the girls to leave the Governor's Mansion for visits home. Slowly the families learned what was going on—and they practically had to kidnap their daughters to get them back!

The Governor and his lady carried on undeterred. They gave Grand Balls in the mansion at which invited guests were required to pay admission. His lordship wrecked taverns by charging in on horseback, demanding drink for himself and water for the horse. Ever skilful at devising money-making schemes, he sold public lands to his close friends. Among the parcels illegally disposed of was one of several thousand acres above Poughkeepsie. In gratitude for such a bargain, the purchaser named his land "Hyde Park" after his benefactor.

In this and other ways Cornbury created a wide breach between governor and people, whom he condescendingly called "twigs belonging to the tree." Meanwhile Lady Cornbury drove around the city in the impressive governor's coach, repaying courtesy calls made on her by local gentry. If she saw any object that she liked in a house, her ladyship carried it home. After leaving, she often recalled a thing of beauty and sent her coachman back for it. In this novel way she accumulated a priceless collection of china, linen, paintings, and objets d'art.

It would seem the Cornburys could sink no lower. Yet one night a city watchman arrested a middle-aged woman who was dancing, with skirts raised high, on the ramparts of the fort. Brought before the nearest magistrate on charges of drunk and disorderly, the dancing beldame turned out to be none other than Lord Cornbury, Her Majesty's governor, attired in one of his wife's dresses. Far from being chastened, his lordship stated that one of his few pleasures in life was donning female garb, and a pox on all who objected! He added that he had often been complimented on his facial resemblance to Queen Anne and considered it his official duty to look as much like Her Majesty as possible. From then on his lordship danced two or three nights a week on the ramparts, coyly waving a fan and dressed like a female, down to silken underthings.

Lady Cornbury died in 1706 and the eccentric Governor gave her the most magnificent funeral New York had ever seen. He then ordered the city fathers to pay for it and was infuriated when they refused. The splendid funeral did much to increase the mountain of debt Cornbury had already accumulated. Two years later his conduct and indebtedness had become so outrageous that England reluctantly took notice. He was removed from office, and on the day his successor arrived, Cornbury was tossed into debtor's prison. He remained there until his father's death conveniently set him free. As the Earl of Clarendon, he magnificently settled accounts and left the New World forever.

Other governors were almost as unsettling as Cornbury, but against them citizens had a strong weapon. The American colonies were small republics, each ruled by an elected assembly. Among other duties, the Assembly controlled the money collected in taxes. Thus the Assembly could both whittle down the governor's power and weaken Britain's hold on the colony. True, the governor had the counterpower of veto, but then the Assembly could retaliate by withholding money for governmental expenses. The Assembly could even refuse to pay a governor's salary—and sometimes did. Governors bombarded Britain with pleas to be paid from home, but the Empire's coffers were always low and the Lords of Trade paid no heed.

A main function of English governors was to make sure that colonies traded only with the mother country. Yet the measures used to enforce this had the opposite effect, and at the same time planted the first seeds of American independence. England decreed that goods from the colonies must be sent first to England, then traded with other colonies. This seemed needlessly cumbersome to Americans, who began smuggling goods direct to their fellow North Americans. Such illicit activity was the basis of nearly all the great New York fortunes. Of the ships that smuggled goods into English possessions, one account says, "They were armed and officered by the flower of New York gentry."

Colonies were also forbidden to manufacture their own goods. This, too, seemed silly to Americans. With beaver skins among the most plentiful articles of export, New Yorkers first held onto a few skins for their own hats. Next, they began making hats for sale. After this came clothing, glassmaking, sugar refining, and the distilling of rum. One English traveler wrote home that on Manhattan's tip he saw "Roperies, distilleries, breweries, and a large iron work." On Wall Street and Queen Street merchants sold home-manufactured goods at warehouses, while artisans labored in small shops.

Through it all Nicholas Roosevelt prospered. He and his family survived a cholera epidemic that killed 700 citizens, driving ordinary New Yorkers to seek refuge in far regions like Greenwich Village, while the rich fled to Westchester and Long Island. Nicholas ran for alderman in 1719 and was elected. His oldest son, Nicholas I, had grown up to display an artistic streak unsuspected in the sturdy stock, and eventually became a gold- and silversmith, disposing of his wares to the rich folk of the town. The daughters of the senior Nicholas made proper marriages into the Schuyler, Low, and van der Huel families.

But of his progeny, the father probably looked with most satisfaction on his sons Johannes and Jacobus, born in 1689 and 1692 respectively. Not the least distinction accruing to these two sturdy men is the fact that Johannes sired the branch which led to Theodore Roosevelt, while Jacobus began the line leading to Franklin—and then Eleanor of the Theodore line married Franklin, her fifth cousin once removed.

There are no portraits of Nicholas Roosevelt and his offspring but sometimes personalities may be sensed from the pages of old records. Thus Nicholas, for all his blondness, seems to have been like Franklin D. Roosevelt, tall and dignified, but humorous withal. On the other hand, both Johannes and Jacobus appear to resemble the traditional Dutch billikin—cheerful, roly-poly, bouncy. They were probably like Theodore Roosevelt as Beatrice Webb later saw him: "thick-set, bullet-headed, with an extraordinarily expressive face, all his features moving when he speaks." One also gets the impression that Johannes and Jacobus were—like Theodore—short of stature for Roosevelts.

In Johannes and Jacobus, as in Theodore, the Roosevelt energy was spectacular. Both married young, with Johannes taking as his bride Heyltje Sjoerts, while Jacobus wed Catharina Hardenbroeck. Both immediately began having children. Inevitably some of their bursting energy was beamed on family and church matters, but most was reserved for business. Working together and separately, the Roosevelt boys found the growing city a happy arena in which to juggle myriad projects. Johannes was in business at the age of twenty, engaged in the manufacture of linseed oil, a smelly substance made from the seed of flax, an ingredient in the paint applied to the hulls of ships. In this activity Johannes was a partner of his brother-in-law, Johannes van der Huel, with a mill on Maiden Lane.

Unlike his father, who stuck to one profession, Johannes was a man of many trades, ready to try anything that promised profit. He repaired sidewalks, erected flagpoles, did general contracting and building. While continuing the manufacture of linseed oil, he also branched out into chocolate and flour. In addition, Johannes was apparently a good man with his hands, for in 1730 he was commissioned to make the ornate tin box in which Governor Montgomerie presented a new charter to the city.

This ceremony began with the ringing of three bells outside City Hall, located in a fine new building on Wall Street. Governor Montgomerie stood waiting for silence, then handed the boxed charter to assembled members of the City Council. One member—serving with others named Philipse, Stuyvesant, Kip, and De Peyster—was Jacobus Roosevelt, younger brother and billikin-twin of Johannes. Now thirty-eight, Jacobus had been the first family member to invest in real estate, a venture which turned out to be the basis of the Roosevelt fortune. In 1728 Jacobus had bought ten lots, 25 by 120, in the Beekman Swamp for 10 pounds each. Next he and Johannes bought the entire swamp, which lay near the present City Hall.

As the area improved, one lane running through it was named Roosevelt Street. The brothers then set about persuading the city's malodorous slaughterhouses and tanneries to move from the foot of Wall Street to the isolated Beekman area, far from the sensitive nostrils of citizens. When this was done, the value of Beekman Swamp rose considerably. For the first time, it has been noted, good business and good citizenship joined hands in a Roosevelt family deal.

"Success is a coy thing," says a guidebook of this early era. Yet the billikin brothers did not seem to find it so. The two now began to make real estate their prime concern. Many years later this type of astuteness was saluted by John Jacob Astor, who, on his deathbed, said, "Could I begin life again, knowing what I do now, and had money to invest, I would buy every foot of Manhattan Island."

The Roosevelt brothers could not buy all Manhattan, but they did the best they could. In time they owned land as far north as Westchester County, becoming joint owners of "Undivided land lying between Rye and Byrom River and blind brook, granted to the Prisbiterian Society in 1729." In 1733 the City Council of New York had offered to rent the land:

Lying at the lower end of Broadway fronting to the Fort, to some inhabitants . . . in order to be enclosed to make a Bowling Green thereof with walks therein, for the beauty or ornament of the said street as well as for the recreation and delight of the inhabitants of the city.

One who rose to this toothsome bait was Johannes Roosevelt. He joined with Colonel Philipse and John Chambers to fence in the land and equip it with greensward suitable for English skittles, the game of bowls. From then on the pleasant spot was—and is—known as Bowling Green. For it, Johannes and his associate paid an annual rent of one peppercorn. After ten years the fee rose to 20 shillings.

In busy lifetimes the energetic Roosevelt brothers never neglected civic affairs. Johannes matched his brother's position in the City Council by serving as assistant alderman and alderman. In business enterprise Johannes slightly overshadowed his brother, and as a consequence, has been described as "the first financier of the family, conservative, hard-headed, upright, philanthropic, shrewd." In this generation the Roosevelts also added intellectual pursuits to other activities, with Johannes serving on a Committee of Five to accept twenty-one cases of books to be housed in City Hall, thus inaugurating the institution that today is called the New York Society Library.

Apart from business, the Roosevelt brothers showed other traits which have become associated with the family. Jacobus served as senior elder of the Dutch Reformed Church, which was slowly losing out to Trinity Church as the town's most popular place of Sunday worship. The main reason for dwindling attendance in the Dutch church was its sermons, which were doggedly delivered in Dutch. Farsighted Jacobus Roosevelt realized the futility of this and led a reform movement which persuaded other Dutch elders to give at least part of the Sunday sermon in English.

The architecture of New York was losing its Dutch solidity to take on the more graceful lines of English. Simultaneously, a growing generation of Dutch youngsters considered it smart to adopt English manners and use English as a first language. Parents fought hard for the old customs, but it was a losing struggle. One result of the town's gradual Anglicization was that on many documents the names of Johannes and Jacobus appear as "John" and "James" Roosevelt.

Johannes Roosevelt also was a devout man—all Roosevelts were! At the same time he displayed an unusual facet. In Johannes the surprising artistic streak found in his older brother, Nicholas I, emerged in a different way. Johannes Roosevelt, bustling businessman of old Manhattan, was one of the first in the city to import paintings and furniture from Holland. He did not do this for profit but for his home which, in decoration if not in size, took a place among the finest in Manhattan.

"His home was viewed as a wonderland by less enterprising fellow citizens," a contemporary wrote.

4

THE REVOLUTIONARY ROOSEVELTS

NICHOLAS ROOSEVELT DIED ON JULY 30, 1742, AT THE RIPE age of eighty-four. Behind him he left at least forty-five assorted children and grandchildren. The number would have been greater had it not been for the many epidemics, plagues, accidents, and health hazards of the time. Between them his billikin sons, Johannes and Jacobus, had contributed twenty-three children to the family tree—Johannes, eleven; Jacobus, twelve—of which only fourteen survived into adulthood.

This, however, was a good average for the day. New York, with its population of ten thousand, was a city of frequent funerals, with the tolling of church bells and sad processions winding over the dusty, half-cobbled streets. The city was so sparsely built that it was dotted with tiny secular graveyards, some of which remain to this day.

In late life Nicholas Roosevelt enjoyed a special distinction. He was the first and only patriarch the family ever knew, for unlike Astors and Vanderbilts the Roosevelts were too independent and individual to cluster around one dominant person. Already the numerous Roosevelt families were notably self-sufficient, while some young members developed an itchy foot which propelled them into leaving New York. A few of these wanderers went to the West Indies, acting as agents there for New York traders. Others headed for a wilder American frontier and ended up by settling in western New York and Pennsylvania. Of these adventurers in the clan, Franklin Roosevelt later wrote: "There are scattered all over the country families of Roosevelts whose origin is quite obscure, either people who adopted the name or have lost all trace of their ancestors."

Daughters of early Roosevelts made excellent marriages which highlight the family's standing in the community. Caterina, daughter of Nicholas I, married Steenwyck de Reimer, son of a mayor. Another Roosevelt daughter married Henry Kip, or Kype, whose impressive mansion by the East River at Thirty-fifth Street brought the name Kips Bay to the entire area. Still another Roosevelt girl married a De Peyster.

The grandchildren of Nicholas—he had so many!—must have given the patriarch much to think about in his later years. What would life in the growing city bring to these children of his six sons and daughters? Perhaps he noted the curious genetic fact that the offspring of his son Johannes, whose home was a wonderland of imported paintings and furniture, were somewhat less flavorsome than the sons of Jacobus, who seems to have found his wonderland in the Dutch Reformed Church. Nicholas may also have observed that Jacobus, son of Johannes, showed a steady disposition, together with a solid determination to get ahead in the world. Jacobus, born in 1724, in time entered the hardware trade, thus founding the business and financial dynasty which cushioned the lives of members of the Theodore Roosevelt branch.

As individuals, the sons of Johannes may have been vigorous—and the activity of at least two of them in the Revolution bears this out. But on the printed page their cousins, the sons of Jacobus, have more identity. Jacobus' son Johannes—both brothers named sons for each other, adding confusion to the family tree—was born in 1715, two years after his father's marriage to Catharina Hardenbroeck. As the first son of a prospering family, Johannes was sent to Yale, thus becoming the first Roosevelt to attend college. He graduated in 1735, married a girl with the fancy name of Ariaantje Lequier, and became a merchant-grocer. His brother Nicholas—again the genealogy becomes bewildering, since both brothers had sons named Nicholas, as did Nicholas I—did not go to college, but also became a storekeeper.

Helena, oldest daughter of Jacobus, was the beauty of the Roosevelt family. In 1737 she married a young Scot named Andrew Barclay whose father was the first Church of England minister in Albany. Barclay's mother was the daughter of a Danish admiral, and from this mixture of bloods Andrew received an unusual drive toward worldly success. He labored long and hard, becoming an outstanding merchant with a warehouse near City Hall where he sold such items as rum, salt, chinaware, and spices. Barclay Street is named for him.

In the years just before his death, Nicholas Roosevelt may have looked with particular pride at Johannes Roosevelt, son of Jacobus, first college-educated member of the family. But if the old man kept his shrewdness to the end, his eyes quit Johannes to move down the line to Jacobus' sixth child. This was Isaac Roosevelt, a stripling of sixteen when old Nicholas died. For young Isaac carried in him a great potential. Not only did he become the great-great-great grandfather of Franklin D. Roosevelt, but for a century he stood forth as the most exceptional man produced by the entire family.

Isaac has been called the first American Roosevelt, and this may be true. Today his portrait by Gilbert Stuart hangs in the living room at Hyde Park, and it is difficult to view this fine colonial gentleman, seated at his desk in a powdered wig, as anything but an aristocrat in the best American sense. His brow is high, nose arched, eyes sharp and serious, jaw slightly underslung like that of Franklin Roosevelt. Isaac's father, Jacobus, left a will written in Dutch, as did his uncle Johannes. Nearly all branches of the Roosevelt family had a continuing custom of speaking Dutch through at least one weekly meal, usually Sunday dinner. Yet it is difficult to look at Isaac's portrait and imagine him ever speaking or writing Dutch. In looks, above all, he *is* the first American Roosevelt.

Isaac's span of years covered the era when New York, together with the other British colonies, became America. He was born in 1726, enjoyed a long life, and died just before the beginning of a new century. His time covered fifty years of the heady turmoil of revolution, crowned by the glorious twelvemonth when George Washington was President of the United States, with the national capital in New York City. Isaac Roosevelt, in a dignified but vital way, was an integral part of all this.

At the age of twenty-one Isaac was already in politics, serving as a freeman of the city. Even in the matter of choosing a lifework—a moment of indecision for most young men—he showed exceptional shrewdness and perspicacity. On the threshold of adult life, he apparently took time to figure out a business Manhattan really needed. He selected sugar refining, and with the financial help of brother-in-law Andrew Barclay opened a wholesale refinery in a stone building in the center of a block on Wall Street. Together with this, Isaac acquired a house fronting on Wall Street. The old Sugar House, as Isaac's place of business came to be called, is usually considered the first refinery on Manhattan Island. If not the first, it was certainly the second, and the first to refine sugar on a large-scale basis. Isaac imported his raw sugar from the West Indies, turning it into lump or loaf. He did so well financially that other refineries quickly appeared in competition. The families which rose to vie with Isaac were top-drawer in business and society—Bayards, Rhinelanders, Cutlers, Van Cortlandts. Soon the Rhinelander Sugar Refinery on William Street, four stories and a loft, was the tallest building in town except for the church steeples.

In 1752, Isaac Roosevelt, then twenty-six years old, journeyed to Dutchess County for the purpose of marrying eighteen-year-old Cornelia Hoffman, daughter of one of the richest men in the area.

The Roosevelts had never lost touch with Nicholas' onetime

home territory of Esopus. No doubt the partriarch Nicholas made a habit of taking his family back to his old trapping ground on summer vacations. In any case, his daughter Rachel married Pieter Low, son of an Esopus storekeeper. Johannes and Jacobus probably continued the family tradition of visiting Esopus with their families. The Roosevelts must also have crossed to the east side of the Hudson, into the region which Edward Hyde, Lord Cornbury, disposed of to his financial advantage. For it was here that young Cornelia Hoffman lived.

Cornelia's paternal grandfather, Martinus Hoffman, had been a young Finnish-Swedish soldier in the Swedish army. He came to this country in 1657, settling in Albany rather than New Amsterdam. In Swedish, Hoffman means Head Man, and life in the New World brought both leadership and prosperity to Martinus. "He was a man of mental and moral force," says the Hoffman genealogy, and these qualities enabled him to become one of the largest landowners in the region, with vast holdings around Esopus and across the Hudson in Dutchess. His son Martinus Jr. married Tryntje Benson, of Swedish descent, and the two settled on his father's acres in Dutchess County. Here a happy combination of wealth and strong character made Martinus a colonel in the local militia, a judge, and a justice of the peace. His estate became one of the finest in the area. If nothing else, ownership of ten slaves raised the Hoffmans high above their fellow settlers.

The marriage of Isaac and Cornelia stands as a milestone in another way. In the third American generation, a Roosevelt was marrying a girl who was not of Dutch or Dutch-German descent. The strains that poured into the line leading to Theodore Roosevelt remained almost entirely Dutch until 1835. In the Franklin line—where Isaac stands—bloods mingle earlier. Cornelia Hoffman brought Swedish-Finnish blood, but it cannot be said this was all she contributed. Years later, from the White House, Franklin Roosevelt wrote somewhat testily to a genealogist who, the President thought, had oversimplified the family tree by attributing pure bloods to its various branches:

My ancestors were, in most cases, not of the pure bloods of any of these nations. For example, my great-great-great grandmother was Cornelia Hoffman. She married Isaac Roosevelt . . . but she herself was about the fourth generation in this country. Her father's paternal ancestor came from Sweden, but he was only one of eight or sixteen ancestors who lived in America. Probably the other seven or the other fifteen (depending on the generation) were of Dutch or Scotch or English or German stock—or a combination of them.

As a bride, Cornelia dutifully left her fine Dutchess County home to become mistress of the small stone house on Wall Street. The years following proved happy ones for the couple, but they were not without tragedy. Two years after the Dutchess County wedding, the hand of Isaac Roosevelt made these entries in the family Bible:

Aug. 13. Monday Morning, one o'clock, our first son was borne, on Wednesday, ye 15th of do August was Baptized and named Abraham. Having for his Godfather and Godmother Jacobus Roosevelt and Catherine Roosevelt, who being his grandfather and mother.

. . . This our first son died in the Lord on Tuesday afternoon at four o'clock on the second day of October in the same year, being seven weeks and one day old, and interred in the family vault in the New Dutch Church Yard.

A year later similar entries in the family Bible marked the passing of Marinus Roosevelt, aged eleven months.

The Roosevelts were never merchant barons like the Waltons, Livingstons, and other families who derived great fortunes from trading, privateering, and even smuggling. Yet for a family that never owned a ship they did exceedingly well. By 1760 the energetic Johannes, billikin son of the patriarch Nicholas, was dead. But his equally energetic brother Jacobus, father of Isaac, remained hale and hearty; he was to live until 1776, thus reaching the same advanced age at which his father Nicholas had left the earth. In 1760 Jacobus, a man approaching seventy, was busily engaged with his friend Philip Livingston in starting a legal lottery. The family Yale graduate, Johannes son of Jacobus, was prospering as a merchant-grocer, a profession of considerable prominence in the town. His cousin Jacobus, son of Johannes, was a hardware merchant on Maiden Lane, chafing because England's strict laws kept him from importing unusual commodities from Holland and other countries.

The poll lists of the early part of the decade show three different Roosevelts with the name of Jacobus, together with an Isaac, Nicholas, Peter, and Oliver. However, the name of Jacobus was headed for oblivion with the Anglicizing of New York. It was becoming James, even in the Roosevelt family, while Johannes turned into John.

Of these Roosevelt males, Isaac possessed in largest measure the dignity and ability that command respect. By his mid-thirties he was already a prominent citizen of New York. If his personality shines correctly from old records, he was a sophisticated type, ever calm and assured. Indeed, it is hard to visualize such an impeccable man running a messy sugar refinery, or even stepping inside such a workaday establishment.

Isaac's name is found on many committees of the day. He was present when a group of merchants formed the New York Chamber of Commerce, the first such body to emerge on the continent. He was also among the incorporators of the city's first hospital. One of the great terrors of the time was fire. When it broke out, neighbors ran to assist in passing buckets of water from hand to hand. But sometimes neighbors failed to respond and the city was in need of trained firemen and equipment. This vital matter was discussed by responsible citizens at a meeting convened in 1762 at the City Arms Tavern. An account of the meeting was subsequently dispatched to Lord Stirling, the current Governor. Isaac Roosevelt wrote and signed this report. Then he personally sent it to the Governor.

Such responsibilities made him a distinguished person, quite worthy of friendship with the Waltons, then the most aristocratic family in New York. Isaac was never on close terms with William Walton, the proud leader of the clan, who was formidable and violently pro-British. But he was a close friend of Abraham Walton, William's favorite nephew. In time, a son of Isaac married a Walton, thus adding the aristocratic Walton blood to the Franklin line.

Following the unhappy death of their first two sons, Isaac and Cornelia had eight more children. One of them died in infancy. The first child to survive was a daughter named Catherine, who lived as a spinster until the age of fifty. In 1760 the couple produced a son, born in excellent health. He was christened Jacobus I, but in accord with the new era grew up James Roosevelt. He attended Princeton and married Mary Eliza Walton. Another son died as a Princeton student, while a daughter died at the age of twenty. Cornelia Roosevelt grew up to marry Dr. Benjamin Kissam. Maria married Richard Varick, who became a mayor of New York. Isaac and Cornelia's last-born was a daughter named Helena, who came along in 1768. She also was a spinster.

For a time this large family inhabited the stone house near the sugar refinery. Then, in 1772, Isaac moved to a nearby home recently occupied by his brother Jacobus I. Roosevelt. This dwelling also backed on the sugar refinery, but faced on Queen (later Pearl) Street rather than Wall.

Jacobus I. Roosevelt had violently broken the family pattern by never taking a bride. Whether this was due to misogyny, rugged independence, or ill-health the record fails to reveal. But the bachelor Jacobus died suddenly in his early fifties, and the untimely event was given important coverage in the *Gazette and Weekly Mercury*:

On Tuesday last Mr. Jacobus Roosevelt, of this city, being in Health, and no otherways heated than by the Weather, which was extremely hot, drank pretty freely of cold Water from the Well in his sugar house yard. He was presently seiz'd with a Pain in the Stomach and Aching in the Bones, which obliged him to go to Bed; Physicians were sent for, and proper Medicines administered, but his Illness continued till next day at 11 o'clock when he grew better and the Doctors had Hopes of his Recovery—But about 12 o'clock he was seized with violent Pains as before, and in a short Time expired; soon after which his flesh turn'd yellow, as in Jaundice. He was a Batchelor, bore an excellent character, was unusually beloved and esteemed, and is generally lamented by all his Acquaintances.

Isaac apparently waited a short interval and then took possession of his older brother's home, which was larger than his own. The new house faced the Walton mansion, a fact duly stressed in the announcement Isaac placed in the *Mercury*:

Isaac Roosevelt is removed from his house in Wall Street to the House of his late brother Jacobus Roosevelt Jr., deceased, near the Sugar House, and opposite to Mr. William Walton's, being on the northwest side of Queen Street.

"A steady widening and quickening of the democratic spirit is the thread upon which to hang the history of early New York," writes Rufus Rockwell King.

Contributing to the city's desire for independence were further repressive trade measures from England and the governors sent from abroad to hold the reins of the colony. Watching the glaring ineptitudes of these governors, New Yorkers realized it would be possible to do a better job governing themselves.

Growing discontent vitalized a Popular party which carried on the tradition of the old Leislerites. In the best spirit of Nicholas, members of the Roosevelt family became stalwarts of the Popular cause. In *The Memorial History of the City of New York*, historian James Grant Wilson puts them first among those who supported the Popular party. Next in line come Bayards, Beekmans, and Stuyvesants. Opposing the liberal Popular party was the so-called Court party, controlled by merchant-aristocrat Tories who sought favors from governors and for reasons of personal enrichment wished to remain friendly with Britain. The two parties waged a seesaw battle for the votes in the Assembly which, because it held the purse strings, was the actual seat of city power. When the Popular party gained power in the Assembly, says one writer,

"It addressed the English officials in language that showed a new spirit among the people."

With tact and firmness the British might have calmed this mounting unrest. For the colonists retained a split personality where England was concerned. No matter how ardent their political feelings, most colonists felt proud to be part of so mighty an empire. True, they had no representative in the British Parliament, but local Assemblies gave the illusion of self-government. More than this, life under a king was the accepted pattern of the day.

Nor were the social aspects of British rule to be discounted. "The gay people of New York are fond of noble names and royal lineage, however tainted or impure," states one writer. Government House was a brilliant social center, with Grand Balls on the King's birthday and on other English holidays. The high panoply of the balls and the sight of his lordship abroad in his handsome carriage always proved a pleasant opiate.

Colonists might fume at laws ordering them to quarter soldiers and sailors in their homes, calling the officers arrogant and the enlisted men dirty. The navy was especially hated, since press gangs grabbed strong citizens from the streets and thrust them into His Majesty's Service. But to counteract this, officers in bright uniforms brought great color to the social life of the town. With the city as headquarters for advance planning for the French and Indian War, as well as for the sea conquest of Madagascar, New York became a London in minature, the gayest of colonial towns.

But even the gaiety changed after George III mounted the throne of England at the tender age of twenty-two. This narrow-minded, erratic, bigoted young man listened closely to admirals and generals who recounted tales of splendid dinners served by liveried Negroes at mansions like the Walton home in New York. Soon he made up his mind that everyone in the North Americas was wealthy and should pay more money into the coffers of the Empire.

The English Parliament, controlled by a group of reactionaries, was perfectly willing to fall in with such a policy. So King and Parliament began imposing new internal taxes on the colonies. The most infamous of these was the Stamp Act, which became the real opening wedge in the break between colonies and mother country. Imposed in 1765, the act itself was not an overly oppressive measure. It merely decreed that all deeds, receipts, and legal papers—including marriage licenses—be written or printed on specially stamped paper by English revenue collectors. To the colonists, however, the act meant more. It had been imposed by Parliament despite the charters between the King and the provinces. Internal taxes were to be voted by the provincial colonies, since the colonies were not represented in Parliament. So here, in truth, was taxation without representation! A resolution adopted by twelve hundred citizens of New York said: "We think it essential to the security of the liberty and the prosperity of Englishmen that no taxes be imposed but by the gift of the people." The words were mild, but behind them lay anger.

In Parliament, William Pitt and Edmund Burke argued for the colonies but others talked of using military force to impose unpopular measures. "Is fighting a people the best way of gaining them?" Burke inquired sardonically. Parliament paid no heed. In the debate over the Stamp Act the term "Sons of Liberty" was coined for the protesting colonists. Intended as ridicule, the phrase soared across the Atlantic to ignite further sparks of rebellion. In October, 1765, as the first shipload of stamped paper arrived in New York, a crowd collected to prevent its landing. To their fury, the colonists found that Governor Sir Henry Moore had unloaded the paper in the middle of the previous night. The moment of protest then became November 1, when the act went into effect. On that day the backgammon boxes and dice at the popular Merchants Coffee House were covered with black cloth. In the morning two hundred merchants—it is to be supposed that Isaac Roosevelt and his cousins were among them—met at Burns' City

Tavern to vote a boycott on all English goods. Both retailers and artisans vowed on the spot to buy nothing sent to this country from England.

This subtle step did little to satisfy the passions of the angry mob. That night a crowd gathered on the Fields, the name now given to the level ground around the present City Hall. After listening to fiery speeches, the crowd—the Tory aristocrats of the Court party called it a rabble—began to march down Broadway to the fort, torches and lanterns lighting the way.

At Wall Street they were met by a group of men who stood across the street with arms locked, barring the way. This was Mayor Cruger and his aldermen, among them Cornelius and Nicholas Roosevelt. Bearing no ill will toward the mayor and aldermen, the mob merely surged left down Wall Street, turning right at Broad, in order to approach the fort from a different direction. As they roared by on the street, bewigged Court party aristocrats looked down on them from lighted windows. At Bowling Green the crowd rapidly demolished the Bowling Green fence erected by Johannes Roosevelt and his associates. On the Green itself they build a huge bonfire, burning effigies of Governor Moore and staff. An attempt to break into the fort was driven back by red-coated soldiers. The mob then plunged northward to sack the beautiful Hudson-side home of Major James, British military commander.

The scene was much different five months later when the Stamp Act was repealed. Pressure from money-minded British merchants, rather than the protests of colonists, had brought about the repeal. Even so, New York had a giant celebration, with every light in the city shining. It was also the King's birthday, so that even those faithful to the crown had reason to celebrate.

But if the King was a year older, he had grown no wiser. He appointed Charles Townshend as Chancellor of the Exchequer. Townshend had voted for the Stamp Act and still favored it, despite its repeal. Undaunted by the Stamp Act uproar, Town-

shend began imposing others on the colonies. The Revenue Act
. . . the Sugar Act . . . the Tea Act . . . the Molasses Act. Each was
accompanied by new turmoil.

The freedom-minded city was kept in constant unrest by the
activities of the Sons of Liberty, informally known as Liberty
Boys, led by Isaac ("King") Sears, a former privateer, and John
Lamb, who rose to be a general in the Revolution. There were
daily scuffles with British troops; incendiary notices posted in the
dark of night; the sudden appearance of newspapers with fighting
editorials. Mobs of patriots freed men arrested by the British;
artisans refused to build barracks for new English redcoats; Tories
were tarred and feathered; and sometimes Tories tarred and
feathered in return. In addition to dashing captains like Sears and
Lamb, the Liberty Boys included the so-called Leather Aprons—
artisans, skilled laborers, dock workers, clerks, sailors, apprentices,
and household servants. To some who favored revolution, the
Liberty Boys seemed rough and raucous. This caused the Popular
party to split into dignified Whigs and more rambunctious Sons of
Liberty. It was said of the two groups that the Whigs sipped
Madeira, while the Liberty Boys guzzled rum or beer.

Isaac Roosevelt became an outstanding Whig, but a few of his
cousins seemed closer to the Liberty Boys. His first cousin, hardware merchant James, was a burning patriot who had long been
blacklisted by the English as a Dutch malcontent. "While so many
Dutch prevail in the Province, I can have little hope of succeeding
in any enterprise," one governor had reported to London. James
was fifty years old, with a son of fifteen as violently patriotic as his
father. Another cousin, Cornelius, belied his sixty years by joining
the foot-soldier militia.

If his cousins seemed to be applying raw emotion to the patriot
cause, sophisticated Isaac was prepared to offer brains and money.
The community was well aware of the fact. In the turbulent days
of 1775 each colony chose a Committee of Observation to make
sure the edicts of the Continental Congress were carried out. Isaac
and his cousin Nicholas Roosevelt were among the sixty men

chosen by New York to serve. From these sixty members eleven were selected as delegates to the Provincial—as opposed to Continental—Congress. Isaac Roosevelt was among the eleven. The names of the men were read aloud at the foot of a liberty pole that had been erected on the Fields, and Isaac must have been there, his feet planted firmly on this hallowed spot.

The date was April 20, 1775. . . .

5

ISAAC THE PATRIOT

ON SUNDAY, APRIL 23, AT FOUR O'CLOCK IN THE AFTERNOON, A horseman galloped furiously down Broadway. The eyes of both horse and rider were bloodshot and the man swayed from exhaustion in the saddle. Pulling up short before the local Sons of Liberty headquarters, he identified himself as a courier from Boston, by name Israel Bissell. Then he shouted news of the battle of Lexington, fought at four in the morning the previous Wednesday.

Bissell had been ordered to alarm the countryside as far south as Philadelphia. He was succeeding. As if he waved a magic wand, quiet towns and villages sprang into frantic life after he passed. Minutemen carrying muskets swarmed to local commons, making preparations to march on Boston. In New York, Bissell paused briefly for food, then galloped on to Philadelphia, where he arrived in twenty-four hours. Throughout New Jersey patriots responded to his news by grabbing up arms.

In New York copies of the dispatch Bissell carried were posted in all places of public meeting. On Monday business practically ceased. Bodies of armed citizens collected to drill and parade in

the streets. Showing rare discretion, the outnumbered redcoats—
General Gage had recently removed his main army to Boston—
confined themselves to barracks, offering no resistance as Liberty
Boys boarded two English ships in the harbor. The ships were
ready to sail for Boston carrying supplies to General Gage. Cargoes
said to be worth 80,000 pounds sterling were lugged ashore and
stored for Continental use.

In a few days emphasis swung from the military to the political
as delegates to the Second Continental Congress in Philadelphia
began passing through the city. Outstanding among them was
John Hancock, Boston shipper and president of the Congress.
Hancock had left a new bride behind to make this journey. Three
miles from New York City he was to be met by a company of
militia and escorted the remainder of the way to town. Gentlemen
on horseback and ladies in carriages, together with hundreds afoot,
followed the militia to this point of meeting.

The cheering throng embarrassed Hancock and the feeling increased when, at the outskirts of town, citizens unhitched his
horses and themselves pulled the carriage to its destination. Accumulating delegates from New Jersey as he went, Hancock proceeded in triumph to Philadelphia, where he ceased to be the
vocal figure of the Revolutionary cause. Colonel George Washington of Virginia was appointed commander in chief of the army
now gathering around Boston, and from then on his stalwart
figure became the symbol of the American Revolution.

New York patriots went wild on July 25 when Washington,
accompanied by Generals Lee and Schuyler, arrived in the city en
route to Boston. Ten companies of militia and members of the
Continental Congress greeted him. Attired in a blue uniform,
with plumes in his hat, the General rode up Broadway in a carriage drawn by six white horses. Curiously enough, Governor
Tryon, the English ruler of the colony, returned from England on
the same day. This put city officials in a difficult position, for New
York was still under British rule, with Tryon its royal governor.
Nearly half the population was as glad to see him return as the

patriots were to welcome Washington. Tryon unwittingly solved the problem by arriving late in the evening. Met at the Battery by a subdued crowd, he slipped quietly into the Governor's Mansion. As days passed, he felt increasing uneasiness and transferred the seat of British government to the man-of-war *Duchess of Gordon,* anchored in the harbor.

Washington remained in the city for several days, discussing with King Sears and John Lamb the equipping and training of several thousand soldiers assigned to New York by the Congress. Shortly Congress convened in New York and appointed Isaac Roosevelt and two other leading citizens to survey local residences and buildings for quarters in which to house officers and troops.

While Isaac scoured the town looking for available space, other Roosevelts leaped to arms. Nicholas II, son of goldsmith Nicholas I, was sixty-one years old when the war began. Nonetheless, this vigorous patriot became a first lieutenant in the Corsicans, a colorful upstate militia company, on whose green shirts red hearts made of tin read "God and Right." On their cocked hats the Corsicans displayed another emblem: "Liberty or Death."

Even more dashing in appearance was John Roosevelt, Isaac's older brother and the first Roosevelt to attend college. He became a captain in the Oswego Rangers, cutting such a gallant figure in uniform of blue coat and white trousers that he was picked as the Ranger spokesman. In 1776 he appeared before the Provincial Congress to offer the services of his outfit. He made such an impression on the Congress that he was chosen as liaison man between Congress and local colonial troops.

The British army remained quietly in Boston during the winter of 1775-76. Washington and his colonials watched them from outside the city. In March, General Sir William Howe's army suddenly quit Boston. Washington had expected his adversary to move on New York and had completed plans to shift the Continental army there. Instead, Howe led his men to Halifax, where he awaited more arms and troops from abroad. Even so, the Continental army marched to New York. Washington knew the British Parliament had decreed the capture of New York as the first step in a master plan for subjugation of the colonies. With New York captured, Generals Burgoyne and Sir Guy Carleton would move down from Canada and divide the colonies. Meanwhile, Lord Cornwallis would ravage Virginia and the southern colonies.

General Israel Putnam led the first division of the Continental army into New York. He made his headquarters in the Kennedy mansion at 1 Broadway. General Washington arrived ten days later, accompanied by his wife and family. He took the famous Richmond Hill House, a mansion at the south end of the area known as Greenwich Village.

It made for great excitement, with troops drilling on the Common, generals on horseback riding importantly through streets, and the intoxicating aroma of rebellion in the air. On July 5, 1776, word arrived from Philadelphia that the Declaration of Independence had been signed the previous day. Washington received a formal copy of the Declaration on July 9, with orders to have it read aloud to all troops. At six that evening the American army drew up around the Fields while each commander read the Declaration to his men. Washington and his staff sat motionless on horseback in the center. In the city below, church bells sounded and cannon roared. At the end of the ceremony onlookers broke loose and did what they had talked of for months. A crowd hauled down the gilded lead equestrian statue of George III on Bowling Green. The heavy statue was then transported to Connecticut to be melted into bullets.

On July 18 the Declaration of Independence was read aloud to civilians from the balcony of City Hall. A huge throng jammed into the area around Wall Street and Broad, greeting each sentence with shouts of approval. At the end mob spirit again took over. One daring group entered the courtroom inside City Hall. Yanking down the royal coat of arms, rioters burned it in the street.

But high hopes drooped on the morning citizens awoke to find the sails of 130 ships whitening the harbor. This was the fleet of Admiral Lord Howe, arrived from Halifax, loaded with veterans and fresh reinforcements. Among the new troops were 8,000 Hessians whose professional-soldier services had been purchased from German dukes at $34.50 a head. Already the English fleet was larger than the Spanish Armada, and before the eyes of astounded New Yorkers it continued to grow. "The ships kept coming like a swarm of locusts escaped from a bottomless pit," wrote an observer.

The full English fleet comprised 37 men-of-war and 400 transports. In the ships was an army of 23,000 British regulars plus the Hessians—31,000 in all—the finest army Europe could muster. For all its menace, the assembled fleet was a spectacular sight. New York City now had 25,000 inhabitants and 4,000 houses, built along both rivers below Chambers Street. Populace and soldiers sat on roofs or lined the waterfront, just to look. Howe landed as many of his men as possible on Staten Island; but even so, provisioning such a force was a huge task. One American, watching the fleet, prayed, "May God increase their wants!"

The American army numbered 28,000 troops. A few had seen action in the French and Indian War, but most were ardent amateurs who had done little more than drill on village greens. Some recruits could not tell right foot from left, causing officers to tie a piece of hay on one foot and straw on the other. "Hay foot—Straw foot!" they then called out. A great number of American soldiers were middle-aged, with others old or Falstaffian. American officers, on the other hand, were young and eager, though largely untrained. Typical of them was Alexander Hamilton, a recent student at King's College, slight of stature, self-confident, quick-witted, and brave.

Though it was summer, army volunteers had fallen sick. Of the 28,000 American troops, only 19,000 stood ready for battle; the remainder were on the sick list. The city itself was as ragtag as the troops. Streets were barricaded with boxes, beer kegs, piles of stones, branches of trees. The only near-professional fortifications lay at Brooklyn Heights and Columbia Heights.

It was brave! It was sad! "I could not get your shoes," volunteer Peter Elting wrote home, "on account of the alarm on the arrival of the fleet, since which almost all business in town is knocked up. The fleet lays very quiet at the watering place waiting a rein-forcement from England, when, they say, they shall little regard our batteries. Our men are in high spirits, and ready to meet them at any hour."

New York City was on the point of becoming a battleground, and the moment had arrived for responsible citizens to shutter homes and take wives, children, and older folk to safety. Men of property first stripped houses of brass doorknockers, sashweights, and anything else that might be melted into ammunition. This was given to the army. Then the exodus began.

Isaac Roosevelt, aged fifty, took his family to his wife's estate near Rhinebeck, in Dutchess County. There he joined the 6th Regiment of New York militia, carrying a rifle in local drills. But Isaac, whose calm good judgment had already been recognized by Congress, could be of more value in other realms. Late in 1776 Congress gave him the complicated task of providing the American colonies with currency. He was directed to turn £55,000 into 213,400 paper bills of varying denominations—an "emission" of currency, it was called. Isaac Roosevelt, heretofore best known as a sugar refiner, performed this feat.

James Roosevelt, hardware merchant, took his wife and family to Esopus. Then the fifty-one-year-old man enlisted as a private in state colonial troops, serving under Captains Hay and Yates. His son, James I, born in 1759, was only seventeen when the war began. Even so, the boy joined the Commissary Department of the army and served—without pay, it is said—through the long conflict. One of the elder James's cousins, Elbert Roosevelt, had married the daughter of Colonel Peter Theobold Curtius, commissary general of the army. It is likely that Colonel Curtius paved the youth's way into his department. Cornelius Roosevelt, middle-aged brother of the hardware merchant, became a private in the colonial troops and rose to the rank of ensign in the 1st Regiment of New York.

On the island of Manhattan, two days of battle led to both defeat and victory for the colonial cause. On September 15, Lord Howe launched a violent attack at Kips Bay, in which his trained soldiers proved superior to the Revolutionary army. With his battle all but won, Howe and his generals paused for tea and cakes with Mrs. Robert Murray, of Murray Hill. While the British army waited for its leaders to reappear, colonial troops from lower Manhattan escaped along a wooded road half a mile away.

Next day the battle of Harlem Heights was fought on a terrain one guidebook calls "charming wilderness." Uneven ground made guerrilla tactics possible and here the Americans excelled. Continental sharpshooters drove the British back from what today is 130th Street to 105th. The decisive moment came on ground now occupied by the campus of Columbia University. This time it was the British who fled in wild confusion, with Americans hooting and jeering behind. It was the first clean-cut American victory of the Revolution and remained a morale booster through the rest of the war.

However, it was too late to recapture lower Manhattan Island. One group of officers wished to steal back and set fire to the city, thus preventing its use as a British headquarters. Congress vetoed the idea. Even so, on the night of September 21, fire broke out in a tavern in Whitehall Street. It spread to destroy Trinity Church and 400 other buildings. The English were convinced that the blaze had been set by patriots and in a fury turned muskets on citizen-firefighters. Up to this moment a few stubborn patriots had thought it possible to remain in British-occupied New York. Now they, too, left the city.

So far as the colonial cause was concerned, New York remained a ghost town for the next seven years. It was an occupied city, under martial law. Trade was at a standstill, with wharves crumbling from disuse. The abandoned homes of patriots rotted away. The English used the unhappy city as a depot for stores and a hospital for British soldiers. But worst of all, it was a prison for captured Americans. Public buildings, among them King's College, were converted into prisons for 5,000 underfed men, while prison ships in the East River were fever-infested hulks.

Except for the city, however, New York State was in colonial hands. As such, it was free to govern itself. Late in 1776 a convention was called in Kingston, or Esopus, to write a state constitution. Isaac Roosevelt was a delegate, representing the displaced folk of New York City. No doubt he stood close to John Jay on April 22, 1777, as that worthy mounted a barrel outside the Kingston courthouse to proclaim the new constitution as law. The first governor of the state was George Clinton, a close friend of Isaac's. Isaac himself was elected to the state Senate, becoming a member of the Governor's inner council.

During the Revolution Isaac's son James, born in 1760, grew to manhood. In spite of the war, he was able to attend Princeton, and graduated in 1780. Three years later he rode at his father's side as the exiled family returned to a New York grudgingly evacuated by the British at war's end. The Roosevelts found scars of the great fire of 1776 still visible. Indeed, the whole city had fallen into a state of decay. Grass grew uncut on lawns and thoroughfares, and a general air of listlessness pervaded the once bustling town. Isaac and his family found that they now resided on Pearl Street; the name Queen Street had vanished with victory. Neither home nor Sugar House had been badly harmed by the English. In this, the Roosevelts were fortunate. The Rhinelander Sugar House, used by the British as part of a prison, had been ruined.

Isaac immediately resumed his place as a prominent citizen of the city. On September 25, 1783, General Washington marched down Broadway at the head of a victorious army. That night he said farewell to his officers at a famous dinner in Fraunces Tavern where strong men wept at parting. A short time later His Excellency Governor Clinton and Council tendered a dinner to Washington. Isaac Roosevelt was the person in charge of all arrangements and he duly submitted a bill for £156 which included:

             120 dinners
             135 bottles Madeira
              36 port
              60 English beer
              30 Bouls punch
              60 Wine glasses broken
               8 Cutt decandters broken
                  Coffee for 8 Gentlemen
               8 dinners for Musick
              10 for Sarvts

For a year afterward Isaac devoted most of his time to teaching his son James the business of sugar refining. Eventually he felt secure enough to place the following advertisement in local gazettes:

Isaac Roosevelt, having repaired his Sugar House, is now carrying on his business of refining as formerly, and has for sale (by himself and Son) at his house 159 Pearl Street, opposite the Bank, Loaf, Lump, and strained Muscovado Sugars and Sugar House treacle. The New Emission Money will be received in full value as payment.

A short time later another notice signed by Isaac Roosevelt appeared. It indicates that he was using indentured servants in his refinery. This practice was frowned upon by some upright citizens of the day who saw it as a form of slavery. However, others found nothing wrong. Though the children of slaves were by city law born free, it was still possible—and would be so until 1826—to buy and use adult slaves in New York City. Indentured servants —who sold their services in order to get to these shores—were often treated no better than slaves. Isaac Roosevelt seems to have been a man of integrity and compassion, but his announcement about two escaped servants reflects the harsh attitude of the times:

Run away, two indented German servantmen, who came here last year, named Peter Sweine and Jacob Rank, neither of whom can speak

English, they were last seen near King's Bridge, and it is supposed
intend for Albany. Eight dollars reward for each will be paid by Isaac
Roosevelt . . .

While Isaac worked to set a new life in order, other Roosevelts
busily did the same. First cousin James reopened his hardware
store at 102 Maiden Lane. Here he was joined by his supremely
patriotic son James I, who had worked without pay in the Commissary Department throughout the war. James I, now about
twenty-five, next married Maria van Schaack, adding another link
in the line toward Theodore Roosevelt. In 1786 Cornelius Roosevelt, uncle of James I, and an assistant alderman, began building a
handsome home on the land where the Woolworth Building now
stands.

But as always Isaac was the prominent Roosevelt. He was still a
state senator, with another career about to open for him. After a
short period of apathy New York responded with renewed vigor to
the era of independence. "The release of energy was terrific," says
one writer about the new spirit of enterprise. One symptom was
the awareness on the part of local businessmen of the need for a
bank. A group of merchants—Isaac among them—set about char-
tering the Bank of New York, with an office in the front parlor of
William Walton's home on Pearl Street. This was the second bank
organized in the country and the first in New York. Alexander
Hamilton wrote its charter and Alexander McDougal, a onetime
Liberty Boy, was first president of the enterprise. Two years later
he resigned and Isaac Roosevelt was elected president of the Bank
of New York.

When this occurred Isaac was sixty. He lived in the Pearl Street
house, comfortably close to the refinery and across the street from
the bank. With him were his wife and his two spinster daughters,
Catherine and Helena. His second son, Martin, had died in 1781.

In the tradition of the times, Isaac rose early and after breakfast
hastened to the Sugar House to discuss the day's work with his son
James, who had married Mary Eliza Walton in 1786 and moved to
18 South Street. This done, Isaac crossed Pearl Street to enter the

one-room Bank of New York, always arriving before ten, the hour of opening. The bank closed its doors to the public at one, at which time Isaac repaired to his home for a hearty dinner. Returning to his office in the bank after this midday meal, he worked with his clerk until sundown on banking and personal matters. From his father, who had died in 1776, Isaac had inherited £650 outright, together with the responsibility of acting as executor of a large estate which included buildings, city lots, farmland, and legacies for the education of grandchildren.

At sundown Isaac might go home for supper with his family, or to an ale- or coffeehouse for a bracing mimbo (rum and loaf sugar) or calibogus (rum and beer) followed by a supper of turtle soup and oysters. Here he might enjoy a stimulating political discussion with friends like John Hancock or Alexander Hamilton. Or he might go to a board meeting of the New York Hospital or a gathering of state senators.

A Whig before the war, Isaac was a Federalist now, a strong supporter of his friend Hamilton in the so-called "party of wealth and talent" which stood for strong national government, a powerful army, and the formality and etiquette of a court. The Federalists had little use for the French, despite the great assistance given in 1776 and after, and would soon view the French Revolution with distaste. The Democratic-Republican party, on the other hand, stood for less complex government, a well-drilled militia rather than a standing army, and a democratic approach to the ceremonies of politics.

At the state convention in June, 1788, held to ratify the Constitution of the United States, the two parties fought bitterly. New York's great commercial advantages, together with the state's territorial size, had always given it a preponderance of power. Yet under the Constitution it would in some ways have no more influence than the smallest state. Eight states had already ratified the Constitution and only one more was needed to bring the national government into being. But the delegates at Poughkeepsie were in no hurry to be the ninth state and thus authorize thirteen states—all equal. Through a hot summer the balance of power seesawed between the Federalists, led by John Jay, and the Republicans, headed by Governor Clinton.

Isaac Roosevelt, like future members of the clan, was a demon letter writer. From the heart of the Federalist camp he wrote to his friend Richard Varick: "We now permit our opponents to go on with their objections and propose their amendments without interruption. When they have got through we may fully learn their intentions." Finally, New York ratified the Constitution long after the majority of other colonies.

In view of this, it is surprising to find the city of New York designated the national capital, site-to-be of the inauguration of the first President. Somewhat surprised themselves, city fathers hastily subscribed $32,000 to transform the City Hall at Wall and Broad Streets into a Federal Hall. The money was turned over to Major Pierre Charles L'Enfant, the Frenchman who later designed the city of Washington. L'Enfant provided a Senate Chamber and Hall of Representatives, lavishing much care on the balcony, then called a gallery, on which the President would take the oath of office.

Hazards of travel kept Congress from convening until April 6, 1789. Then it unanimously elected George Washington first President of the United States. He began a triumphal journey to New York City, arriving on the 24th.

Inauguration Day was April 30 and never, citizens said, had such a crowd filled the city. Visitors arrived from town, hamlet, and village for hundreds of miles around. At nine in the morning of the great day every bell in the city pealed, then suddenly stopped. Traffic was barred from the streets near Federal Hall, allowing the crowd to fill the area. Then church bells tolled again, summoning people to religious services. Soldiers in military array stood before the Cherry Street mansion chosen by Washington as his residence. To the sound of martial music, the General proceeded along Pearl Street to Broad and up to Wall. The personage who held the head of Washington's horse during this march was, according to family legend, none either than Isaac Roosevelt.

Before Federal Hall the military opened ranks, allowing Washington and escorting dignitaries to enter. He next appeared on the balcony, where State Chancellor Robert Livingston administered the oath of office. It is said that not a whisper came from the crowd during the ceremony. At the end of the oath Livingston turned to the crowd and shouted, "Long Live George Washington, President of the United States!" The crowd responded with a thunderous roar, while bells all over the city pealed and cannon boomed from fort and ships.

That night the city was lighted in every possible way. At eight o'clock the boom of thirteen cannons summoned crowds to the harbor for a fireworks display commencing with thirteen rockets shot at the sky. Most of the assembled people had never seen such wonders and gasped with astonishment over rockets, fountains of fire, and Roman candles. Finally a second salvo of thirteen rockets closed the display. People then walked or rode in carriages to stare at the illuminated mansions where balls were in full swing. Taverns remained open all night and were patronized to capacity.

For a year New York showed the gaudy trappings of a royal town, with ceremony outdoing the days of the English governors. A court was the only precedent in government, and as a Federalist stronghold New York was only too willing to follow the established pattern. Never have such figures appeared on the sidewalks of New York! Alexander Hamilton, a familiar sight, was joined by Vice-President Adams, Secretary of State Thomas Jefferson, and Chief Justice Jay, together with Cabinet members, senators, and representatives from the thirteen states. Even more dazzling were the foreign dignitaries, led by Count de Mousier of France, a gentleman who wore earrings and high red heels.

Washington himself, a commanding six-foot-three figure, could often be seen striding along downtown streets, for distances in the city were so small there was no point in riding. The President also had a striking canary-colored state coach, shaped like a half pumpkin and ornamented with cupids, emblazoned with the Washington coat of arms and drawn by four white horses. On Sundays he liked to ride in it with his family, taking what came to be known as the Fourteen Mile Ride. Driving up the good roads on the East River side of Manhattan, he traveled as far north as 110th Street, then swung west and returned home by the good roads of the Hudson side.

Washington and his wife both held weekly levees, or receptions. The President's were late-afternoon affairs to which government officials, foreign diplomats, and local merchants were invited to exchange a few words with the Chief Executive. Members of the Republican party were critical of these gatherings, describing guests as "the fashionable, the elegant, and refined." They also complained that many of the wealthy New Yorkers invited were former Tories. In addition, the levees came under criticism for being stodgy to the point of dullness.

Mrs. Washington's levees, held on Friday nights, were no better. The President attended and, as nine o'clock approached, the First Lady raised her voice to say, "The General always retires at nine and I usually precede him."

Of the winter of 1789, a lady of fashion wrote, "It was a burst of splendor that has never been surpassed." And a Mrs. Iredell, wife of a Supreme Court justice, wondered, "Where shall I get the spirit to pay all the social debts I owe?" New York fully expected to continue as capital of the United States, and there was talk of cutting off the lower end of Manhattan from river to river to build "magnificent parliamentary buildings, each with a fine ocean view and surrounded by spacious grounds ornamented by shade trees and shrubbery."

But New York did not remain the presidential city. The usual reason given is that neither state nor city would cede the ten miles of territory requested by the federal government. A better reason, however, is that local-son Alexander Hamilton, in need of votes to pass his Funding and Assumption Bills, gave in to Southern legislators who—like President Washington—wanted the governing city on the Potomac. In any event, at the end of a year, Congress moved to Philadelphia to be nearer the projected seat of government.

Through all this Isaac Roosevelt, bank president and state senator, played a muted part. His wife Cornelia died on November 13, 1789, at the beginning of New York's winter of social glory. In death, Mrs. Isaac Roosevelt achieved a special distinction, for President Washington used her funeral as a means of circumscribing the duties of office. In his diary the conscientious Chief Executive wrote:

Received an invitation to attend the funeral of Mrs. Roosevelt (the wife of a Senator in this State), but declined complying with it, first, because the propriety of accepting an invitation of this sort appeared to be very questionable, and secondly, (though to do so in this instance might not be improper), because it might be difficult to discriminate in cases which might thereafter happen.

In 1791 Isaac Roosevelt reached the age of sixty-five. He decided to retire and quit his position at the bank, keeping only his presidency of the Society of the New York Hospital. His son James already had three children, one an Isaac. Isaac's cousin James was equally satisfied. His son James I had joined him in the hardware business which was now called Roosevelt and Son. Freed from the yoke of Britain, the firm began importing glass and other commodities. In addition, daughters of both Isaac and James had married well, producing families of suitable dimensions.

Looking around—as he must have—Isaac could see some fifty Roosevelt families in New York City, all stemming from Claes Martenszen and the six children of the patriarch Nicholas. Among them all he was known as Isaac the Patriot. There had been many sorrows in his life, probably the sharpest being the death of his second son. But there had been pleasure and fine accomplishment as well. In the Revolution he had been outstanding among those who governed rather than fought in battle. His had been a full, satisfying life, but now it was drawing slowly to a close.

On October 17, 1794, at the age of sixty-eight, he summoned a scrivener and dictated a will which filled seven parchment pages in the tight, shaded handwriting of the time. The will shows Isaac as both God-fearing and a man of property. He left the Sugar House, the ground it stood on, and his gold watch to son James. To his oldest daughter, Catherine, went the Roosevelt home. To daughters Catherine and Helena went carriages, horses, and servants. Having disposed of this private property, he takes up rents, income, interest, and real estate—the last an intricate detailing of parcels of land in spots like Old Slip, New Slip, Water Street, Front Street, Cherry Street, Peck Slip, and Roosevelt Wharf.

But most of all, Isaac's last will and testament shows a God-fearing man. He begins it with fervent invocation to Almighty God:

In the name of God Amen. I, Isaac Roosevelt, of the City of New York Merchant being now by God's mercy continued in life though in bodily weakness but of sound and disposing mind memory and understanding and being sensible of the uncertain time of this frail and transitory life and knowing that it is appointed for all men once to die Do make and I do by these presents make and publish & declare this my last will and Testament in manner and form following that is to say First and principally I recommend my soul into the merciful hands of Almighty God having a well grounded hope of being justified from all sin in and through the imputed Righteousness of Jesus Christ my Lord and redeemer by whose active and passive obedience he hath merited a pardon from all Sin and a right to eternal life for all who believe in him and obey his everlasting Gospel on which alone I trust for a glorious and happy Immortality to everlasting life And my body I commit to the Earth to be interred in the family Vault in such decent manner as my Children shall think proper expecting a joyful resurrection to eternal life when my redeemer shall come in his Glory to judge the world in righteousness at the last day And as it hath pleased God in his Holy providence to bless me with the enjoyment of a temporal estate I do give devise and bequeath . . .

Two years later Isaac died. Tributes from friends and associates stressed his contribution to the Revolution. "He was," wrote one friend, "beloved and honored as a tried, true, and constant patriot."

6

THE FAMILY PERSONALITY

SO THE ROOSEVELTS ENDED A CENTURY AND A HALF IN THE LAND TO which Claes Martenszen van Rosenvelt and his wife Jannetje had journeyed from Holland.

In those years Roosevelts, male and female, had married into families named Hardenbroeck, Comfort, Tappan, de la Montague, De Peyster, Lounsbury, Low, de Reimer, Thurman, Van Vleeck, Provost, Schuyler, Walton, Burke, Duffie, Varick, Kissam, Bayley, Van Schaack, and other fine lines. Bolstered by such bloods, the family in each generation displayed a remarkable ability to swim in the mainstream of American life: farmer to fur trader, to buyers of real estate, to merchants and importers, to a man of distinction in the person of Isaac.

Yet with this ability to thrive on contemporary life, the Roosevelts never lost sight of the family motto. Claes Martenszen had been one of the planters of the New World, and his descendants believed in caring for it. Freemen . . . assistant aldermen . . . aldermen . . . members of the City Council . . . Revolutionary Committees . . . each Roosevelt generation boasted members who promoted civic affairs and engaged in city politics.

As a group, the Roosevelts prospered. If there were any poor relations among them in 1800, the printed record hides it well. Instead, a contemporary account calls the family "more than prosperous, capable, prominent." The Roosevelts never accumulated money on the scale of the Vanderbilts or Astors. Describing his ancestors in his Harvard sophomore thesis, Franklin D. Roosevelt states: "None were poor, yet none were ever exceptionally rich or founded great fortunes." Still, from Nicholas on, the family waxed comfortable and became more so with each generation.

The family also showed a happy ability to marry well. Roosevelt girls married into prosperous, established families, while males of the clan showed rare skill in choosing girls who were congenial partners, willing bearers of children—a child every two years was the usual pace—and at the same time brought into wedlock helpful contributions of money and property. Roosevelt marriages offer still another pattern. Males of the family either married young, taking brides of seventeen or eighteen, a year or so younger than themselves, or remained bachelors until the arrival of middle age, then wed young girls.

For second marriages, Roosevelt widowers usually picked women of their own vintage. Once married, Roosevelt men made excellent husbands who cherished wives and children. When James Roosevelt's wife, Mary Eliza, died in 1810, the bereaved man wrote that she had been the "most affectionate, best of wives, and most tender of mothers." The same words could be applied to most Roosevelt helpmates. Yet James followed still another family pattern after his beloved wife died. He did not pine for his dead Eliza or otherwise fall into a decline. While continuing to cherish her memory, he married twice more before death claimed him. It was always seemly for a man—a Roosevelt especially—to have a spouse!

By 1800 Roosevelt money had become as tangible a part of life as the air the family breathed or the food it consumed. Writing later of Theodore Roosevelt, Professor Howard Beale says, "An important influence on [his] life was his forebears' long-established enjoyment of more than comfortable means and, in some cases, great wealth, that created a sense of security."

By the same year the era of comfortable means and great wealth had already begun. At the same time the family had developed a strong cultural curiosity, for the strain which turned Nicholas I into a silversmith and made the billikin Johannes an extravagant importer of art was never absent in any generation of Roosevelts. Among future members of the family were many supervoracious readers and some early Roosevelts seem to have had the same interest. There is evidence of it in the musty records of the New York Society Library. In a single year James Roosevelt, son of Isaac, read the following books:

Gordon's History of the American War, 3 volumes; Tour through France; Bachelor of Salamancha, 2 volumes; Smyth's Tour in the United States, 2 volumes; Hayley's plays; Hume's History of England, 8 volumes; Smollet's History of England, 7 volumes; Cotton Mather's works; Emmeline, 2 volumes; Arundel, 2 volumes; Brydone's Tour through Sicily and Malta; Political magazine, 5 volumes; Fair Syrian, 2 volumes; Caroline of Litchfield, 2 volumes; Modern Times or Gabrial Outcast; Cook's Voyages, 4 volumes; Life of Putnam; Hawkesworth's Voyages, 2 volumes; Johnson's Anecdotes; Henriade: Zoriada; Lady Luxborough's letters to Shenstone; Beauties of magazines; Pliny's Epistles; Emma Corbett; Temple's Works; Wilson's Pelew Islands; Herring's letters; Power of Sympathy, 2 volumes; Marriage Act, 2 volumes; Rowe's callipaedia; Cotton's Works; Smith's Universalist.

James Roosevelt was a Princeton graduate and might be expected to be a scholarly man. But his cousin Cornelius, a busy man with no particular educational advantages, read almost as many books during the same year. The library charged a fine of a penny a day for keeping books over a week, but no Roosevelt ever paid it. In their prodigious reading James and Cornelius were doing somewhat more than displaying mental depth. The two Roosevelts were again proving the family knack for being an integral part of the times. In this remarkable era, men of affairs devoted long hours to work, wrote letters in laborious longhand, and kept intimate diaries. At the same time they managed to read great numbers of books. Even in his year of reading, James Roosevelt failed to match the number of books devoured by John Jay, who averaged three heavy tomes a week. Lawyer Aaron Burr took out nearly as many from the library. So did Alexander Hamilton, but he showed a dismaying partiality for novels.

Having established themselves as part of the time, the Roosevelts next began to make the world aware of an unusual amount of family energy. It was as if, following one hundred fifty years of behaving with Dutch doggedness and devout godliness, family members had reached a point of throwing off conformity to step forth as highly individualistic persons.

But their most remarkable feature was always the unusual amount of energy possessed by the family as a group. In time members of the clan themselves poked fun at this, declaring that at family gatherings everyone talked at once in loud voices, without listening to what others said. In the world outside Roosevelts enjoyed encountering other Roosevelts. In any large group they gravitated toward each other, to converse with zest and vehemence, oblivious to others around. From generation to generation an extraordinary ebullience is apparent, as if freedom from money worry and confidence in the New World permitted family members to lead the fullest possible lives. Instead of remaining conformists, the Roosevelts began to flex muscles and become conspicuous.

In New York the family had even become so prominent that people gossiped about them. One tale of Little Old New York concerns a young lady named Janet Roosevelt, described as clever and extremely lovely. Her story is to be found in a series of books called *The Old Merchants of New York*. Despite this staid title, the books are gossipy and often malicious.

As detailed therein, the life of Janet Roosevelt might have come from the intricate pen of novelist Henry James. In 1795 she married one Jansen Inderwick, a merchant who owned a fine city residence at 22 Cortlandt Street and a country estate set in the midst of twenty uptown acres. At first Inderwick only wanted to marry Janet, but once the knot was officially tied he dreamed of a child by her. No offspring arrived and Jansen became "morose, dejected, almost cruel." Janet must have found him totally cruel, for in September, 1803, she departed the Cortlandt Street mansion to take a suite of rooms in a respectable boardinghouse run by a Mrs. Riggs, on Broadway.

Here the Jamesian touches begin. For the separation between Jansen Inderwick and his wife Janet was a peculiar one. Each morning Jansen sent a carriage from his stable to the boarding-house on lower Broadway. With it went the young Negro slave girl who had been Janet's maid when she lived at Cortlandt Street. Once a week the maid brought a supply of money for Janet's living expenses. If the need for extra money arose, Jansen always handed it over—"whether it was one hundred dollars or five hundred dollars, he sent the amount required to her in Bank of New York notes."

Even as he did all this, Jansen Inderwick made a solemn vow never again to speak to his wife. At the same time the wealthy gentleman liked to give dinner parties. Every successful dinner requires a hostess, and on nights when Jansen entertained, a splendidly attired Janet returned to Cortlandt Street to act as her husband's hostess. Through such evenings neither husband nor wife spoke to the other. New York society was a trifle bewildered, but continued to invite the Inderwicks to outside dinner parties as a pair. Jansen and Janet made appearances together, enjoyed themselves, then retired to their respective beds without exchanging a word.

This odd state of affairs lasted until one Richard Rupert, described as a merchant from Nova Scotia, took a suite at the Riggs boardinghouse. Janet was, of course, lovely to look at; Rupert was a fine figure of a man. Proximity wove its spell and the handsome couple fell in love. "It was observed that he boldly entered her private apartments," reports the gossipy *Old Merchants*. On Sundays the attractive couple flaunted their love by riding out to-gether in the Inderwick carriage.

About a year after the appearance of Rupert, Janet and her young Negro maid suddenly vanished from New York. Richard Rupert also disappeared, apparently in another direction. Word soon began to circulate that Janet was visiting in Sussex, New Jersey, where she had unhappily contracted yellow fever. Two months later she returned to the boardinghouse, looking pale and haggard. Then it was noted that the Negro girl made daily visits to a brick house on Maiden Lane. On one floor resided William and Milly Seymour, just arrived from out of town. The Seymours were the parents of bouncing, newborn boy-and-girl twins. Curiously, the Seymours did not dress particularly well but the twins were always attired in smart baby clothes. Over the following months, the maid kept up her daily visits, though Janet Roosevelt was never observed near the Seymour home. Then the girl twin died. The boy survived, and gradually it became known that he bore the name Rupert Roosevelt Seymour.

A year later, in 1805, Jansen Inderwick died. Janet was still his wife, and his last will and testament did nothing to alter this lucra-tive status. The widow promptly moved back to the Cortlandt Street mansion and a few days later was driven to the Seymour quarters on Maiden Lane. She reacted with outrage at the condi-tion in which she discovered little Rupert Roosevelt and accused the Seymours of neglecting and mistreating the child. As a climax, she slapped Milly Seymour hard across the face. Departing, she promised to return the next day and take the boy away with her. When she did, the Seymours and the child were gone.

Janet was a wealthy widow, so it would seem that she could easily track down the fleeing family. Yet she was never able to find them. First, she put advertisements in city newspapers offering $1,000 reward for information about the child's whereabouts. Pre-sumably she also used the services of such private investigators as the era offered. All to no avail. Nor did Richard Rupert ever reappear to claim the hand of the wealthy widow Inderwick. Probably he was a philandering married man, with wife and family in Nova Scotia.

This story baffles students of Roosevelt family history. Can it be true? There are indications that it isn't. No record exists of a marriage between a Janet Roosevelt and Jansen Inderwick. Nor is there a Janet Roosevelt on the family tree at this moment. Yet some factors indicate at least partial truth. In other pages of *Old Merchants* the Roosevelts are spoken of with such respect that it scarcely seems likely that an author would suddenly switch to lies and libel. When the five-volume series was published, the Roosevelts were rich and powerful folk, in a position to fight any printed untruths. This opens the possibility that the sprightly author of *Old Merchants* knew of a skeleton in the Roosevelt closet and protected himself by changing the names of the principals.

While developing a family personality the Roosevelts inevitably produced a few members who, if not outright eccentrics, were at least original thinkers and stimulating characters. Foremost among them was Nicholas Roosevelt, who was born in 1767 and died eighty-seven years later, in 1854. Nicholas was an inventor, and every self-respecting Roosevelt son and daughter considers him the man who really invented the steamboat.

Nicholas was the youngest son of the hardware merchant James; his older brother was the stripling who worked through the Revolution in the Commissary Department of the American army. Nicholas himself was nine years old when the war began and sixteen when it ended. He went along when James took his wife and younger children to the safety of Kingston before the British attack on New York. Father and older son then went off to fight, leaving Nicholas to attend school and spend his off time in the barn-workshop of a tolerant neighbor named Joseph Oosterhaudt.

On summer days the boy fished and rowed on the Oosterhaudt pond. Young Nicholas had the type of inventive mind which can-

not do things without figuring ways of improvement. While rowing, he was struck by the idea of propelling the boat by means
other than human strength. A wheel of paddles perhaps, one
wheel over each side of the boat. Nicholas was only fifteen—"a big,
burly farm boy"—when this smote him. He was sure no one else
had ever thought of side wheels on a boat before, and he may have
been right.

Nicholas found a pair of old carriage wheels with an axle wider
than the boat. To each spoke he fastened a wooden paddle that
dipped into the water as the wheel turned. The job took over a
month to finish, and then the attempt to make it work was a
dismal failure. Far more muscle power was needed to turn paddle
wheels than to row a boat!

So Nicholas had only his idea of paddle wheels over the sides of
a boat. But how to turn the wheels? He was still pondering when,
after the Revolution, the family returned to its New York home at
62 Greenwich Street. Nicholas set about finishing his schooling in
New York, only to find that his parents expected him to enter the
hardware business. He rebelled—young Nicholas was more interested in learning how to forge heavy metals into new shapes and
balances. He became a blacksmith and by the age of twenty-one
had mastered the trade well enough to supervise other smithies.
Although Nicholas was no fanatic, dreaming and talking endlessly
of his paddle-wheel idea he kept mulling it and, according to one
story, made an attempt in Collect Pond to drive a boat with
paddle wheels turned by hickory and whalebone springs that un-
wrapped a cord bound around the axle. This, too, was a failure,
and he quit experimenting.

However, dreams rekindled when he—together with the rest of
the country—learned what a Philadelphian named John Fitch had
done with the condensing steam engine recently invented abroad
by Scotsman James Watt. Fitch placed the engine in a small boat,
fixing its piston to drive six paddles placed Indian-style over the
side. Nicholas was instantly impressed by the idea of a steam engine driving the boat, though not by the paddles. "My idea is

better than Mr. Fitch's." he reputedly told a friend. "Side wheels are better than side paddles."

Nicholas was apparently that rarest twig on the family tree: a *shy* Roosevelt. His own father was a well-to-do hardware merchant. His father's first cousin, Isaac, was one of the prominent men in New York, friendly with other important men. When Isaac died, his son James became a man of wealth and property. Yet Nicholas apparently hesitated to ask any of these Roosevelts to finance his dream. Or was he another rare type of Roosevelt—an unlucky one? Perhaps Nicholas did approach his family only to be rebuffed by those hardheaded businessmen who called his idea fanciful. Whichever, he kept on working with iron and copper. Four years later he learned that John Fitch had improved his initial invention. A Fitch boat with a new paddle was running regularly on the Delaware River between Philadelphia and Burlington, a distance of thirty miles. An awestruck committee of Congress stood on the riverbank to watch, and as a result the inventor got a patent on steam-driven craft.

Nicholas Roosevelt was a hard-working fellow in his mid-thirties when he learned that the Schuyler copper mine on the Passaic River near Newark was for sale. This was the sort of common-sense venture that might have been of interest to the other Roosevelts, and Nicholas may have raised the purchase money from relatives. Or possibly he had saved the amount over fifteen years of diligent work. In any case, he bought the mine and over it built a foundry and machine shop patterned after the famous Boulton and Watt works in England. He named this the Soho Works after the English counterpart. Here he planned to manufacture sheet copper to sheathe the hulls of ships. Under him were twelve workmen, two of whom had actually worked for James Watt in England.

Work turned out by the American Soho Works proved exceptionally good. So good, in fact, that it drew the attention of Chancellor Robert R. Livingston, the majestic figure who had administered the oath of office to George Washington. Among many other enterprises, Livingston owned the largest iron foundry in the New York area. The Chancellor was described as imperious and bull-headed, but at least he was farsighted enough to see possibilities in steam navigation.

At first, the Chancellor gave Nicholas Roosevelt a routine work order. Then the two men bumped into each other on the day in 1796 when John Fitch brought a boat to New York for an exhibition on Collect Pond. Fitch's Philadelphia steamboat suffered so many mishaps that the inventor had abandoned regular trips. Now he was trying to raise new funds in New York and for this had constructed a small engine with a screw propeller which drove an 18-foot yawl hardly bigger than a rowboat. Thousands of New Yorkers gathered to watch this latest wonder of the world. "What do you think of all this, my boy?" the Chancellor asked Nicholas when they met in the crowd. "I don't like the propeller," Nicholas answered. "I think there's a better way."

A year later Nicholas got an order from the federal government to sheathe the hulls of three new 74-gun frigates. He went deep into debt to buy the necessary copper and to hire additional men. Then Congress suddenly canceled the project. It was a shattering blow, but Nicholas' slipping world righted when Chancellor Livingston appeared with plans for a steam engine to be placed in a sailing vessel. Nicholas, however, was to build only the engine. All planning on the project was to be done by Livingston and an associate who was two years Nicholas' senior. The man's name was Robert Fulton.

In accounts of the invention of the steamboat from the angle of Nicholas Roosevelt, Robert Fulton appears as the villain. Yet the real villain may well be Livingston. During most of his adult life Fulton was a painter living in Europe. He met Livingston while that impressive figure served as American minister plenipotentiary to France. Fulton had a true inventive flair, but his real interests were submarines and canal navigation.

Livingston immediately began pushing the artist-inventor toward steamboats. The tie between them pulled closer when Fulton married Livingston's younger sister. It is possible to surmise that—in dealing with Nicholas Roosevelt, at least—Fulton acted mainly as a front man for the redoubtable Livingston. Nicholas and Fulton had many arguments over whether paddles on the new boat should be on wheels over the side or on a vertical axle at the stern. In advocating the latter course, Fulton supposedly pressed his own theory. But possibly he acted on orders from Livingston. Inevitably the Livingston-Fulton team won out. The craft was equipped with paddles in the rear; its trial run was a failure.

At this point Nicholas Roosevelt sat down and, seemingly for the first time, made a real attempt to promote his idea of paddle wheels over the side. He wrote Livingston an impassioned letter which has been called "the first record in America of the practical suggestion of the combination which eventually made [steam] navigation a practical success." Livingston replied with a curt note saying paddle side wheels were out of the question. By now Nicholas had his Dutch up. With his men he constructed a boat sixty feet in length, putting a one-cylinder engine inside. Over the sides he put saddle wheels of his own design. Again he wrote Livingston, advising him of the date when a trial run would take place. Livingston replied that he was interested only in working with Fulton, then in France in quest of inspiration and money. On the designated date Nicholas' boat pushed through the water at six miles an hour, but Livingston was not there to see it.

Nicholas Roosevelt had lost money on the canceled government contract. He lost more on his steamboat. Now he was forced to sell the Soho Works and travel to Philadelphia to work for the famous architect-engineer-builder Benjamin H. Latrobe on construction of the Philadelphia Water Works. Here his primary job was building pump engines, but he and Latrobe worked so well together that he stayed on as a partner. The Roosevelt luck shone further on Nicholas when he fell in love with Latrobe's young daughter Lydia. He was forty-one when he married her.

History fails to reveal whether Nicholas Roosevelt stood on the banks of the Hudson on August 17, 1807, as the Fulton-Livingston steamboat *Clermont* made its maiden voyage. The *Clermont* traveled at five miles per hour and was driven by paddle wheels over the side—precisely what Nicholas Roosevelt had advocated from boyhood and outlined to Livingston in his letter. No mention of Nicholas was made in the jubilation after the successful voyage, nor did Fulton or Livingston ever really give him credit. Even so, the relationship between the trio continued, and in 1809 Livingston engaged Latrobe and Roosevelt to construct a steamboat which would navigate the Ohio and Mississippi Rivers from Pittsburgh to New Orleans. This craft was designed by Fulton. It was 116 feet long, with a 20-foot beam, a 34-inch cylinder engine, boiler and other parts in proportion. Despite the success of the *Clermont*, Fulton and Livingston stubbornly insisted that the new craft have paddle wheels at the stern.

Before construction began Nicholas took a flatboat trip down the rivers to make sure such a steamboat could navigate the waters. He decided it could. Timber cut from nearby forests was floated along the Monongahela to Pittsburgh, then piled near the shipyard. On September 27, 1811, the boat, christened *New Orleans*, was ready. On its flat deck were two cabins, a large one forward for men, a smaller one in the stern for ladies. To the consternation of Pittsburghers, Lydia Latrobe Roosevelt stated that she and two maids would occupy the ladies' quarters during the voyage. It was bad enough to take women on such a hazardous trip, but Lydia was pregnant! Nicholas was implored not to take his wife for fear of endangering her life and that of the unborn child. He cheerfully replied that, pregnant or not, Lydia wished to make the trip. That was enough for him!

Pittsburgh gathered en masse to watch as, with a stupendous blast of its steam whistle, the *New Orleans* started down the Ohio. Aboard were the two Roosevelts, a captain, pilot, engineer, six deckhands, Lydia's two maids, waiter, cook, and a large Newfoundland dog named Tiger. All hands felt complete confidence in the boiler-driven craft. As described later by John H. B. Latrobe in *A Lost Chapter in the History of the Steamboat*: "The regular working of the engine, the ample supply of steam, the uniformity of the speed, all inspired confidence. . . . The very crew of unimaginative men were excited by the novelty of the situation." The Roosevelts themselves, fully equipped with imagination, were too excited to sleep on the first night out. They spent it together, wide awake, on deck.

Along the river the sound of escaping steam frightened entire towns in daytime and woke the slumbering at night. Crowds lined the banks to wave, and the voyagers waved back. In two days the boat reached Cincinnati. No dock on the river was big enough for her, so the *New Orleans* anchored off the city while flatboats and riverboats clustered about. Though shy in pressing his own schemes, Nicholas was a Roosevelt, hearty and enthusiastic with the rest of the human race. He invited prominent citizens to row out from shore and gave dinner parties on the open deck at night.

The two-day trip to Louisville was equally pleasant. The *New Orleans* arrived at midnight, and Nicholas displayed his robust Roosevelt humor by ordering the engineer to pull down the safety valve. The sound of the steam whistle shrieked through the silent night and inhabitants of Louisville leaped in terror from their beds. There was much talk of the Comet of 1811 at this time, and citizens were sure the comet had made a target of their city. Next day all was forgiven when the curious lined the bank to pass opinions on the unusual craft.

As at Cincinnati, Nicholas found that those who saw the *New Orleans* were convinced she could proceed downstream but not up. A few nights later he invited a group of proper citizens aboard for dinner. During the meal the crew upped anchor, allowing the boat to drift downstream. There was consternation until the engine shook into action and began to push the craft back upstream. Nicholas had contrived this small crisis as proof that the *New Orleans* could operate against the current.

Up to this moment the trip had been carefree as a Sunday picnic. Now trouble set in. The falls of the Ohio below Louisville were running too shallow to allow the passage of the big craft.

This kept the boat anchored in Louisville for two and a half months—not altogether a misfortune since it allowed Lydia to have her baby in comparative comfort. By late November waters had risen to permit five inches of clearance. An impatient Nicholas decided to take the risk. Full speed ahead, with all the steam-pressure boilers could provide, safety valve screeching, the boat—with Lydia and the baby aboard—hurtled toward the falls. Nicholas stood on deck with arms around wife and child as the craft twisted dangerously over the hazardous drop.

After this safe passage there came what Lydia called "days of horror." The Comet of 1811 had in fact passed overhead, leaving in its wake great upheavals of nature. Suddenly the atmosphere seemed to change. "The air grew musty and dull," writes J. H. B. Latrobe, "and though the sun was visible, like a glowing ball of copper, his rays hardly shed more than a mournful twilight on the surface of the water." That night the heavens opened for a driving rain, while a fierce wind seemed to make the riverbanks bend and buckle, churning the river into turmoil. In the morning those aboard could see that the buckling on land was no illusion. There had been a severe earthquake, one of a giant series of tremors that shook the Mississippi Valley to its center, oscillating down the courses of rivers and passing over the Alleghenies to die away in the Atlantic. The settlements of New Madrid and New Prairie were worst hit along the Mississippi, with log cabins overturned and streets inundated. The *New Orleans* passed these towns during the day.

On the riverbanks Indians, driven from homes, watched the steamer pass and decided it had caused the quake. Racing alongside, they cursed the big "Fire Canoe." Afternoons the *New Orleans* fastened to the bank while the crew went ashore to chop trees for furnace wood. They were besieged by homeless white settlers who begged to be taken aboard ship. The terrible convulsions of the earth also brought problems to the pilot, for river channels had been changed by the quakes. Where he expected to find deep water, roots and stumps projected above the surface.

Tall trees that had served as navigation markers were gone, while islands had changed shape or vanished altogether. Through all this the water continued to churn and boil, with sky overcast and air heavy.

"We lived in constant fright," Mrs. Roosevelt later told her brother. "No one seemed disposed to talk, and when there was any conversation, it was carried on in whispers almost." After fourteen such days the *New Orleans* reached Natchez, where at least one ray of brightness appeared. The captain of the boat had fallen in love with Mrs. Roosevelt's maid. At Natchez a clergyman was piped aboard and the two were wed.

At New Orleans the boat was greeted by a huge crowd that included Edward Livingston, younger brother of the Chancellor. An able lawyer and onetime mayor of New York, Edward had found life in New Orleans congenial. The Chancellor had vanished from the steamboat picture, but Edward proceeded to take his place. Fired with enthusiasm, he joined with his nephew John in negotiating with states for a monopoly to navigate the Mississippi. Commencing this complex task, he, no less than the Chancellor, forgot Nicholas Roosevelt, who took himself, wife, and child back to the bosom of the Latrobe family.

From then on Nicholas made intermittent efforts to press his claim for a patent on the side-wheeler steamboat. Robert Fulton, holder of the first such patent, died in 1815, which may be the reason Nicholas was given a patent in that year signed by President Madison. United States patents lasted fourteen years. In 1828 Nicholas Roosevelt—supported, as always, by the Latrobes—decided to renew his patent. It cost $100, and according to some accounts Nicholas was so poor he did not have this sum. Nor did the Latrobes. Yet the Roosevelts in New York were approaching new peaks in prosperity and earning power. So again the question arises—was Nicholas too shy, or too proud, to ask relatives for a hundred paltry dollars? Or did he ask, only to be rejected again by family members who continued to distrust so original-minded a man?

Yet the story of Nicholas' poverty may be untrue. Rather than poor, he may have been fed up with steamboats and patents. Support is given this theory by the fact that the nation's superintendent of patents, sensing the huge rewards in steam navigation, had himself revived the claims of John Fitch, dead for many years. This brought hopeless confusion to the whole matter. By one account, "the business had grown so tangled that everyone at last gave up in disgust."

Still, the filing of affidavits in support of Nicholas' claim had one interesting offshoot. In his affidavit Benjamin Latrobe, Nicholas' father-in-law, revealed that in 1809, during negotiations for the building of the *New Orleans,* he had found himself alone with Fulton. Latrobe took the inventor of the steamboat to task for pilfering Nicholas' idea of wheels over the side. Nicholas Roosevelt, rather than Fulton, Latrobe declared, should be holder of the first patent for the steamboat. Fulton, the affidavit states, became defensive, saying he did not sign his application for a patent. This raises the possibility that Livingston signed it for him.

"I have no pretensions to be the first inventor of the steamboat," Fulton continued. "Hundreds of others have tried it and failed. . . . That to which I claim an exclusive right is the so proportioning the boat to the power of the engine and the velocity with which the wheels of the boat, or both, move with the maximum velocity attainable by the power, and the construction of the whole machine." Asked where Nicholas fitted in all this, Fulton answered, "I regard him as a noble-minded, intelligent man and would do anything to serve him that I could."

By now Nicholas was in Skaneateles, New York, where he lived out the rest of his long life. Of his nine children only three reached maturity. Roosevelt Hall, the Latrobe home in Skaneateles, has been called the finest edifice ever built by a member of the Roosevelt tribe, which seems to disprove stories of Nicholas' poverty. But whatever his financial condition, Nicholas Roosevelt remains a stimulating footnote in American history as well as in the family. Years later another Nicholas, a diplomat and journalist born in 1893, summed him up: "He belongs among the pioneers of the industrial revolution. . . . Had he possessed in a higher degree the acquisitive instinct so strong in others of his tribe, he might have become a powerful figure in the industrialization of America."

Like the sad history of Janet Roosevelt Inderwick, the life of James Henry Roosevelt, born in 1800, might have been etched by Henry James.

James Henry was a grandson of Cornelius, younger brother of Isaac Roosevelt. Thus James Henry was a great-grandson of Jacobus, the family's pioneer purchaser of real estate. Through his father—another James!—James Henry inherited a small amount of the real estate purchased by Jacobus. His patrimony was part of the Beekman Swamp, the original real-estate purchase in the family. At first the possession of this neat packet of real estate failed to loom large in the life of James Henry. From the female side of his branch he had inherited a dash of French blood. It made him clever and personable, a man bountifully equipped for the battle of life. James Henry graduated from Columbia in 1819 and immediately undertook the study of law. He also fell in love with Julia Maria Boardman, daughter of an old New York family. The pair had marriage in mind from the first, but decided to wait until James Henry's law career started.

Such was the cloudless state of affairs as James Henry achieved his twenty-first year. He had passed his law examinations and was beginning to build a practice. Simultaneously he and Julia made plans for a wedding. Then this most fortunate young man was stricken by infantile paralysis. It left him—as it did a future Roosevelt—without use of his legs. But, unlike the Roosevelt of the future, James Henry decided that anything resembling a normal life was impossible. Marriage, especially, was out of the question. Julia Boardman agreed. In true Henry James fashion, she vowed never to marry anyone else and remained James Henry's devoted friend throughout his life. When he died, his will named her executrix.

Having decided—without bitterness, it would seem—that he could never practice law or enjoy a social life, James Henry began to devote all time and energy to turning his small inherited estate into a large one. The stricken young man turned out to be something of a financial genius, and by the time of his death in 1863 he had accumulated over a million dollars.

During his illness he had realized how little doctors knew about treatment of paralysis. This led him to develop an interest in medical matters and a deep sympathy for people in need of medical attention. In his will the interest in money-making merged with interest in medicine. James Henry left the faithful Julia Maria an annual income of $4,000. The rest went for "the establishment in the City of New York of a hospital for the reception and relief of sick and diseased persons, and for its permanent endowment." At first this bequest involved only money, for James Henry left his Beekman Swamp real estate to a nephew named James C. Roosevelt Brown. But he died childless a month after James Henry whereupon the real estate reverted to the hospital endowment.

Roosevelt Hospital, on Ninth Avenue between Fifty-eighth and Fifty-ninth Streets, opened in 1871. It is there today.

7

JAMES MAKES A MOVE

IN THE YEAR 1819 JAMES ROOSEVELT, ONLY SON OF ISAAC THE Patriot, took an important step.

James was now fifty-seven years old. In his career, no less than in his portraits, he was something of a shadow of his exceptional father. James had carried on the work of the family sugar refinery, operating it with steady profit. He had managed the parcels of real estate that had come down from Jacobus and been nurtured by the canny Isaac. Like his father before him, James was an officer of the Bank of New York, but a director rather than president. In the family tradition of public service he served in the State Assembly in 1796-97 and as a city alderman in 1809.

Only in one respect did his career differ from that of his father. James studied law, but apparently did so only to manage his affairs better, for he never practiced. Like his father, James was a stanch, God-fearing member of the Dutch Reformed Church. He lived with his family in a pleasant home at 18 South Street at the tip of the island. In 1810 his wife, Mary Eliza, by whom he had ten children, died at the age of forty-one. James waited two lonely years, then married Catherine Eliza Barclay. By her he had two more children. Catherine Eliza lived only four years after the marriage, so in 1819 James Roosevelt was again a widower whose household included two young children.

James was a prosaic-looking man. At Hyde Park his portrait hangs at the opposite end of the living room from the handsome Gilbert Stuart painting of his father. James's portrait makes him as colorless as the steel spectacles he wears. An over-all pedantic look indicates that his pleasures were mild and conventional. Indeed, James seems to typify what Gerald Johnson has written of these early Roosevelts: "They were simply worthy people, intelligent without genius, decent without saintliness, educated without erudition, not slothful in business, but not titans of industry—in short, admirable, but not inspiring."

Yet James Roosevelt, however sober his exterior, was feeling the simmering juices that were beginning to change the Roosevelts into a unique family. The man who in his portrait appears the typical New York merchant nursed an inner yearning for the soil and the outdoor life. Under his dry surface lay a love of the land, horses, farming, and the raising of cattle. As his life lengthened James thought back increasingly to boyhood years spent during the Revolution on the rolling Hoffman acres at Rhinebeck and Tivoli in Dutchess County. While his beloved Mary Eliza was alive, James was able to curb these desires and remain satisfied by city life. But after her death the good man began attempts to satisfy inner urges.

The first thing he did was purchase a 400-acre farm north of the city in the area known as Harlem. His chunk of property began at what is now Fifth Avenue and ran over to the East River, from 110th Street north to 125th. Today the mind reels at the value of such an area, but well-to-do James Roosevelt did not buy the land as an investment. True, it was largely covered by timber, some of which he sold to regain part of the purchase money. But this was a sideline. James wished to become a gentleman farmer, and on his Harlem acreage made strenuous efforts in this direction until he became convinced the soil was too rocky. On the land he also built stables and bred fine horses. Sundays he rode back and forth in a spanking carriage from South Street to his farm. Yet all this was far from satisfactory to the near-elderly man who yearned to be close to the land. In 1819 he sold the Harlem property for $25,000.

James's thoughts still went back to Dutchess County, and this time he did something about it. After many trips around Pough-keepsie, he purchased a hilltop and surrounding acreage north of the town. On this hill he built a large, square, comfortable home which he named Mount Hope. On the grounds were stables for horses and barns for livestock.

In 1821, when he reached the age of fifty-nine, James took as a third wife Harriet Howland, a member of a Yankee-trader family represented in New York by the powerful firm of G. G. and S. S. Howland. In honor of his bride James disposed of the South Street residence and bought a better home on Bleecker Street, two blocks south of vernal Washington Square. Possessed of a New York town house, a Poughkeepsie estate, and a third wife, James Roosevelt stood ready to enjoy the longevity allowed most Roosevelts of his line. He did this with eminent success, living on until 1847, when he died at age eighty-eight. By this time Poughkeepsie had become his number one residence.

Thus James Roosevelt became the first major member of the family to break the pattern of urban living. For him, however, the move to rural regions was only a half step. As long as James was active he retained the Greenwich Village town house and passed summers in Poughkeepsie.

But if James took just a semistep toward becoming a country squire, his son Isaac, born in 1790, took a full one. In many re-spects Isaac, one of James's ten children by Mary Eliza Walton, was an unusual Roosevelt. For with him the family deviated for the first time to produce a near-weakling. Most Roosevelts were enthusiastically beamed on success in the world, but Isaac was shy, studious, retiring. "He was of delicate constitution, with refined tastes," a contemporary wrote. In describing Isaac, others fell back on the slang of a past century to call him an odd duck. One of them goes so far as to brand him ineffectual.

Isaac, who graduated from Princeton in 1808, was a Roosevelt who never showed a flicker of interest in business or politics, both of which engaged his predecessors. Instead, he announced that he wished to be the first medical man in the family and enrolled in the College of Physicians and Surgeons at Columbia. But on graduation he reverted to being a queer duck. He informed relatives he had no plans to practice his new calling. "I cannot stand the sight of blood and human pain," he astoundingly explained. Instead of practicing medicine he undertook what a later era called medical research. At first he detoured into fields of physics and botany, but slowly his interest swung back to the history of medicine.

When his father scoured the Poughkeepsie countryside in search of suitable property for a home, Dr. Isaac, who appears to have been James's favorite son by Mary Eliza, rode with him. Dr. Isaac assisted in choosing the Poughkeepsie acreage named Mount Hope. When elderly James Roosevelt returned to New York, young Dr. Isaac remained in Dutchess County to supervise the building of the house. With Mount Hope completed, he moved in as a permanent resident.

The marriage of James to Harriet Howland did nothing to alter this pleasant arrangement. No less than his father, Isaac loved the land, horses, and the gentlemanly aspects of farming. While James and his wife spent winters in New York, the doctor-son lived the full year in Poughkeepsie. Having filled the shelves of a comfortable library with rare books on medical history, he balanced his life between reading and supervising breeding, gardening, and farming on the estate.

Dr. Isaac's portrait shows a man with a lean face and straight, thin, patrician nose. His mouth is almost quizzical, eyes somewhat bemused. Over his whole personality lies an aura of frailness, but he appears a pleasant, erudite, and humorous man. Some relatives were baffled by Dr. Isaac's lack of interest in the great world beyond Mount Hope. To a few it appeared that with this fragile, well-mannered bachelor doctor, deeply immersed in medical studies, the Jacobus line of Roosevelts was going to seed in the manner of other early Dutch families, among them the once mighty Stuyvesants. "He spent his time puttering around the gardens and tending livestock," says one account of Dr. Isaac's mild existence, "leading the life of a reclusive bachelor, taking great care of his health and interesting himself in the affairs of the old Dutch Reformed Church in Poughkeepsie."

But people like Dr. Isaac have a way of surprising the world. Just when he appeared hopelessly set in his ways he roused himself. At the mature age of thirty-seven the quiet man suddenly came alive to woo and win the heart of Mary Rebecca Aspinwall. A girl of eighteen, she was the niece of Isaac's second stepmother, Harriet Howland Roosevelt.

Taking into consideration the pallid Dr. Isaac and the subsequent history of the Dutchess County Roosevelts, Mary Rebecca appears to be the first member of an outside clan to give a perceptible boost to Roosevelt blood. This is made even more likely by the tremendous vigor of the Aspinwalls.

Where Roosevelts had always been merchants, content to purchase and sell goods transported to these shores by adventurous traders, the Aspinwalls were themselves adventurous Yankee traders. They had, indeed, been in this country longer than the Roosevelts. The first Aspinwall arrived in Massachusetts from England in 1630 on the ship *Arabella*. Colony records call him an unusually well-educated man, but a stormy petrel. "He seemed to have the faculty of continually getting himself in trouble," a descendant observes wryly. He supported Anne Hutchinson and for this was accused of sedition and banished to New Haven. Returning a few years later, he became one of the founders of the town of Brookline, then known as Muddy River.

By this time other Aspinwalls had arrived from abroad. One was Peter Aspinwall who settled in Muddy River and married a girl with the blithe name of Remember Palfrey. Joseph, son of the pair, was the first Aspinwall to run off to sea as a youth. Eventually he worked his way upward to become captain of a Yankee clipper. Next he became a shipowner and made New York his home. He also established the tenor of a breezy Aspinwall family personality, for he is remembered as "very passionate, very gay, facetious, good company and always loose and exceeding careless of his own and children's affairs." In his old age he was respected as a testy sea dog.

Joseph's son, John, also ran away to sea as a boy. He, too, became captain of a Yankee trader, then shipowner. "His vessels knew every port in the world," says one history. He was the real founder of the family fortune, for in addition to being an outstanding trader-merchant he built and bought docks and warehouses along the East River. Under his guidance the Aspinwalls reached the stature of merchant princes. As such they were one of a pair of great shipping dynasties in New York City. The other was the Howland family, whose ancestors had been aboard the *Mayflower*. It would seem almost too much for an Aspinwall son to fall in love with a Howland daughter. Yet this happened when John Aspinwall, Jr., married heiress Susan Howland.

Neither the huge prosperity of both families nor this fortuitous union changed Aspinwall habits. The first child of the young couple was William Henry Aspinwall, born in 1807. Where other families, including the Roosevelts, might have sent such a son to college, William Henry Aspinwall was apprenticed to the countinghouse of the Howland firm. After this humble beginning he climbed to the status of partner at the age of twenty-five. The firm was then renamed Howland and Aspinwall. With his riches William Henry built a splendid home on University Place. Of it Philip Hone, onetime mayor and hard-to-please diarist, wrote, "A more beautiful and commodious mansion, or in better taste in every particular, I have never seen."

Mary Rebecca Aspinwall—a girl who preferred to be called Rebecca—was the younger sister of William Henry. She married Dr. Isaac Roosevelt in 1827, possibly choosing a quiet older man in rebellion against her dynamic, money-minded family. Yet there is no record of personality clashes between Roosevelts and Aspinwalls. On the contrary, Isaac and Rebecca often used the University Place mansion as a town house or visited Barrytown, on the Hudson north of Rhinebeck, where the Aspinwalls had a gigantic estate.

Nor did city-bred Rebecca chafe at country life. In 1828, one year after marriage, she gave birth to a son who was christened James. The young couple still lived at Mount Hope with James Roosevelt and his third wife, Rebecca's aunt. But after the birth of the child they decided on a home of their own. Isaac bought a large parcel across the Post Road, north of his father's property. Here, in leisurely fashion, he supervised construction of a gabled house which was named Rosedale. In 1832, when little James was four, the family moved there. Eight years later another son, John Aspinwall Roosevelt, was born. The older boy James, who was twelve at the birth of John, became the father of Franklin Delano Roosevelt.

New York City, which in the day of the original Claes Martenszen van Rosenvelt had been the brawling colony of New Amsterdam, was now the domain of only one major line of Roosevelts. These were the descendants of the billikin Johannes, eldest son of Nicholas.

During the Revolutionary era the Johannes Roosevelts had been overshadowed by the high-echelon activities of cousin Isaac of the Jacobus line. Until 1820 unimaginative hard work had seemed to be the characteristic of this bough of the family oak. Since Johannes Roosevelt had astounded contemporaries by importing paintings and furniture from Holland there had been little color in family members, who seemed uniformly pleasant, industrious, and dull. The inventor Nicholas contributed an inventive, original mind to this part of the family, but his relatives seemed unimpressed by him. The hardware merchant James and his son James I fought hard in the footslogging war of the Revolution. They had returned to Maiden Lane to reactivate the business which soon became Roosevelt and Son, Hardware Merchants. These two established the pattern saluted many years later by William T. Cobb in his book *The Strenuous Life: The Oyster Bay Roosevelts in Business and Finance:*

The practices which were ever after to guide this branch of the family were even then cast in the mold. In successive generations one son was always to head the financial and commercial interests of this branch through the firm; and it is probable that James I was even then helping to care for the real estate interests of his father, James, then seventy-three years old, who had inherited them in turn from Johannes of the Beekman Swamp.

However, the inertia afflicting Dr. Isaac caused a shift of balance in the Roosevelt family. The energy currently absent in the Jacobus line suddenly sprouted up in the Johannes. It became the turn of this group to be wealthy and prominent. This branch of the Roosevelt line had no interest in Dutchess County and eventually picked the locality of Oyster Bay, Long Island, for country living. It was this New York, or "Knickerbocker," family that gave the world the first famous Roosevelt—Theodore, twenty-sixth President of the United States.

Before producing a President, though, the Johannes line offered one member as exceptional on his side as Isaac the Patriot had been on his. This was Cornelius Van Schaack Roosevelt, elder son of James I and his wife, Maria Van Schaack, a lady described as every bit as Dutch as her husband. Cornelius Van Schaack was born in 1794, and if Isaac Roosevelt was the first American member of the family, C.V.S.—as family records call him—can be considered the last Dutch one.

Until his death in 1871, Dutch was rigorously spoken at Sunday dinner in his home. C.V.S. also looked Dutch—or at least oddly foreign. Here at last was a short-of-stature Roosevelt, his body topped by a face almost ugly. Over a high forehead and broad brow the hair was reddish, tight, and curly. His lips were wide and thick; eyes shrewd, bright, and myopic behind gold-rimmed spectacles. Altogether C.V.S. Roosevelt was a man of whom a contemporary wrote, "His appearance always reminded me of a Hindoo idol, roughly carved in red porphyry." Yet Hindoo idol or not, C.V.S. was packed tight with the vim, vigor, and vehemence of a Roosevelt.

He was also clamped in the family mold of business. For a time he attended Columbia, but with a position in the Roosevelt firm awaiting him education seemed pointless. "Business calls me with its imperious beckoning," he confessed. Soon he was applying all his bustling energy to Roosevelt and Son. Under his management the firm made further contact with export companies in Europe. He also guided the firm toward finance. C.V.S. increased the import of plate glass, in which the firm achieved a virtual monopoly in the United States.

In only one way did small, redheaded C.V.S. swerve from the family pattern. In 1821, at the age of twenty-eight, he married Margaret Barnhill of Philadelphia, whose Quaker forebears had come to America on the ship that carried William Penn. Margaret's blood was a mixture of English-Welsh-Irish-German. One of her ancestors was the Lord of Drombaugh, an Irish peer. She was the first non-Dutch bride in the Johannes line of Roosevelts.

The union of C.V.S. and Margaret Barnhill was notable in another respect. For seldom has a girl been courted in such a pragmatic way. In later years C.V.S. wrote tender love poems to his wife, but as a suitor he confined himself to letters that showed a businesslike approach to life and love. "Economy is my doctrine at all times—at all events till I become, if it is to be so, a *man of fortune*," he warned his beloved. As the wedding day approached he became more realistic. "You know that I hate extravagance in young folks," he wrote, "and the only things in which I shall be extravagant will be carpets for the two lower rooms, a sideboard, and sofa. *Our* chairs will not be mahogany. My idea is that of little or nothing for ornament alone, but of that which is useful to be ornamental, if possible."

Only once, at this emotional time in the average young man's life, did C.V.S. lapse from his hardheaded view of life for a bit of soul-searching: "I sometimes say to myself, oh could I tear myself from that absorber of every gentle and every noble feeling of the soul—business—and fly away and be at rest in the midst of the more enchanting pursuits of the mind." But he quickly checked these dreamy thoughts. In the next sentence he reminded himself that those who loaf through life usually "complain of ennui, of want of occupation, and speak enviously of business."

C.V.S. lived up to his realistic conception of matrimony by waiting until after the wedding to buy the family silver. Only when the young couple knew exactly what was required did he give his wife the necessary money. For Margaret, whom he adored, C.V.S. built a large house at the corner of Broadway and Fourteenth Street—the city was indeed expanding northward! Over the next fifteen years Margaret gave birth to five boys, four of whom survived. At home with his family a complete transformation occurred in dry C.V.S. Despite his overmastering passion for business, he was a fine husband and father, implanting in his sons the independence and strong self-confidence that were a conspicuous family trait. Though stern and unrelenting at work, C.V.S. was warm and relaxed as a parent, allowing his home to ring with vigor, fun, and rampant individualism. After a hard day at the office, the Hindoo-like little man unbent to engage with his boys in horseplay that would have astounded his commercial associates.

Yet to the outer world C.V.S. remained all business. The dreamed-of opportunity to become a man of fortune arrived with the Panic of 1837. C.V.S. had inherited $250,000 from his father—his younger brother received only $150,000. In addition, he had made large profits from Roosevelt and Son. In the 1837 panic companies failed, banks closed, and land values fell. Large numbers of businessmen panicked, but not C.V.S. Roosevelt. Retaining total faith in his country and the city of his forebears, he sank patrimony and profits into New York real estate. Since he did not know what property would become valuable, C.V.S. bought all over town. This won him a listing as one of the ten top real-estate owners in New York City, with property valued at $1,346,000.

Still, real estate was only a sideline with this volcanic little man. He also became a director of the new Chemical Bank, and perhaps it was his influence that made the Chemical an institution of towering probity which paid all obligations in gold. In time C.V.S. earned another exceptional honor: he was named one of the five richest men in New York. "No family shines more honorably in the ancient Dutch annals of this province than the Roosevelts—venerated burgomasters of their day," wrote Moses Y. Beach of this honor.

C.V.S. Roosevelt was a man whose dream came true—he was irrefutably a man of fortune. But success in business never led him to neglect his family. C.V.S. firmly believed that long outdoor summer vacations away from the dirt and noise of the city were beneficial to growing boys. He and Margaret made valiant efforts to find a place where the family could set down summer roots. For years they tried various spots along the then fashionable New Jersey shore. These never proved fully satisfying, and C.V.S. branched out in other directions. Even after his boys were grown and married, he continued to search for the ideal summer spot. At last he found it in the quiet town of Oyster Bay on Long Island Sound.

The verisimilitude so baffling to those who try to generalize about the Roosevelts is strikingly apparent in C.V.S. and his brother James J., a man who chose a *J* for Junior instead of the customary Dutch *I* for a middle initial.

Between these two brothers runs a clean line of personality cleavage. C.V.S. inherited in abundance the business acumen and financial drive of the family; James J. inherited political instincts. In a long life, the wealthy C.V.S. never sought political office or apparently considered the idea. James J., on the other hand, thrived in the world of politics. The two men differed in appearance as well. While C.V.S. was a gnarled little man, James J. was stout and bluff.

James J., born in 1795, graduated from Columbia and studied law. For ten years he had his own practice, occasionally assisting father and brother with special problems in the hardware business. During this time he served as an assistant alderman. The Roosevelts were deep-dyed Democrats; for not until the Civil War would a family member switch to the Republican party. Up to now they had been Democrats in the dignified Hamilton-Federalist mold set by Isaac the Patriot. But in 1828 James J. Roosevelt upset relatives by espousing the rambunctious cause of Andrew Jackson. James J. compaigned vigorously in New York, and after this enlivening experience embraced politics wholeheartedly.

To make matters worse, he became a Tammany man. To the sachems of Tammany Hall his services were of special value because his social and business connections allowed him to act as liaison man between Wall Street and Fifth Avenue without attracting undue attention. In true Tammany fashion, James J. was rewarded by election to the state legislature and to the house of Representatives in Washington. Thus he became the first Roosevelt to serve in the nations's capital. His unabashed union with Tammany made him a second Roosevelt who was called a traitor to his class. The diarist Philip Hone thought him, "the leader of the blackguards, in whose person . . . our poor city is disgraced."

James J. also loved society. "He was a gay young man, quite aware of his social standing, and a familiar figure at the balls and parties of the era," says a contemporary account. At one point early in life he was something of a poseur. Or was this the robust Roosevelt sense of humor? At any rate, James J. went abroad in 1830, when he was a member of the State Assembly. In preparation for his arrival in France, he ordered a set of expensive calling cards:

James J. Roosevelt
Membre du Consiel de New York et Attache
a la Ambassade des Etates Unis

This distinguished-looking pasteboard eased his way into inner French court circles. There he met an outstanding beauty of the era. She was an American—Cornelia Van Ness, daughter of Cornelius Van Ness, onetime governor of Vermont and United States senator. Van Ness was an unusual Vermonter who preferred life in Washington and Paris to the rigors of his home state. In Washington, Cornelia had been considered one of the most beautiful girls in America. Abroad, she was "celebrated as a belle and noted for her fascinating social qualities, her exquisite grace, sprightliness, and elegance of style."

James J. Roosevelt promptly fell in love with her, and lovely Cornelia reciprocated. The two were married in a ceremony replete with European magnificence. The bride was given away by the Marquis de Lafayette, a close friend of her cosmopolitan father. After a European honeymoon, the pair returned to New York where James J. resumed the practice of law and the life of a Tammany stalwart.

Gorgeous Cornelia fell into the proper Roosevelt groove by producing eleven children in twenty years. Married life for the couple was happy, though at one time Cornelia apparently decided her husband was stingy with her. She made an arrangement with the A. T. Stewart department store whereby the monthly bills sent to James J. were padded, the extra money given to her. In this way, the family believes, Cornelia earned $30,000 in spending money over the years.

James J. was a hearty character who sometimes signed himself James I. Roosevelt, in the Dutch tradition. Then he was asked what the *I* stood for and the question never ceased to infuriate him. "It stands for I—I—I. ME!" he would bellow. Yet in time his name proved no problem. A grateful Tammany appointed him to the New York State Supreme Court in 1851. So he became Judge Roosevelt and was called by that title even after resigning to take the more exciting job of United States attorney for the Southern District of New York.

James J. and Cornelia were always as much at home in Europe

as in the United States. After the judge retired from politics, the couple lived abroad for fifteen years. When James was eighty, they returned to New York. He died a short time later. The once radiant Cornelia survived him by a year.

Judge James J. was not the only well-known Democrat among Knickerbocker Roosevelts. Clinton Roosevelt, descended from another son of Johannes, also was politically minded. This second cousin of C.V.S. and Judge James was a retiring author and intellectual, active among Locofocos, as left-wing Democrats were called. The ideas advocated by Clinton Roosevelt were radical for his—or any—day. But though he wrote with clarity and vigor, few people of his time paid heed. In numerous pamphlets and books he branded the bankers enemies of the people and urged a curb on their powers. He was elected to the State Assembly in 1835 and, following his term in Albany, demanded greater reforms, among them controlled prices and regulated currency.

Clinton Roosevelt was especially annoyed by the incongruity of poverty amidst plenty. He called the frequent financial panics of his era "the delirium tremens of trade, arising from that stimulant, bank paper, by the credit system."

But, most of all, Clinton adds to the bewildering variety of the Roosevelt family. Though a member of the Theodore line, he advocated theories that were precursors of Franklin's New Deal. Clinton Roosevelt even wrote of the "rubber dollar," a phrase later used by Franklin.

8

THEODORE THE FIRST

THE BUSTLING CITY IN WHICH C.V.S., JUDGE JAMES J., AND CLINTON Roosevelt displayed prominence was now a teeming metropolis.

The events and discoveries that made it so had come about rapidly. The first were the great forward strides in shipping. As long as a tight Fulton-Livingston monopoly stifled development in steam navigation, only big ships with sails left New York harbor to cover the seven seas. But when the Fulton-Livingston monopoly ended, steamboats began to move up the Hudson to Albany, then to California, and finally, in 1855, to France.

Aiding initial expansion in shipping was the Erie Canal which carried to the docks of the metropolis the products of the northwestern United States. The opening of the canal in 1825 provided a moment without parallel in the history of the city. New Yorkers were aware of this and insisted on knowing the exact instant that Lake Erie water touched waters of the canal. No telegraph existed at the time, and state officials ingeniously devised a method of relaying the news to New York. Leftover cannon from the Revolution and War of 1812 were placed at 8- to 10-mile intervals from Buffalo to Albany, then down the Hudson to Sandy Hook. As Erie

water was let into the canal, cannon number one fired. The crew
of the next cannon down the line heard its boom and fired. In this
fashion it took one hour for the booms of successive cannons to
reach Albany, and exactly twenty-one minutes more for the sound
to travel down the Hudson to New York. There a tumultuous
celebration began.

Seven years later, in 1832, the Erie Railroad was chartered. This
left the canal a major waterway but no longer in the first rank of
commercial transportation. Another American era had begun!

Steamboat . . . canal . . . railroad. With these was one additional
development, less dramatic perhaps but equal in long-range effect.
In the 1820's illuminating gas was introduced in New York City,
commencing the Gaslight Era of nostalgic song and story. In retrospect this may appear amusing, but at the time gas was an in-
novation which assisted education, business, and culture—not to
mention the elimination of untold strain on the human eye. Gaslight crept slowly through New York. At first its installation in
homes was a contemporary status symbol. Among the first to
embrace the flickering brightness were the theaters of the town.
BRILLIANTLY LIGHTED BY GAS, posters advertised.

Up to now Manhattan's population growth had been sluggish.
In 1763 the population was 23,000—an average increase of a mere
183 persons a year since the days of Peter Stuyvesant! By 1810 the
annual increase was somewhat better—2,666. From 1810 to 1820
this jumped to 32,532. Foreign immigration began in the decade
1820-1830, but at first totaled only 90,077 newcomers annually.
Then, wildly, the dam burst. Over the next ten years the yearly
increase was 342,517. From 1840 to 1849 the figure was 1,161,664.
In the next decade Ireland and Germany alone contributed
2,000,000 immigrants to America. In 1860 the population of the
city stood at 813,669, one fourth Irish. Native-born whites numbered only 310,000, or less than half the city population.

This teeming influx forever changed the temper of the town.
Among other things, it introduced racial bigotry and religious
prejudice. But the greatest change was visible in city politics. Per-

haps the first to discover this was aristocratic Cornelius Van Wyck Lawrence, elected mayor of the quiet city in 1837. As a rich man, Lawrence followed the custom of previous wealthy victors by flinging open his mansion to constituents on election night. In the past such victory celebrations had been lively but friendly. Now such an ill-behaved horde descended on his home that Lawrence summoned police.

The episode had further shadings. Mayor Lawrence, prosperous merchant, was the type of man who had always governed the city. He was a Democrat, and the Democrats were now opposed by the Whigs. The two parties were almost evenly matched in the city. At election time both factions put up candidates of such high moral fiber and ability that mayorality races were close. Between Lawrence in 1837 and Jacob Westervelt in 1854 there had been five Democratic mayors and five Whig mayors—a balance almost too perfect to contemplate!

For Lawrence, Westervelt, and others, politics had been only a part-time interest, a civic duty to be engaged in while running a business. Now the civic scene began to encampass men whose full-time occupation was politics. The tribe increased after 1846, when all city offices, including judgeships, became elective. Politicians concentrated on wooing the Irish, luring most of them into the Democratic party. Thus control of the party slipped from prosperous merchants and dignified businessmen into the hands of professional politicians. One more era had dawned!

Other changes testified to city growth. The wealthy families who clung to mansions on the lower end of the island had at last been forced uptown by the spread of commerce. Reluctantly they moved northward to Washington Square, lower Fifth Avenue, Fourteenth Street (where C.V.S. Roosevelt pioneered), and lower Second Avenue. Madison Square, the post-Civil War hub of the city, was still too far uptown for dwellings, but a few builders were already eying Riverside Drive with its splendid view of the Hudson River.

There was much construction of commercial buildings and

residences in the city, bringing high profit to the glass-importing division of Roosevelt and Son. Nearly every respectable urban family had its own home, for as yet no apartment houses had been erected. Immigrants were jammed tight into tenements provided by venal builders. In these rabbit warrens of humanity, sanitary facilities were few and opportunities for squalor great. Only a few citizens rose to protest the dreadful existence that was the lot of the newly arrived immigrants. In those days Americans held the convenient belief that anyone with the ability to rise above his fellow men had a God-given right to exploit them. This philosophy was amplified by rugged Commodore Cornelius Vanderbilt, a man worth vast millions. "What do I care about the law? Hain't I got the power?" he demanded.

Even society was in flux. No single powerful leader like Mrs. Astor or Mrs. Stuyvesant Fish had as yet appeared. But beside such social pre-Revolutionary families as Van Rensselaer, Van Cortlandt, Kip, Beekman, Nicolls, and Murray, there were new ones like Astor, Lawrence, Bache, Remsen, Belmont, and Morgan.

High and low, the populace was fascinated by finance and politics. To most citizens these two were like sporting events played in a giant arena. The city's Stock Exchange had first been started under a buttonwood tree on lower Wall Street. By 1817 its members, weary of meeting in the open air, moved themselves indoors. The new quarters were "to furnish exchange rooms and other facilities for the convenient transaction of the business by its members." Into this pleasant atmosphere stormed the robber barons who would dominate the nation's finance during the latter part of the century.

In politics Tammany Hall began a rise to power by cultivating voters at the precinct level. On election day crowds stood around the polls to watch the fun. Electioneering continued until the moment a voter lifted a pencil to scratch his vote. Pressures were on him to the very end, a process inviting fist fights and bloodletting. Men with beards and mustaches were especially popular on election day. After voting, they were hustled by ward heelers to nearby barbershops. Beards and mustaches shaved off, they were marched back to vote under new names.

In this new type metropolis the Roosevelts continued to flourish.

The money inherited over four generations, and increased in each, had brought the family to a level of living enjoyed by few Americans of the day. This unostentatious accumulation of wealth also served to illuminate another aspect of the family personality. The Roosevelts stood forth as true American aristocrats. Yet they differed from others of the breed in that they were neither money-mad nor society-mad. Male Roosevelts acted as if possessed of all the money they would ever want, and each seemed completely satisfied to operate within the confines of that money. Even C.V.S., to whom business beckoned imperiously, did not appear overly concerned with the actual accumulation of wealth. Rather it was the exciting game of business that enchanted him.

It was the same in the social sphere. James J. Roosevelt may have cut a social swath in New York and married his international beauty abroad. But having done this he relaxed to enjoy the benefits of solid social standing and never strained for more. Comfort rather than luxury, satisfaction rather than worldly success—these were the inbred instincts of the tribe. C.V.S. loved his business; James J., his politics and social life; in Dutchess County, Dr. Isaac, his medical research, farming, and animal husbandry. Each appeared completely satisfied with what God had given him. To a remarkable degree the Roosevelts as a family were geared to obtain the most from life, with the side benefits of wealth more interesting than wealth itself. Pleasant moderation in all things became the Roosevelt credo. It is summed up by Gerald Johnson, who writes, "No Roosevelt ever died a martyr to some great cause, and none was ever shot in a quarrel over a trollop."

The first males to reap full rewards of this comfortable existence were the sons of C.V.S. These four boys were brought up in the house at Broadway and Fourteenth Street, facing Union

Square. It was a large house, almost a mansion, with black and white marble on the floor of the entrance hall. This hall rose regally to the roof, with a winding staircase at the side that provided an excellent place for games of tag. Margaret Barnhill Roosevelt was a devoted and tolerant mother. C.V.S., so unbending in business, was high-spirited at home. The result was an unusual upbringing for the boys. In an era when children were supposed to be seen and not heard, the Roosevelt offspring were visible and audible. One family friend who saw Margaret Roosevelt out walking with her yeasty brood, said, "There goes that lovely Mrs. Roosevelt and those four horrid boys!" The boys themselves realized that their unbridled home was likely to astound the unprepared. One son tells of the bafflement of guests at "the sudden fits of irony, cordiality, conceit, affection, nonsense, and sense, which succeed each other without any apparent connection or warning approach."

C.V.S., last of the Dutch Roosevelts, had somehow absorbed the aristocratic British attitude that a well-to-do man need not work provided he keep busy with philanthropy, reform politics, or humane good works. He offered to settle on each of his sons a life income that would permit such an existence. Yet each unhesitatingly chose work. His oldest boy, S. Weir, attended Columbia and studied law. In middle age he became a member of the Board of Education of the city of New York. James Alfred, the next son, took after his father, deciding to skip college in order to enter the family business as rapidly as possible. When C.V.S. retired, James Alfred dropped hardware and plate glass from Roosevelt and Son, to turn it into an investment and brokerage company.

James Alfred married an Emlen of Philadelphia and became a director of several banks. He loved outdoor life and got to be a well-known yachtsman. With this went a fondness for dinner-party society. One of his daughters married a Lowell of Boston, while another wed a grandson of Nicholas and Lydia Latrobe Roosevelt, to make the first family union between close cousins.

Robert Barnhill Roosevelt, the third son, also became a lawyer.

At the same time he responded with force and vigor to the freedom offered by the family money. Writes Karl Schriftgiesser, "He could afford to do the things he wanted to do without having to worry at the same time over the vulgar problem of earning a living." Born in 1829, he studied law without going to college, which in those days was often done. In time Robert Barnhill became the first Roosevelt since Isaac the Patriot to press the family name deeply into the public consciousness. Where Isaac was intelligent but quiet, Robert was colorful and flamboyant. "An Elizabethan survival in the Victorian era," his great-nephew Nicholas calls him. "He lived life with open hands. . . . He was a man who loved laughter and to make people laugh."

Others salute Robert Barnhill as a mixture of the irascible and lovable and say his dynamic energy was coupled with stubborn Dutch persistence. Everything he did was performed with gusto, together with a salting of humor and a peppering of eccentricity. The number of his accomplishments is staggering. Robert Barnhill was reformer, editor, naturalist, diplomat, politician, public servant, author, banker, and indefatigable friend of the great, near-great, and not-so-great. Above all, he was a pungent conversationalist, fond of lamenting what he called "the inborn cussedness of human nature." Nothing seemed to faze him. For some reason newspapermen decided that his middle name was Barnwell, not Barnhill. To him, this was a matter of supreme unimportance—another instance of man's inborn cussedness. If newspapers wished to call him Barnwell—well, dammit, Barnwell he would be! It became the middle name he used for the rest of his life.

For many years Robert Barnwell Roosevelt was owner-editor of the New York *Citizen,* a newspaper devoted to literature, politics, and exposure of civic corruption. Barnwell and his crusading paper were a potent force in toppling Boss Tweed, the postwar Tammany Hall chieftain. As a leader among the so-called Seventy Honest Men who drove Tweed to jail and disgrace, Barnwell was offered the post of sachem of the laundered Tammany. He refused. What he really wanted was to run for mayor on a Reform

Democratic ticket. But this one great wish was always denied him.

However, he had other careers. He was a member of Congress; minister to the Netherlands during the first Cleveland administration; author of four books and countless pamphlets. At the age of twenty-one he married Elizabeth Ellis, daughter of a New York banker. When she died in middle life he married Marion O'Shea Fortescue, a widow born in Ireland. By each wife he had two children.

Barnwell was also the first president of the Holland Society and vice-president of the Sons of the American Revolution. He served as treasurer of the Democratic National Committee and was twice mentioned by the Democrats as a presidential possibility. He was a member of a three-man committee for the construction of Brooklyn Bridge and a much-in-demand speaker at banquets and political rallies. As an orator he was said to possess "a surpassing command of irony, sarcasm, and vitriolic invective, combined with a powerfully paternal method of appealing to one's better nature."

Few men of the time displayed more facets than Barnwell, but his main preoccupation gradually became conservation. A dedicated naturalist as a boy, he eagerly hunted and fished as a young man. Then he suddenly realized that he was helping exterminate the nation's wildlife. Simultaneously he learned that America's beautiful lakes and rivers were being polluted by sewage, sawdust, and industrial refuse. Lastly, he discovered that commercial fishermen were using nets and other devices that hampered the procreation of fish.

All this assisted Barnwell in finding his number one lifetime Cause. He had himself appointed New York State fish and game commissioner, but slowly his interest channeled exclusively into the sphere of fish. "Up guards and at 'em!" the robust chap liked to roar when facing a knotty problem. Now he rushed pell-mell into the job of preserving America's lake and river fish. He persuaded Albany legislators to appoint a Fish Commission. Naturally, he was chairman of this three-man board, whose two other members held down full-time jobs elsewhere. This was entirely to

Barnwell's liking, for it allowed him to labor without interference, only reporting to the others in order to have his expenditures approved without question.

For twenty years he restocked the state's rivers, fought for fish hatcheries, campaigned against fish nets across the Hudson, and reacted with pleasure when newspapers referred to him as the "Izaak Walton of America" or the country's "Piscatorial High Priest." European countries begged him to bring his know-how to their shores, but usually Barnwell was too busy. So Europe sent men to the United States to study his methods.

Barnwell was also one of the world's great letter writers. His teeming mind fired off letters—in longhand—to a multitude of friends and strangers everywhere. Among his correspondents were General Custer, John Hay, Oscar Wilde, Gilbert and Sullivan (Barnwell himself was tone deaf), Horace Greeley, Joaquin Miller, Bret Harte, and Admiral Dewey.

Because of his turbulent New York activities, Barnwell was not often away from the city he considered his private domain. He had a lordly custom of sending gifts to distinguished foreigners arriving in this country whether he knew them or not. Visitors from Sarah Bernhardt to the Prince of Wales received welcoming presents from Robert Barnwell Roosevelt. If any were surprised, it is not apparent in hundreds of thank-you letters Barnwell received from celebrities. Most of the recipients seemed to know Robert Barnwell Roosevelt and to realize that this was just the sort of gesture he would make to newcomers on American shores.

Theodore, youngest son of C.V.S., was born in 1831 and appeared to share all the characteristics of his older brothers. S. Weir was a jolly man; Theodore had a sense of humor. James Alfred followed the footsteps of C.V.S. into Roosevelt and Son; Theodore, too, went into the family business. Robert Barnwell devoted his life to good works and reform; Theodore did the same with much less bombast, functioning on a local rather than a world scale. The brothers were, in various ways, sporting men. So was Theodore, who liked to ride or drive his four-in-hand around Central Park and over the dirt roads of Harlem at such speed that—in a contemporary expression—the grooms fell off at the corners.

Theodore grew up in the big house on Union Square among his outgoing, uninhibited brothers. As a youth his only complaint was that he was forced by his parents to wear the hand-me-down attire of older boys. Once, on hearing his father and mother discuss what might be trimmed down for him, Theodore burst into tears. The young man did not go to college but at the age of twenty joined father and older brother in Roosevelt and Son. He was given the plate-glass division to handle and did this diligently until C.V.S. retired. When the family business became a banking and investment firm, Theodore was a partner. His last job in the plate-glass field was a large one. Roosevelt and Son supplied the glass for rebuilding Chicago after the fire of 1871. Apparently convinced that this marked the end of a prosperous road, the firm quit the importation of glass.

If Theodore's full personality borrowed from his brothers, his romantic life stemmed directly from C.V.S., first in the line to marry a girl who was not Dutch. C.V.S. had found his treasured helpmate away from New York—in Philadelphia. His two older sons married Philadelphia girls, but up to now no Roosevelt had gone farther afield to find love.

Theodore did. His older brother, S. Weir, had married Mary West of Philadelphia. Her brother, Dr. Hilborne West, was engaged to Susan Elliott from a fine plantation at Roswell, Georgia, nineteen miles north of Atlanta. One evening Hilborne regaled a gathering of the Roosevelt clan with the beauties of Roswell: the white-columned dignity of the mansion, the courtly manners of its occupants, the velvety air, the gentle crooning from slave quarters in the rear, the loveliness of the Southern belles who descended on Roswell for balls and sweet flirtations. The imagination of Theodore, then only nineteen, promptly fired. He asked permission to accompany Hilborne on his next visit to Georgia.

In the summer of 1850 the two young men set off, and to young Theodore Southern plantation life fully lived up to expectations. Of course, from his point of view the Deep South could never take the place of New York but it provided a pleasant interlude for a young man preparing to enter the commercial life of a great city. The Southern belles especially matched his dreams, and with increasing frequency Theodore found his eyes resting on the girlish figure of fifteen-year-old Martha Bulloch.

Martha was a half sister of Susan Elliott, Hilborne's fiancée. She was beautiful, fragile, willowy, a girl with the gift of laughter. Her lovely complexion was later described as "more moonlight-white than cream-white, and in the cheeks there was a coral, rather than a rose, tint." Her blood was mixed Scotch, English and Huguenot French.

Martha's first American ancestor was the Reverend Archibald Stobo, a Scotsman who joined an ill-fated expedition to colonize Darien on the Isthmus of Panama. By his side, as he crossed the rough Atlantic in 1699, stood a young bride. When the Darien colony failed, the Stobos sailed on a fever-ridden ship to Charleston, South Carolina, where Archibald was importuned to act as preacher for Scottish residents of the colony. He and his wife had a daughter Jean who married a Scottish minister named Bulloch and moved to Savannah. Their son, Archibald, prospered as a Georgia planter. He built Roswell, an extensive plantation in the uplands above Atlanta. His son, James Stephens, inherited the wealth and plantation. He married a widow named Elliott, who was already the mother of Susan.

At the end of his visit, Theodore Roosevelt bade farewell to the hospitable South and returned to New York. There he went to work in the office of Roosevelt and Son. Two years later he paid a visit to Dr. and Mrs. Hilborne West in Philadelphia. He found another guest—Martha Bulloch, now aged seventeen. The old attraction flared into love, and when the Southern belle left for Roswell, Theodore followed. By May, 1853, when he returned again to New York, he was engaged. On the day following his departure, Martha wrote him tenderly:

New Amsterdam was a tiny, rambunctious Dutch colony when Claes Martenszen van Rosenvelt and wife Jannetje set eyes on it in the late 1640's.

In Little Old New York of the 1830's, the Roosevelts were known for energy, good humor, the ability to lead full lives.

Isaac Roosevelt (1726-1794), most distinguished limb of the family tree for three hundred years. This Gilbert Stuart portrait hangs in the living room at Hyde Park.

Isaac's son James was a carbon copy of a dynamic father. First of the family to leave New York, he moved to Dutchess County.

Dr. Isaac studied medicine, never practiced. A rare Roosevelt introvert, he lived placidly in Dutchess County.

Dr. Isaac's son was James, father of F.D.R. Some called him a snob, but he lived life exactly as he wished.

A widower with a grown son, James married Sara Delano, beautiful daughter of another Hudson River family.

In New York, cousin C.V.S. turned into the first Roosevelt millionaire. He found the ideal summer spot in Oyster Bay, Long Island.

Theodore Roosevelt, son of C.V.S., never failed to heed a call from his fellow man. He was active in numerous philanthropies.

Theodore Jr., born sickly, furiously exercised his way to rugged health. He loved animals, was also a sportsman-hunter.

Theodore followed grandfather C.V.S. to Oyster Bay. He built Sagamore Hill, the house he loved until death.

Theodore adored his wife and six children. The offspring were almost as energetic as he was.

Theodore was restless as Vice-President. While working off frustrations by mountain climbing, he learned President McKinley had been shot.

The newfangled auto was made to order for President Teddy. He used it at every opportunity, let daughter Alice drive her own car.

In final years hatred and bitterness set in. He died in 1919, aged 60, his body so depleted by exercise that it had no resistance.

Theodore was powerful enough to put over the election of William H. Taft. Later he regretted it, ran against Taft and

Life was pleasant in the Hudson River house where F.D.R. grew up. Springwood was remodeled to its present stateliness in 1915.

Franklin was cheerful, abrim with fun. Cousin Eleanor (Teddy's niece) was inhibited. Yet F.D.R. fell in love, enjoyed teasing the girl.

Franklin could be serious. He ran for the State Senate as a Democrat in Republican Dutchess. He won, here occupies his new seat.

Franklin D. Roosevelt Library

Life had opened up! Franklin was happy as Assistant Secretary of the Navy; Eleanor was losing fears; the children were full of family vigor.

Bachrach

Few men were as addicted to family history as F.D.R. Here he peruses old family Bible on which he took oaths as Governor and President.

A *New Yorker* cover that never ran. Solemn state of nation and recent assassination attempt prompted last-minute decision to discard it.

"Mother, Wilfred wrote a bad word!" Cartoonists had field day with "hate Roosevelt" feelings. Reproduced by permission of *Esquire Magazine.*

Brown Brothers

Franklin's ability to laugh and turn serious matters into jokes helped him bear enormous burdens. Laughing too, James A. Farley.

The icy finger of death pointed at F.D.R. in Yalta. Yet he returned to proclaim himself refreshed by travel, as Roosevelts always were.

Franklin D. Roosevelt Library

United Press International

T.R.'s niece, F.D.R.'s wife, Eleanor was named First Lady of the World. Her energy, patience, wisdom, unshakable good humor, won universal love.

Thee, Dearest Thee:

I promised to tell you if I cried when you left me. I had determined not to do so if possible, but when the dreadful feeling came over me that you were, indeed, gone, I could not help my tears from springing and had to rush away and be alone with myself. Everything now seems associated with you. Even when I run up the stairs going to my own room, I feel as if you were near, and turn involuntarily to kiss my hand to you. I feel, dear Thee,—as though you were part of my existence, and that I can only live in your being, for now I am confident of my own deep love.

Theodore was in his office when this reached him. He immediately shoved aside work to answer:

How can I express to you the pleasure which I received in reading your letter! I felt as you recalled so vividly to my mind the last morning of our parting, the blood rush to my temples; and I had, as I was in the office, to lay the letter down, for a few minutes, to gain control of myself. I had been hoping against hope to receive a letter from you, but *such* a letter! O, Mittie, how deeply, how devotedly I love you! Do continue to return my love as ardently as you do now, or if possible love me more. I know that my love for you merits such return.

Later she wrote:

I long to hear you say once again that you love me. I know you do but still I would like to have a fresh avowal. You have proved that you love me, dear, in a thousand ways and still I long to hear it again and again.

The two were married at Roswell in December, 1853, at the end of a full week of gay receptions, parties, and sundown-to-sunup dances. After a honeymoon they moved into a trim, narrow, four-story home at 28 East Twentieth Street in New York. Robert Barnwell and his wife were ensconced in an identical house next door, while C.V.S. and his wife lived six short blocks to the south.

As a girl from the lazy South, Martha may have found the big city bewildering. Yet life with a Roosevelt was never dull and she must have been diverted by the activities of her beloved Thee in his own habitat. For young Theodore Roosevelt differed from most New Yorkers of his background. He was big, with a leonine face, its warmth hidden by a forbidding set of whiskers. Like his brother Barnwell, Thee was able to do a prodigious number of things at once. He adored his new home and spent much time in it. At the same time he worked long hours at Roosevelt and Son.

This would be enough for the average husband, but Theodore Roosevelt was not average. "One must live for the living" was his credo. While Barnwell devoted himself vigorously to Causes, Thee was ever on the alert for a call from the rest of humanity. "He had a strong sense of obligation to society," writes his great-nephew Nicholas. "If he became convinced that something had to be set right, he shouldered the burden himself and enlisted the aid of friends." Indeed, friends became accustomed to Theodore's charitable appeals. Seeing him approach with a glint in his eye, they automatically inquired, "How much this time, Theodore?"

The sight of a newsboy shivering in the cold was enough to arouse Theodore's interest in the plight of the city's lost and homeless children. He helped organize a Newsboys' Lodging House and every Sunday night left home to spend the evening there. As generous with money as with time and counsel, he found foster homes for many boys or paid railroad fares back home for runaways.

Theodore's charities only began here. New York City was commencing its humanitarian and charitable endeavors, and he became involved in nearly every one. He was a pioneer in the city's helpful work with the blind; a founder of the Children's Aid Society; vice-president of the State Charities Aid Association; member of the board of United Charities and the State Board of Charities; a founder of the Orthopedic Hospital. And still he had time to be a sponsor of Miss Slattery's Night School for Little Italians. Theodore was also a founder of the Society for the Prevention of Cruelty to Animals and—on a different echelon—of the Metropolitan Museum of Art, the Museum of Natural History, and the Union League Club.

As the Roosevelts became more American and less Dutch, some members of the family left the Dutch Reformed Church for other denominations. Theodore broke away to attend the Presbyterian Church on Madison Square, where he conducted a Mission Bible class for young men. He was interested in every kind of humanitarian effort, but his main preoccupation was the poor and unfortunate. The busy man spent every Monday visiting slum families. Yet with all this he was no pompous, humorless reformer. His wife was considered one of the belles of New York society and he delighted in dancing through the night with her at balls. His friend Louisa Lee Schuyler would recall: "Who more than he enjoyed a four-in-hand drive in the Park or a waltz in the ballroom? . . . I can see him now, in full evening dress, serving a most generous supper to his newsboys in the Lodging House, and later dashing off to a party on Fifth Avenue."

With this great interest in his fellow man, which increased rather than diminished as he grew older, Theodore Roosevelt neglected none of his family responsibilities. A year after marriage to his Mittie, the two became parents of a girl christened Anna. Four years later Martha was again pregnant, and this time she and Thee prayed for a boy. During this period of pregnancy the young Roosevelts of Twentieth Street seemed the most fortunate of couples. The husband had an unusual amount of charm, vim, and vigor. The wife was sweet and delicately beautiful. The two led a life of ease and comfort, for they had more money than most couples.

Indeed, the young Roosevelts might be living out the happy ending to a Victorian romance in which a brisk young man from the North boldly captures the dainty hand of a cloistered Southern belle. The birth of a male heir should do no more than write a glowing finis to this fragile love story. It did not seem a moment for Destiny to appear. . . .

9

❦

BOYHOOD OF A ROOSEVELT

A BOY WHO BECAME PRESIDENT OF THE UNITED STATES WAS BORN to the Theodore Roosevelts of East Twentieth Street at 7:45 on the evening of October 27, 1858. His weight was eight pounds and he was christened Theodore. The child was given no middle name, nor did the father and mother see fit to avail themselves of the Dutch middle initial I or J of family custom. In later years young Theodore sometimes added "Jr." to his name to distinguish himself from his father.

But at first this was not necessary, since the Roosevelts were much given to nicknames. Theodore Sr. was already "Thee," while his wife was "Mittie." Anna, the oldest child, was "Bamie" or "Bye." As soon as he was able to make sounds, little Theodore became "Teedie." Two other Roosevelt offspring followed Teedie at intervals of eighteen months. Of these Corinne became "Conie" and Elliott was inevitably called "Ellie." As the eldest by four years, Anna always seemed to belong to the generation of grown-ups. The younger children, banded so tightly together in nursery play, called themselves "We Three."

The elder Roosevelts' satisfaction in their brood was somewhat alloyed by the fact that Bamie grew up with a spinal curvature, while Teedie was the victim of attacks of asthma. Of the other children, Corinne had occasional bouts of illness, but Elliott was blessedly robust. However, Theodore's asthma was terrifying and, because of it, he required much parental attention. During the attacks the child gasped frantically for air. He could sleep only when propped high in bed or wrapped in blankets in a big chair. Even so, the attacks continued. Holding Teedie tight in his arms, Theodore Sr. spent long nights pacing around the house. Sometimes he dispatched a servant for a horse and open buggy. Then, with Teedie bundled in robes beside him, he raced through city streets in the belief that this forced helpful air into the boy's lungs. When Teedie was grown, he once dictated staccato recollections of his father's ministrations:

My really great father—a gentleman and a sport—he was the first American to drive four horses handsomely through New York—in style, in the good old English style, with everything that belonged—he worked for, he saved, my life. I was a weak-lunged, asthmatic child, and I remember—I think I remember—him carrying me in my distress, in my battles for breath, up and down a room all night. Handsome dandy that he was, the thought of him now and always has been a sense of comfort. I could breathe, I could sleep, when he had me in his arms. My father—he got me breath, he got me lungs, strength—life.

For fear of increasing the asthma, Teedie was ordered to remain quiet for long periods. He grew into a wan, wistful child, with a wide mouth, large teeth, unruly hair, and spindly legs. Huddled in a chair with a book, he looked pathetic, but this was deceptive. "Some minds are cisterns, others are fountains," a writer has said. From the beginning, Teedie's was a soaring fountain. He liked to talk and be talked to, and he joined freely with grownups in any conversation. He was able to read at a precocious age and especially enjoyed books about animals and the African jungles. In the nursery he kept the other members of We Three enthralled by imaginative, serial jungle sagas predating Rudyard Kipling. After telling a story the gifted child took a pencil and tried to write it down, for he seemed to find writing as pleasurable as talking. Then he took a new grip on the pencil and made illustrations for the text.

Problems other than the children's health assailed the Roosevelt household. As clouds of civil war gathered, Mittie Roosevelt, former Georgia belle, remained loyal to the Southern cause. After the birth of her children Mittie had become "delicate" and exerted only the gentlest pressure on her family. To help, her sister, Anna Bulloch, came to New York. She, in turn, was followed by matriarchal Mrs. Bulloch, the duchess of Roswell. These three Confederate ladies set up an unlikely beachhead of Southern sympathy on East Twentieth Street.

Theodore Sr. never permitted this to bother him. A steadfast Northerner in his sympathies, he first joined with other New York merchants in efforts to head off the conflict. One reason was that the South had taken at least $5,000,000 worth of Northern goods on credit. With other New York businessmen, Theodore petitioned Congress to make every effort to prevent war. Then he helped promote a huge antiwar mass meeting.

With the firing on Fort Sumter, however, Theodore Sr. became a passionate supporter of war. Out of deference to the Bullochs, he did not volunteer for service in the Northern army. Indeed, the Roosevelts—so redoubtable in Revolutionary ranks—were oddly passive throughout the Civil War. Only one member of the obscure Pennsylvania branch actually fought; he lost a leg at Gettysburg. Yet the Roosevelts made their feelings unmistakably known. Male members of the family had been stanch Democrats since the early days of the city. Now they shattered this strong family tradition by turning Republican or becoming so-called Lincoln Democrats. Theodore Sr. turned into an outright Republican, as did his brothers, S. Weir and James Alfred. But Robert Barnwell was a Lincoln Democrat. In Dutchess County, Dr. Isaac Roosevelt and his two sons were the same.

Having become a Republican, Theodore Sr. felt he should do

still more. "I would never feel satisfied with myself after this war is over if I do nothing," he informed Mittie. During his work in the slums Theodore noted that many men marching off to war were leaving behind destitute families. His sympathetic mind immediately began to grapple with this problem. With the aid of two other men, he thought up the idea of allotments—small amounts of money voluntarily withheld from a soldier's pay to be sent home to dependents. Theodore took his idea to Washington but found Congress unable to believe such a plan could be carried out without hidden personal gain. Three months were needed to allay these fears, and during that time Theodore became friendly with President and Mrs. Lincoln. The First Lady took a special liking to the ebullient young New Yorker and often invited him to accompany her on afternoon carriage rides. Sometimes they went on shopping expeditions, and he helped her choose a new bonnet.

Finally Theodore Sr. was appointed one of three United States allotment commissioners, acting under orders from the War Department. Rugged days followed. During the winter of 1861-62, Theodore toured battle lines urging his voluntary allotments on a suspicious soldiery. Riding horseback into a camp, he alighted to stand behind a table and deliver a speech, trying to persuade the men to part with some of their army pay—in most cases, money ordinarily allotted for liquor and women.

Often Theodore arrived late at night, and in one letter wrote home, "I could not help thinking what a subject for a painting it would make as I stood out there in the dark night, surrounded by the men with one candle just showing glimpses of their faces— tents all around us in the woods." His opinion of the Union army was not flattering, for all too often the officers who greeted him were drunk and the men sullen. Yet there were bright spots. One soldier, after signing up for an allotment of $5 a month, reappeared to say, "My old lady has always been good to me, and if you please, change mine to ten."

As he progressed from one camp to another, Theodore wrote letters home signed "YOUR LOVING HUSBAND WHO WANTS VERY

MUCH TO SEE YOU." Two of Mittie's brothers, one a boy of sixteen, were fighting in the Confederate navy and her feelings were truly torn. Yet she bravely responded with homey items, like the news that Teedie had come downstairs one morning to say, "I've got a toothache in my stomach."

Theodore's efforts to sell the Union soldiers on allotments took him as far north as Niagara. Then he turned the field work over to others and returned to New York to become resident allotment commissioner. He also went back to his desk at Roosevelt and Son but, as always, did far more. He raised money to equip the first Negro regiment to fight for the North and helped the ladies of the awkwardly named Sanitary Commission, a precursor of the Red Cross, collect funds to send bandages and other supplies to the fighting lines. He next realized that the government was not keeping its promise to disabled soldiers, so he organized a Protective War Claims Commission which channeled a million dollars in benefits to deserving veterans. At war's end the indefatigable man set up a Soldiers' Employment Bureau.

Despite all his outside activity, Theodore Sr. remained dominant in his own home. Grandmother Bulloch died in 1864, spared the knowledge that General Sherman had sacked Roswell. Anna Bulloch stayed on, more of a mother to the children than Mittie. For Mittie Roosevelt's delicate health was accompanied by an increasing vagueness which left her unable to keep household accounts or remember appointments. In addition, she developed peculiarities, among them such a mania for cleanliness that she kept furniture covered by sheets. Yet Mittie was still a person of beauty and social charm. The children loved her and in recognition of her helplessness around the house called her Little Motherling.

It was a happy household, with the youngsters somehow aware of the good fortune of their birth. "We had the most lovely mother, the most manly, able, and delightful father, and the most charming aunt, Anna Bulloch . . . with whom children were ever blessed," Corinne wrote years later. But if the children loved mother and aunt, they adored Theodore Sr. "My father was the best man I ever knew," Teedie later wrote. "He combined strength and courage with gentleness, tenderness, and great unselfishness. I never knew anyone who got more joy out of living than did my father, or anyone who more wholeheartedly performed every duty."

Theodore Sr. had in full the family talent for parenthood. "My father was the most intimate friend of all his children," Corinne writes, "and we all craved him as our most desired companion." To her father she applies the adjectives *sunny, gay, dominant, unselfish, forceful,* and *versatile*. She has a word for another quality that set him apart as a father. It was, she says, the quality of Charm: "One of his delightful rules was that on the birthday of each child he should give himself in some special way to that child, and many were the perfect excursions which he and I took together on my birthday." On these perfect days father and daughter drove out into the country behind a pair of fine trotters. After unhitching the horses, the two consumed a picnic lunch under a tree, then passed the afternoon reading poetry to each other.

The Roosevelt home was a mixture of rare freedoms and Victorian stiffness. We Three were allowed liberties unusual for children of the time, but aside from the nursery the house was uncomfortable. Horsehair furniture, when not covered by Mittie's sheets, scratched the bare legs of children. The first-floor parlor, boasting a chandelier of cut-glass prisms, was kept resolutely shut except on Sundays. Each day began with prayers read by Thee, the children struggling for the privilege of sitting beside him during the reading. After this formal beginning to the day, Teedie was often sent to a market on Broadway to buy fresh strawberries for breakfast.

On one of these trips he spotted a dead seal, caught in the harbor the night before, stretched out on a board in the center of a store. "The seal filled me with every possible feeling of romance and adventure," he later recalled. Specifically, it fired him with the desire to grow up to be a naturalist, and, despite many triumphs in other fields, he remained primarily a naturalist all his life. So long as the seal lay in the store, Teedie haunted the premises. At one point he took its measurements, laboriously using a child's pocket rule. Then he ran home to begin writing a book on natural history. That night he dreamed happily of owning the seal and stuffing it, a vision that almost materialized when the storekeeper presented him with the bony skull. With it he began a Roosevelt Museum of Natural History in his bedroom. "My mother and father encouraged me warmly in this, as they always did in everything that could give me wholesome pleasure or help to develop me," he writes.

The Roosevelt children never attended school. At first they were taught at home by Mittie and Anna Bulloch who themselves had received only the education necessary to create Southern belles. For a time a French mamselle brought instruction to the household. Sometimes Theodore Sr. guided the education of his offspring; then, as Bamie matured, she took over the job. But for the most part We Three were taught by Teedie and his voracious reading.

In 1869 a new type of education loomed for the children. In the spring of that year Mittie persuaded her husband to take the family abroad to visit her two Confederate brothers who had settled in England. Bamie was fifteen; Theodore, eleven; Conie, nine; and Elliott, seven. None wished to go abroad, which meant missing the usual summer holiday. For Theodore, no less than C.V.S., believed an unfettered out-of-town vacation necessary for growing children. "We were always wildly eager to get to the country when spring came," Teedie later remembered. Corinne says, "Summers were the special delight of our lives. The days never seemed long enough, the hours flew on joyous wings. Groups of joyous children invented and carried into effect every imaginable game, and, as ever, our father was the delightful collaborator in every scheme of pleasure." Where C.V.S. had already settled in Oyster Bay, Theodore Sr. was still testing other vacation spots. He tried Madison, New Jersey; Riverdale, New York; and Barrytown in Dutchess County, where he rented the John Aspinwall estate.

Faced with a long tour of Europe, We Three were also appalled at the thought of missing Christmas at home. "Christmas was an occasion of literally delirious joy," Teedie writes. "I never knew anyone else to have what seemed to me such attractive Christmases." But the mutterings of childish mutiny dwindled as they set sail on the paddle-wheel steamer *Scotia*. After visiting the Bulloch brothers in Liverpool, the family proceeded to the Lake District of England, to Holland, Belgium, Germany, Switzerland, Austria, Germany, and finally to Rome, where Christmas proved almost as rapturous as at home.

The Roosevelts never relaxed when traveling and, despite his frail appearance, Teedie was the most tireless and energetic of them all. In true Roosevelt fashion he had already begun a daily diary in which he made such jottings as: "England is not nice at all" . . . "Scotland on the whole very nice." In addition, he set down critiques of cathedrals, paintings, and out-of-doors scenery. He also seized every opportunity to collect birds, mice, and snakes —much to the annoyance of Elliott, who had to share his hotel rooms.

Teedie wrote reams of letters home, for writing was still as effortless to him as talking—and would be so all through life. Anna Bulloch had remained in the United States to marry James King Gracie, and Teedie wrote her often. He also corresponded with aunts, uncles, and cousins, as well as friends of his younger sister. Among these was a girl named Edith Kermit Carow, whose family lived next to C.V.S. in Fourteenth Street. Often he added his inimitable pencil sketches to the letters and signed himself Teedie or T.D., but seldom Teddy—a name he never liked.

One reason for the European trip was the hope that sea air and foreign climes would help Teedie's asthma—"asmer" as he wrote it in his unschooled spelling. But the trip was little help. He was still sickly despite his unusual energy of mind and spirit. The glint of eyeglasses was a new feature of his appearance, for it had been discovered that the boy was nearsighted. Yet asthma remained his worst affliction. During attacks he fought desperately for breath. The condition was better by day, worse by night; less troublesome in summer than in winter. This much the family learned from agonizing experience, and it was about as much as doctors seemed to know.

Finally, Theodore Sr. decided to take his son's health in his own hands. Medical men thought Teedie's frail physique was caused by the asthma. But was it? Theodore asked himself. Suppose the reverse was true—with bodily weakness causing the asthma? If the boy could first build his body, the father reasoned, the asthma might vanish. The vigorous man decided to cure his son by exercise.

At a time when most people feared fresh air and slept with windows closed, Theodore Roosevelt, Sr., was a fresh-air fiend. All Teedie's exercising, he decided, must be done in the fresh air. Such a regime might kill as well as cure a boy with Teedie's affliction, but Theodore Sr. had no doubts. He remodeled the rear room of the second story of the Twentieth Street house into an outside porch, stocking it with barbells, horizontal bars, punching bag. "You must *make* your body," he lectured Teedie. "It is hard drudgery to make one's body, but I know you will do it." Teedie promised, and celebrated the event by turning his beloved diary into a "sporting calendar" which recorded chin-ups and time spent punching the bag.

Still he did not pursue physical rehabilitation with the same gusto that he put into talking, reading, and writing. A good part of the time he only daydreamed about exercising. Teedie had mastered taxidermy and found the mounting of birds and animals fascinating. In fact, during his youth he usually gave off a foul odor of formaldehyde and the guts of dead animals. Yet his parents never complained. "I suppose that all growing boys tend to be grubby," he later wrote, "but the ornithological small boy, or, indeed, the boy with a taste for natural history of any kind, is generally the very grubbiest of all."

Now came an episode impossible to underestimate in writing of the nation's twenty-sixth President. For it changed his entire life. At the age of thirteen, after a particularly severe asthma attack, he was sent alone to Moosehead Lake, Maine, where the pure air promised relief. In the stagecoach en route to the lake, he found himself facing two boys his own age. Teedie wore glasses, he was owl-eyed, pallid, and wispy. In addition, he was precocious and eager to start conversations. The boys didn't like him and began to torment him—"a foreordained and predestined victim," he later saw himself. The boys said such ugly things that Teedie lost his temper and tried to fight with his fists. The boys mockingly kept him at arm's length and tormented him more—"I found that either one singly could not only handle me with easy contempt, but handle me so as not to hurt me much and yet to prevent my doing any damage whatever in return."

It was an experience that seared his Roosevelt-Bulloch pride, at the same time miraculously fusing his father's recent advice about exercise into the wellspring of Roosevelt energy. From now on Theodore Jr. was a changed personality. He was a boy whose guiding drive was a belief in the efficacy of strenuous physical exercise. Or did he spend the rest of his life running madly from the vision of his humiliation by the two rough boys?

In any event, as he wrote later, "the episode taught me what probably no amount of advice could have taught me." If, as his father declared, physical prowess was the means to avoid such disgrace in the future, why, he would gain physical prowess. To get it, he would exercise as few people in the world ever exercised— "Having become quickly and bitterly conscious that I did not have the natural prowess to hold my own, I decided I would try to supply its place by training."

At Twentieth Street he began to spend hours in the outdoor gym. "For many years one of my most vivid recollections is seeing him between horizontal bars, widening his chest by regular, monotonous motion," writes Corinne. He also took boxing lessons from a pugilist named John Long. Slowly results became visible. The faithful diary proudly records an improvement of five-eighths of an inch in chest expansion—his chest was now 34; weight, 124. Like his father and other Roosevelts, Teedie was developing an ability to do many things at once. Though he exercised in the gym a large part of each day, his wide reading and natural history studies never seemed to be neglected. Nor his diary.

In the autumn of 1872, when Teedie was fourteen, his father decided that a winter in the heat of the Nile would benefit the family. Again, the younger children objected to the trip, but by the time of arrival in Egypt young Theodore was in a state of churning excitement over the new specimens of animal, vegetable, and mineral life to be found there. On the Nile his father bought a houseboat with sails and engaged a native crew that towed it from the banks when no wind came along. At each tie-up Teedie plunged ashore in search of specimens for his collection. Even Theodore Sr. found it hard to match his dervish son. "I walked through the bogs with him, at the risk of sinking hopelessly and helplessly, for hours," he wrote home. "I felt I had to keep up with Teedie!"

Teedie discovered yet another skill—he was a hunter. "I killed two pretty little finches," he confides to the diary. His joy was unconfined at Christmas when his father gave him a double-barreled breech-loading shotgun. With it he shot storks, ibis, owls, pelicans, and doves. Most of these he skinned and stuffed before the admiring eyes of family and crew. "I have almost two hundred skins," he wrote.

How the dedicated naturalist in him reconciled the demon hunter is a question. Teedie suffered a few qualms over shooting birds and nondangerous animals but never stopped hunting. The answer seems to be that, even as a boy, Theodore did what he liked, acting first and thinking afterward. When really enjoying something, he might never think about it at all. The role of hunter fitted the active personality he was busily developing and there seemed no reason to curtail it. Rather than the Dutch stubbornness which might be expected in his character, this may have been part of an eternal boyishness still visible when he was the nation's chief executive. "You must always remember," his friend Cecil Spring-Rice wrote then, "that the President is about six."

While combining the roles of hunter and naturalist, fourteen-year-old Teedie rode the desert astride a donkey, with a gun slung over his shoulder. When not hunting, he explored ruins, furiously taking notes. "I think I have enjoyed myself this winter more than ever before," he wrote Edith Kermit Carow. After the Nile, where one night the houseboat tied up near another carrying Ralph Waldo Emerson, the Roosevelts took a horseback tour of the Holy Land, then went by steamer to Rhodes. After that, Athens and Constantinople.

All this took a full year. Then Theodore Sr. felt obliged to return home on family business. Among other things, Thee had decided that the house on Twentieth Street was too small and proposed to build a more commodious residence in the desolate uptown region of Fifty-seventh Street just west of Fifth Avenue. Until this new home was ready, the rest of the family remained in Europe.

We Three could speak French but not German. To remedy this the children were deposited in Dresden with a family named Minckwitz, while delicate Mittie repaired the ravages of the year by taking the Carlsbad cure. Left alone, We Three joined other expatriate children in starting the Dresden Literary American Club, whose members wrote stories, poems, and plays for mutual edification. Teedie, now fifteen, let his hair grow long in the manner of a German poet, "*a la* mop" he called it. His dynamic personality grated on a few members of the literary club, one of whom said, "he always thought he could do things better than anyone else." He continued to be a naturalist, still annoying Elliott by keeping dead owls and dissected mice in their room. He also formed an admiration for the German character which lasted until 1914. But above all, he was energetic, writing home to his father:

When I am not studying my lessons or out walking, I spend all my time in translating natural history, wrestling with Richard, a young cousin of the Minckwitz' whom I can throw as often as he throws me, and I also sometimes cook, although my efforts in the culinary art are really confined to grinding coffee, beating eggs, and making hash, and such light labors.

The humanitarian efforts of Theodore Roosevelt, Sr., never abated. Doctors had been helpless when, in early years, his daughter Bamie developed a spinal curvature. Now, in New York, the father met Dr. Charles Fayette Taylor, who had begun to pioneer in orthopedic work. What the city needed, the forceful Thee decided, was a hospital devoted to Dr. Taylor's work. When his family returned to occupy the new home at 6 West Fifty-seventh Street, he persuaded the hospitable Mittie to invite a group of wealthy friends to an afternoon reception. Rather than tea and cakes, the assembled ladies found crippled children from the slums lying on the dining-room table and elsewhere. Nearby were braces and walking aids advocated by Dr. Taylor. Thee and his children volubly demonstrated how the appliances could be used. Among the first to be impressed by all this was Mrs. John Jacob Astor, who exclaimed, "Theodore, you are right! These children must be restored and made into active citizens again, and I for one will help you in your work!" Enough money was collected on this afternoon to begin construction of the New York Orthopedic Hospital, the second city hospital for which a Roosevelt was responsible.

In the summer of 1874 Theodore Sr. at last followed his two brothers to Oyster Bay. C.V.S., who discovered the sleepy little town on the Sound, had died in 1871. But his two older sons had bought summer residences in the Cove Neck section of Oyster Bay.

Robert Barnwell had inexplicably chosen nearby Sayville. Now Theodore joined this family colony. To the delight of his boisterous progeny, he rented a house named Tranquility, which looked like a small-scale copy of the Roswell plantation house. With the Roosevelts, the residence seldom resembled its name. "Countless cousins, assembling there with their friends, fairly rocked the old walls," writes Corinne. To date, the Roosevelt offspring had rapturously enjoyed every summer passed in America, but apparently had never really known the meaning of holiday happiness. Oyster Bay proved perfect.

"An enchanted spot," Corinne calls it, christening it The Happy Land of Woods and Waters. She goes on: "Every special delight seems concerned with Oyster Bay. We took long rides on horseback through the lanes then so seemingly remote, so far from the broad highways which are now traversed by thousands of motors, but were then the scenes of picnics and every imaginable spree."

Teedie, no less that Corinne, reacted passionately to Oyster Bay. Here he found one more love that lasted a lifetime. The first love of his life was his family; the second, natural history; a third, strenuous exercise. His new love was Cove Neck, Oyster Bay.

At sixteen Teedie was filling out, beginning to look more like a normal boy. Constant gymnastics, plus boxing, walking, swimming, and riding, had brought him closer to good health. His teeth shone when he smiled, his eyeglasses glinted in the sun, and he was a tireless, dynamic talker. Cove Neck offered a horde of growing cousins and neighbor children, among them Edith Carow. In early childhood days Elliott, healthy, neat, good-looking, had been leader of outdoor games. But suddenly Teedie was the leader. Bursting energy combined with a vivid imagination and increasing self-confidence to make cousins and friends look up to him as the dominant figure on hikes, picnics, horseback and boat rides.

Yet Teedie still found time for solitary nature study. "Days full of ornithological enjoyment and reptilian rapture," he called Oyster Bay summers. He observed a rare Ipswich sparrow and a fish crow and sent his notes to an ornithological magazine which gratefully printed them. He also hunted. The voracious boy-reader had not skipped poetry and he enjoyed standing alone atop Cooper's Bluff, near a hill the Indians named Sagamore, declaiming Poe and Swinburne into the teeth of the wind.

Only in education did he lag behind other boys. In his favorite field of natural history he could hold his own with experts; in literature and American history he was unusually well read. But otherwise his education was lopsided. His spelling was spotty, arithmetic poor, and other subjects weak. Delicate health had been a reason for keeping him out of school, but this excuse was no longer valid. Now his parents decided that Teedie must go to college. Brushing aside Princeton and Columbia, heretofore Roosevelt strongholds, they chose Harvard. A young tutor was hired, and with his help Teedie crammed three years of formal education into two. In the spring of 1876 he passed entrance examinations.

With this rose another question: What should he prepare for? Nature had always been Theodore Jr.'s burning enthusiasm, suggesting a career as a teacher or a conservationist, the latter in emulation of Uncle Barnwell. In truth, Teedie resembled Barnwell more than he did his own father. Like Barnwell, he always seemed propelled by a superabundance of explosive energy, while Theodore Sr. appeared to harness his dynamism, using it unobtrusively but to best effect. Again, Barnwell and Teedie seemed to prefer *things,* while Theodore Sr. was beamed on people.

But, however one looked at the matter, Teedie's talents did not promise large remuneration. In view of his special interests in ornithology and zoology, he might not be paid at all. At this point Theodore Sr., acting in the family tradition, promised his son a small income for life if he decided to devote himself to science. But, the father pointed out, if Teedie chose this road he would never have much money himself and the income of the elder Roosevelts would be diminished accordingly.

No decision about the future had been reached when Theodore Roosevelt, Jr., the name he now used, arrived at Harvard. Freed from family supervision, he blossomed overnight into a dude. In addition to fancy clothes, he grew full sideburns which reached to his chin and turned out a surprising red. Still slight, his outsize teeth and wide mouth made him even more conspicuous than in later years. Theodore had traveled so widely and spent so much time with adults that professors failed to awe him. He seemed completely sure of himself, and in some classes acted as if he knew more than the teacher. Theodore Jr.'s branch of the family was innately conservative and he followed tradition by deploring the efforts of Charles W. Eliot, the new young president of Harvard, who was striving to modernize the curriculum. Before Dr. Eliot, the eight hundred students of the college had studied the same subjects. "Eliot turned the whole university over like a flap-jack," commented Oliver Wendell Holmes. Theodore was one who didn't like it.

Still the conservative mind that opposed Dr. Eliot managed to appear eccentric by Harvard standards. Theodore Jr. liked to study and rose at 7:15 on Saturdays to study more. In class he listened to what professors said and often stood up to dispute their teachings. He did not endear himself to fellow students by complaining, "Now few fellows have come here with any idea of getting an education." Harvard men affected a pose of bored sophistication—a satirical poem called them "indifferent spectators to the world." Said Henry Adams, "If Harvard College gave nothing else, it gave calm." In the midst of calm Theodore Roosevelt, Jr., was turmoil. One undergraduate wrote, "It was not considered good form to move at more than a walk, [but] Roosevelt was always running."

Yet he enjoyed himself. Indeed, the Theodore Roosevelt who had been an unusually mature boy seemed at Harvard to be turning into a happy though somewhat immature man. He lived in private lodgings, away from the college, presumably to benefit his health. The walls of his rooms at 16 Winthrop Street were decorated with mooseheads, while menageries of live snakes and mice covered tables and chairs.

Because of his family background, he mingled with boys of Harvard's upper crust and mixed in Boston society. His close friends were named Saltonstall, Minot, Bacon, Weld, and Hooper. He liked the girls he met through classmates and the girls liked him—that is, until he began to discourse on natural history. He made the ultra-exclusive Porcellian Club, and one day shattered precedent by taking a pretty girl to lunch there. He tipped the scales at 135 pounds and dreamed of becoming lightweight champion of the college. In the ring he contrived a terrifying scowl, but without his glasses could not see his opponent well enough for knockout blows.

Inevitably he became a member of the Natural History Club.

He joined the staff of the *Advocate*, but the youth who always wrote as naturally as he talked made surprisingly few contributions. He still felt close to his family and wrote frequent letters to "Darling, Beloved Motherling," and others in West Fifty-seventh Street. His father, Conie, Edith Carow, and cousin Maud Elliott were invited to Cambridge for his freshman Class Day. Not another boy in college, he wrote home, "has a family who loves him as well as you all do me, and I am *sure* there is no one who has a father who is also his best and most intimate friend."

Theodore Roosevelt, Sr., had remained a member of the Republican party after the Civil War, though his brother Barnwell and the Dutchess County Roosevelts returned to the Democratic fold. When Thee was interested in a cause he worked hard for it, and he labored hard for the Republicans in each election. He did so for principle rather than reward. Hence he, no less than others, was astounded when Rutherford B. Hayes unexpectedly appointed him to the post of collector of customs for the port of New York. Among others surprised were Senator Roscoe Conkling and powerful New York State Boss Tom Platt, both of whom had expected to dispense this patronage plum themselves. The two exploded in fury and plotted a strategy of postponement. "We will foil the President," Platt swore. He kept the appointment bottled up in Congress for two years.

As he awaited the results of this political strife, Theodore Sr. continued as before. He was forty-seven years old, still much in love with his Southern wife. His rare quality of charm was still apparent in relations with his children, and in the fall of 1877 he accompanied Bamie to Bar Harbor for a vacation. A pleasant trip was made especially so by social attentions from parents of boys Teedie knew at Harvard.

In this happy atmosphere Thee took up mountain climbing, doing it with full Roosevelt gusto. The vital man may have climbed too much, stirring up latent trouble in his intestines. He returned to Fifty-seventh Street in pain and was put to bed by doctors. He remained bedridden, in increasing agony, for three months. Doctors diagnosed his trouble as cancer of the bowel, but feared to operate. Early in February Thee took a turn for the worse. Theodore Jr., in his sophomore year, was not told of his father's illness for fear of interrupting his studies.

However, New York City knew it. As word spread that the elder Theodore Roosevelt was sinking, the rich arrived in carriages to pay respects, while the poor he had so long befriended collected on the sidewalk outside to await word from the sickroom. Among them were newsboys from the Home and little Italian girls from Miss Slattery's school. Others came from the Orthopedic Hospital or the homes for the blind. On February 10, 1878, Theodore died. The New York *World*, never a newspaper to pay unearned tribute, headlined the story of his burial: FUNERAL OF HIM WHO WAS EYES TO THE BLIND, FEET TO THE LAME, GOOD TO ALL.

Theodore Jr. was, of course, desolate. "I have lost the only human being to whom I tell *everything*," he lamented, "never failing to get loving advice and sweet sympathy in return. . . . With the help of my God I will try to lead such a life as he would have wished."

He vowed to keep all his father's letters forever—as lifetime talismans against evil.

10

JAMES AND SALLIE

ONE NIGHT IN MAY, 1880, MRS. THEODORE ROOSEVELT, SR., GAVE A dinner party at her home at 6 West Fifty-seventh Street. At the table, in addition to the hostess, were her daughters Anna (Bamie) and Corinne. Also present was Miss Sara Delano, a close friend and contemporary of Bamie. Among the gentlemen were a Mr. Crowninshield of Boston and James Roosevelt, Esq., of Hyde Park, New York.

The James Roosevelt who wended his way to Fifty-seventh Street on that night was not a stripling who might be expected to display interest in any of the young ladies present. Rather, he was fifty-two years old, and thus three years older than the late Theodore Roosevelt, who had died two years before. In addition, James himself was a widower of four years standing and a recent grandfather to boot. If this James Roosevelt paid attention to any of the ladies at the dinner, it would undoubtedly be to his hostess, the ever-charming Mittie Roosevelt, five years his junior. There was also the possibility that Mr. Roosevelt might not pay particular attention to any of the ladies. He had already lived a full life, and might be content to spend the rest of his days as a comfortable widower.

This fifty-two-year-old James was the older son of Dr. Isaac, the Roosevelt recluse in whom the family blood appeared to grow thin. James Roosevelt had been born in 1828, when the President of the United States was John Quincy Adams. The mainspring of James's life was a deep love of Dutchess County and the area around Poughkeepsie where he had grown up. Yet this attachment to the Hudson Valley had not confined him to the existence of a country squire. He was a man of manifold outside interests, and as a gentleman-capitalist had ranged far from the proscribed life of Hudson River gentry.

Courteous, even-tempered, fastidious, James Roosevelt held himself with a calm, upright dignity and always looked most at home when carrying a riding crop. On his long face the sensitive, fine-honed features of Dr. Isaac had been given new strength, no doubt by his Aspinwall mother. From early manhood James wore heavy muttonchop whiskers which brought a severity to his refined and handsome face. In all, he was a squire-businessman-sportsman who, after Dutchess County, most loved English manorial life. Some relatives found this annoying and called him a snob. Years later one said, "He tried to pattern himself on Lord Landsdowne, sideburns and all, but what he really looked like was Landsdowne's coachman."

For all his air of dignified aristocracy, James Roosevelt was a pleasant fellow. He had a hearty, ready laugh and a fund of amusing anecdotes to punctuate his conversation. One business associate recalled that the atmosphere in the office always brightened when he entered the door.

James was also one of the well-educated Roosevelts. Born at Mount Hope, the Poughkeepsie home of his grandfather James, he moved with his parents to the newly built Rosedale at the age of two. Mount Hope and Rosedale were close together, so that James Jr., as he was sometimes called, sat under the thumb of Grandfather James who was determined to give him a superior education. As a boy he went to Poughkeepsie Collegiate, a private school for the sons of Hudson Valley gentlemen. Later he was sent to Dr. Hyde's Academy at Lee, Massachusetts. Both Grandfather James and Dr. Isaac Roosevelt had gone to Princeton, but James was ready for higher education at such an early age that he was sent to New York University. Thus he could live at the Bleecker Street home of his grandfather or at the University Place residence of his mother's family. At N.Y.U. James won a gold medal for debating but otherwise did not excel. In 1848 he switched to Union College in Schenectady, then considered one of the finest small colleges in America. He graduated from Union at the age of nineteen, after joining Delta Phi, the nation's first secret fraternity.

The wealthy man's pattern of the day next required James to make a Grand Tour of Europe. His grandfather had died in 1847, leaving him under the full control of Dr. Isaac, a fussy parent with a morbid fear of sickness and accident. His mother's Aspinwall determination at last untangled the young man from his father's terrors of a transatlantic trip, and in the company of a Dutchess County neighbor James embarked in 1850 on a tour that was truly grand.

Lasting almost two years, it began in England where James mingled with landed gentry and developed his lifetime admiration for the noble breed. He then traveled through France, Germany, Greece, and Italy, there proving that hot fires flamed beneath his calm exterior. Surprisingly tossing off all bonds of young gentlemanly restraint, he enlisted in the fighting legions of Garibaldi. In a red shirt, with feathered hat atilt, he stood prepared to fight for Italian independence. But James had the bad luck—or was it the good?—to volunteer at a period when the fiery legions rested between battles. After a month of boredom he tore off the red shirt and continued on his Grand Tour.

Returning to the United States, James took a two-year law course at Harvard. He graduated on his twenty-third birthday. The young man had inherited Mount Hope on the death of his grandfather, and he began to spend as much time as possible there. He also became associated with the New York office of the well-known lawyer Benjamin Douglas Silliman. The firm did corporation work and within a year James found himself a director of the Consolidated Coal Company of Maryland. It was his first exposure to the business world and he found it more stimulating than law. At the same time he fell in love with his cousin, Rebecca Brien Howland, a plump, pretty, bouncy girl of twenty-two—James was twenty-five—daughter of Gardiner Greene Howland of the firm of G. G. and S. S. Howland. By marrying Rebecca, James became the third of the Roosevelt clan to take a Howland wife. His grandfather had been the first and his father second—for, of course, James's mother's mother was a Howland. So, in bubbling Rebecca, James married the daughter of his mother's first cousin.

Through life James displayed an admirable gift for keeping the various portions of his life separate. Dutchess County was his main love, and there he and Rebecca lived happily, surrounded by thoroughbred horses and farm acres, displaying a squirelike interest in local affairs. James had imported an Alderney bull and several cows to make one of the first Alderney herds in this country. Now he began to cross his stock with Jersey and Guernsey. He raised corn and other crops and made his Mount Hope farm pay. The local citizenry applauded his efforts, calling him a "gen-u-wine farmer."

This, however, was only part of this well-integrated man's existence. An appetite for business had been whetted by his coal-company directorship. His grandfather had been associated with Matthew Vassar in promoting the Hudson River Railroad as well as the Delaware and Hudson. James had this stock and he also invested heavily in the Pennsylvania and Cumberland, becoming vice-president of the line. Over the years he served as president of the Louisville, New Albany and Chicago Railroad; as president of the Champlain Transportation Company; as an incorporator of the City Trust Company; as a trustee of Farmer's Loan and Trust; and bought large interests in West Superior, Wisconsin.

To round out a busy life, he was also a father, for Rebecca gave birth to a son two years after their marriage. Apparently James himself had disliked being called Junior, even in honor of a grandfather. For he christened his first son a resounding James Roosevelt Roosevelt, confident that no one else would ever be given a similar name. Through a long life James Roosevelt Roosevelt, whose cheery disposition resembled his mother's, was called "Rosy."

In 1865 James and Rebecca made one of their frequent trips to Europe, leaving Mount Hope rented to a New York family. One night the house caught fire and burned to the ground. Destroyed were many Roosevelt family records that might have cast light on the personalities of Roosevelt ancestors from Claes Martenszen down.

Yet the fire was not a total tragedy. James and Rebecca had never really liked the family homestead, but lived in it largely out of a sense of duty. Both wished to be closer to the Hudson—why live in the Hudson Valley without a view of the beautiful river? The state had recently bought the land around Mount Hope for the Hudson River State Hospital and now offered James $45,000 for his property. He accepted. James and Rebecca then discovered a colonial clapboard house called Springwood a few miles north of Mount Hope in the small township of Hyde Park. Springwood had been built in 1826 and last occupied by one Josiah Wheeler and family. Now it stood vacant. At first James planned to tear down the house and build a new residence. Yet, on close examination, Springwood proved so sturdy that he decided to add a stone wing and live in it. The interior of the house was spruced up, new furniture purchased, and the Roosevelts moved in during June, 1867.

Springwood thoroughly satisfied both Roosevelts. They loved house and grounds, especially the roses which Rebecca gathered by the armful in summer. "It would be difficult to imagine a more serene spot," a writer says of the Hyde Park estate at the time. The house stood high above three quarters of a mile of virgin oak and hemlock forest, running to the Hudson. Through these woods cascaded a merry brook. Over treetops the far side of the river was visible, while to the southwest the forest parted to show the river again. Squire James Roosevelt preferred to keep the estate rural. Practically the only formal landscaping was a 20-foot hemlock hedge between the house and the stables where James housed his thoroughbred horses and carriages.

Bit by bit the squire purchased surrounding land until he owned nearly a thousand Hyde Park acres. This made him one of the prominent men in the township and he was elected a supervisor of the town of Hyde Park. To James the job was no sinecure. His strong Roosevelt sense of community obligation drove him to visit the local schoolhouse at least once a month, sitting in on classes. Another of his responsibilities was the local jail. And after completion of the State Hospital—known to townsfolk as the Lunatic Asylum—James Roosevelt sat on its Board of Managers. When at Hyde Park he made almost daily visits to the hospital to make sure inmates were well treated. On June 8, 1874, he noted: "Ward 8 overcrowded, twenty-eight in this ward intended for fifteen. . . . Number in the home, women 87, men 85."

With all this he never neglected his business affairs and reputedly accumulated $300,000 in addition to his own inheritance from father and grandfather and that of his Howland wife. Because of his interest in railroad stocks, James had grown to be an expert in transportation problems. At the end of the Civil War he became president of the Southern Railways Securities Company, formed to speed reorganization of the former Confederate railroads.

Up to now the Roosevelts had been notable for living carefully within their means and getting the most out of the money they had. But at least three times James broke the pattern by trying for a financial killing that would skyrocket him into the ranks of America's multimillionaires. One attempt was a huge bituminous coal combine; another, a railroad network in the South; the third, a canal across Nicaragua. Each time financial panic or national recession blasted his ambitions. These setbacks did not make James Roosevelt bitter, nor did they visibly affect him financially.

Life at Hyde Park went on as before, with James spending as

much time as possible at Springwood. If his presence was required in New York he hitched up a trotter and drove himself the seventy miles to the city. When Hyde Park grew cold in winter, the family moved into a house at 15 Washington Square. All in all, James Roosevelt—with his muttonchop whiskers, alert mind, infectious laugh, country-squire dignity, cheerful wife and robust son— seemed a most contented man.

A long shadow fell across this pleasant life in 1875, when Rebecca Howland Roosevelt showed signs of a heart condition. A year later she died, leaving James in the role of widower. Business continued to occupy him, and he became a board member of more corporations than before. At Hyde Park he remained the gentleman farmer, proud that the produce grown in his gardens, together with the milk given by his herds of cows, more than paid the upkeep of the estate. He loved every tree on the Springwood acres and planted numerous new groves.

Two years after his wife's death James was agreeably caught up in wedding preparations as his son James Roosevelt Roosevelt made the most spectacular marriage ever contracted by a Roosevelt. In 1878 Rosy married Helen Schermerhorn Astor, daughter of *the* Mrs. Astor, New York's supreme social arbiter. With this new bride Rosy not only won a charming young lady but a $400,000 trust fund and a mansion at 372 Fifth Avenue. Yet, like his father, Rosy had Dutchess County in his blood. He and Helen bought a house next to James at Hyde Park. By 1880 James had a grandson, another James who was nicknamed Taddy.

Even so, the older James Roosevelt, embarking on his fifty-second year, was essentially a man at loose ends. He was to be sure, a member of the Holland Society, Delta Phi, the Metropolitan, Century, and Manhattan Clubs in New York, the Metropolitan Club of Washington, and a yacht club. Then, too, his new in-law, Mrs. Astor, invited him to many of her functions, as did lesser hostesses like the widowed Mrs. Theodore Roosevelt. With it all James Roosevelt may have been busy, but there remained a desolate gap in his life. . . .

... Such was the man who arrived at 6 West Fifty-seventh Street on that night in May, 1880. After dinner, with the guests scattered, Mittie Roosevelt and her daughters went upstairs. As they prepared for bed Mittie called out, "Did you notice how James Roosevelt kept looking at Sallie Delano? Why, he never took his eyes off her ... he kept talking to her all the time."

The Sara Delano to whom James Roosevelt devoted so much attention—received by her with pleasure rather than embarrassment—was twenty-six years old. Thus she was only half as old as James himself, the same age as his son Rosy. She was tall, dark-eyed, and brown-haired, with exceptional dignity of carriage. Her father, Warren Delano, had nine children, among them four daughters called "the beautiful Delano girls." James Roosevelt knew Warren Delano, having served with him on corporate boards. Besides, the Delanos lived on the Hudson at a handsome estate called Algonac, on the west bank, two miles north of Newburgh. From the porch of Hyde Park it was almost possible to see downstream as far as Algonac.

Sara's paternal forebears were Norman French and Flemish, the common ancestor of the clan being Jehan de la Noye, a Knight of the Golden Fleece. The blood of Charlemagne, William the Conqueror, and other warriors made a proud and prosperous Huguenot clan. Around 1600, Jean de la Noye and his wife Marie quit France for Leyden, Holland. Then, in 1609, a woebegone group of a hundred men and women fled religious persecution in England, taking refuge in Leyden. Jean and Marie de la Noye, a wealthy couple, made the unusual gesture of offering these pilgrims twelve houses in which to live.

For eleven years the Puritans waited, and their tribe increased to three hundred. In 1620 they set sail on the *Mayflower*. Aboard ship was attractive Priscilla Mullins, a girl who had fallen in love with Jacques de la Noye, oldest son of the family. Jacques had failed to return her devotion. In fact, he married a Dutch girl as soon as the *Mayflower* got out of sight.

But his younger brother, Philippe, nursed an unspoken passion for pretty Priscilla. He vowed to follow the *Mayflower* on the next boat, to carry word of his brother's marriage and declare his own love. This he did, becoming the first Huguenot to set foot on American soil. Otherwise Philippe did not fare well. Both he and Captain Myles Standish were rejected by Priscilla on the day she urged John Alden to speak for himself. The blow was a harsh one to proud Philippe de la Noye. For years he led a solitary existence, refusing to notice any other girls. At last he succumbed to the charms of Hester Dewsbury.

Like Roosevelt, the name de la Noye was much mangled on colonial records. It was written Delano, Delaneaux, Delanow, De Lano, Dellanow, and Delannoy. Gradually Delano and Delannoy were favored. Jonathon Delano, seventh son of Philippe, married Mercy Warren, to found the line leading to Sara. His son, Ephraim, went to sea, commencing the family tradition of sea captains, whaling masters, and shipbuilders. Ephraim's son Warren became the swashbuckling captain of a Yankee clipper trading with the Orient.

The Delanos owned trading and whaling ships sailing out of New Bedford and also invested heavily in other voyages. Slowly they became rich. Warren, Jr., born in 1809 at Fairhaven, made his first trip to China on the clipper *Commerce*. Soon he was captain of his own ship. He liked the East and became associated with the exporting firm of Russell Sturgis and Company, powerful Yankee traders in the Orient.

Commanding clipper ships might be expected to toughen rather than broaden a man's mind, but then—and forever—Captain Warren Delano had varied interests. Writing of him, one author mentions his "warm-hearted promptings of every kind of kindness." As a group, the Delanos were called "Ever restless, ever imbued with the itch to make the world over *their* way." Warren Delano's penetrating mind quickly made him a partner in Russell Sturgis. He also served as American vice-consul in Canton.

In 1843, at the age of thirty-four, Warren, Jr. returned to the United States, where he married eighteen-year-old Catherine

Lyman, whose ancestors were among the founders of Hartford, Connecticut. Immediately after the ceremony the newlyweds stepped aboard a clipper. A voyage of one hundred four days brought them to Warren's magnificent estate in Macao. Over the next three years Warren made so much money in the tea trade that he decided to return to the United States.

For a time the family, already increased by two children, lived in New York City. As a boy Warren had been taken by his father to the opening of the Erie Canal. He had never forgotten the majestic beauty of the Hudson and began the quest for a proper home on its banks. He found one in Algonac, a stately mansion on a hill two miles north of Newburgh. After engaging an architect to enlarge the house to forty rooms, he moved there with his family in 1848. More children were born. Then, on September 21, 1854, came a girl, Sara, soon known to the family as Sallie.

Algonac was more formal than Hyde Park. The sprawling, verandahed house was brick and stucco, with overhanging eaves. Grounds were impressively landscaped with drives, sloping lawns, gay flower beds. In high-ceilinged rooms, Victorian rosewood furniture vied with Oriental art startling in a Hudson River bracketed mansion. Among these Chinese treasures were priceless porcelains and two large Buddhist temple bells. Ever present, to take care of all this, were what a Delano aunt called "a class of respectable American women [who] did the family work."

At first Warren Delano flourished in the United States. His ships, by one account, were still the envy of the maritime world. In addition, he had branched out to purchase valuable land around New York harbor, together with coal mines in Pennsylvania, copper mines in Tennessee, and money-making properties in Maryland. He became so important that towns were named for him. Therefore, it would seem hard for so prosperous a man to go broke, but Warren Delano managed in the Panic of 1857. Things got so bad that he actually put a FOR SALE sign outside Algonac. He found no buyer, for most of his fellow millionaires had lost money and none could afford the handsome acreage.

The distracted man could think of only one solution. At the age of fifty he must return to China to build another fortune. In 1859 he left a pregnant wife and six growing children to sail for the Orient. Three years later his wife leased Algonac and sailed with the family in the square-rigger *Surprise*. Four months and six days later the Delano brood arrived in Hong Kong.

By then Warren was in the opium trade, a field more lucrative than tea. At the time there was nothing shameful or illicit about opium. It was used in America for medicine—especially during the Civil War. Warren was still prodigiously active, and the legend of his energy traversed the Pacific to Washington. President Lincoln now delegated him to draw up a pioneering trade agreement with China. Warren and his family continued to live on the estate in Macao, vivid with gardens of palms and exotic blooms. In these odd surroundings his Hudson River children cavorted happily.

The Delanos were ever in flux. Two years later Sallie, with a brother and sister, was sent home by way of Egypt, France, and the Atlantic Ocean. Algonac was still rented, so they stayed with relatives in Fairhaven, Massachusetts. The family reunited in 1866 to visit the Paris Exposition, where twelve-year-old Sallie was thrilled at seeing the Empress Eugénie and the Empress Carlotta. Following this, the elder Delanos returned to the United States with some children, while Sallie and two others were left in Germany under the general supervision of an uncle and aunt.

Sallie returned to America in 1870 at the age of sixteen. One of her older sisters was already married, while younger children were being taught in a schoolroom at Algonac. Sallie, who spoke perfect French and German, began to study drawing and singing. The family was close-knit. Her father's brother, Franklin Delano, had been a shipbuilder. After marrying Laura Astor, an aunt of Mrs. Rosy Roosevelt, he retired to manage his wife's millions. The two resided at Steen Valetje, a magnificent estate seventeen miles up the Hudson from Hyde Park. The wealthy Franklin Delanos were childless and became a bountiful set of second parents to the Algonac children.

As she reached eighteen, then twenty, Sallie became a beauty, tall, slender, aristocratic, aloofly charming. In truth, she was so dignified that her younger sister Cassie loved to play tricks on her. "She never lost her temper, but when annoyed only became more dignified than ever," reports a biography. Sara had developed into a strong-willed girl, at times an outspoken one. But, like all the women of the family, she gave unquestioning obedience to Papa Delano. The elder Delano was a relentlessly Victorian parent, forbiddingly stern at some times, tender at others, always brimful of emphatic opinions. Delano males voted Republican and prayed Episcopalian—in that order, it was said. Warren Delano stated his politics bluntly. "I will not say that all Democrats are horse thieves," he pontificated, "but it does seem that all horse thieves are Democrats."

Young Sallie's regal beauty attracted the attention of a few tentative suitors, several of them cadets from nearby West Point. But none met the high standards set by Papa Delano. In Father-Knows-Best fashion, he told Sallie to discourage the attentions of any who persevered. Dutifully the girl wrote notes breaking things off.

"Life at Algonac was joyous," says one description. The Delanos were a musical family, far more so than the Roosevelts, and sweet girlish voices raised in song were heard around the huge house. In summer there were polite sports like archery and croquet on the sweeping lawn, together with saddle horses, all-day picnics, boat rides. In winter came taffy pulls, church socials, and dances. For reading the family had new books by Dickens, Thackeray, and Henry James. West Point still provided potential suitors for the beautiful Delano girls, but Warren Delano seemed to prefer members of the Russell Sturgis firm as mates for his daughters. Dora, the oldest, was already married to a partner and lived on the estate at Macao. Other Delano daughters would wed men in the China trade.

The years passed, and Sallie found no man greatly to her liking. She met Bamie Roosevelt and formed a close friendship with her.

When she visited the Roosevelts at Oyster Bay, Theodore Sr. enthusiastically showed her around. In winter months Sallie made frequent trips to New York, staying with Bamie or other girls. She attended symphony concerts and the opera; her nights were a succession of dinner parties, balls, cotillions, and *tableaux vivants*. She saw *Pinafore* and Edwin Booth in *Hamlet*. Of the two Roosevelt boys, she preferred pleasant, outgoing Ellie, for Teedie always seemed to have his nose in a book. But Sallie was a true daughter of the Hudson. Returning to Algonac, she never failed to heave a sigh of pleasure. "How much nicer it is here than in New York," she fervently said.

In 1876 Sallie accompanied her married sister and brother-in-law back to Macao. The trio stopped in London and Paris, then passed through the recently opened Suez Canal. In China another suitor for Sallie's hand appeared. Warren Delano was not present to veto him, but Dora Delano Forbes did. "I do not think he is the right person for you, dear," she informed Sallie. Once again, the girl wrote a note.

Back in the United States, Sallie resumed her life at Algonac. She was twenty-five years old and, as an older sister, began to take some household responsibility. When Warren Delano traveled, it was Sara who supervised the men working on the estate. Judging from a remark in later years, the thought of living out life as a Victorian spinster had already entered her mind.

Then she received the invitation to dinner at West Fifty-seventh Street and for the first time met courtly James Roosevelt. He may have reminded the girl of her father or she may have loved him for himself alone. In any event, she was delighted by his show of interest. Hyde Park was twenty miles from Algonac, with a ride across the river on the Beacon-Newburgh ferry. James Roosevelt immediately began to visit her.

Courtship in those days resembled a minuet, and next James invited Sallie to Hyde Park for a week while Mittie and Bamie Roosevelt were guests. One day during this week he asked her to arrange the flowers on the luncheon table. From this she knew his

intentions were serious. The only hurdle remaining was Warren
Delano, aged seventy-one, who labored under the delusion that
James Roosevelt visited Algonac to see *him*. The visits pleased the
old man. "James Roosevelt is the first person who has made me
realize that a Democrat can be a gentleman," he declared.

The courtship of James and Sallie moved forward. A little over
a month after they first met, James asked Warren Delano for his
daughter's hand. No details of this provocative interview remain,
but Warren Delano may have feared that his stately daughter was
headed for spinsterhood—or realized that Sallie had a whim of
iron and was at last prepared to use it. He granted permission, and
James and Sallie were engaged.

One of Sallie's aunts died a few days later, so the wedding at
Algonac on October 7, 1880, was a restrained affair. One hundred
twenty-five relatives and friends attended, with the guests from
New York met at the ferry landing by hospitable carriages. The
weather was warm and beautiful, with the foliage autumn-red.
The bride wore white brocade with ruffles of old lace. Around her
neck hung a five-strand pearl necklace just given her by James.
After the ceremony some guests wandered out on the lawn for a
catered collation, while others examined the wedding gifts which,
a newspaper said, "were magnificent, embracing, in addition to
the usual routine of table service, many rare and valuable heir-
looms and art treasures."

At 4:30 the newlyweds climbed into the Delano family victoria
drawn by the matched horses Meg and Pet and driven by French,
the faithful coachman. They trotted north to Milton, the midway
point between the two estates. There Hutchins, the Roosevelt
coachman, waited with a T-cart, a small vehicle with a high
rumble seat in the rear. Hutchins remained at the horse's head
until bride and bridegroom were comfortably seated. Then he
jumped into the rumble. James Roosevelt lifted reins to drive his
bride toward the Highland-Poughkeepsie ferry and thence to
Hyde Park and Springwood.

A month later the newlyweds boarded the White Star liner

Germanic for an idyllic European honymoon. In ten months they covered the face of the Continent, sightseeing, visiting friends, and encountering relatives, including the Delano clan, which arrived in Paris to take an entire floor of the Hôtel du Rhin.

In September they returned to Springwood and on January 30, 1882, in an upstairs room, a child was born. In the family diary the father wrote, "At a quarter to nine my Sallie had a splendid large baby boy. He weighs 10 lbs. without clothes."

Next came the question of a name. James wished to give his son the family Isaac—and it is interesting to speculate on the baby's future if this had happened. However, Sallie felt that any child of hers would be more Delano than Roosevelt. She wanted to name the child Warren Delano for her father. But a child of her brother's who bore that name had just died. Sallie felt she must ask her brother's permission before using the name again. His reply was a surprise. "No—I could not bear it," he stated flatly.

Sallie was only momentarily nonplused. "Then we shall name him after Uncle Frank," she said. This was the bountiful Franklin Delano of Steen Valetje.

So the child was christened Franklin Delano Roosevelt. Elliott Roosevelt, Sallie's favorite male of the New York-Oyster Bay branch of the family, was invited to Hyde Park to officiate as godfather.

11

TRAGEDY

ON THE DAY FRANKLIN D. ROOSEVELT WAS BORN, THEODORE ROOSE-
velt had been happily married a year and a half.

For the bustling young Harvard student had fallen head over
heels in love at the beginning of his junior year at Cambridge.
Theodore liked to say he fell in love at first sight. "I first saw her
on October 18, 1878, and loved her as soon as I saw her sweet, fair
young face." But perusal of his diary indicates it took six months
for the twenty-year-old student to realize that this was the girl for
him.

She was seventeen-year-old Alice Hathaway Lee, who had such a
happy disposition that friends called her "Sunshine." Alice was
winsome and utterly fetching. "Beautiful in face and form, and
lovelier still in spirit," declared a smitten Theodore. She was a
proper Bostonian—at the moment Theodore was associating with
few others. Her father was George Cabot Lee of Chestnut Hill,
Brookline. Her cousin was Richard Saltonstall, one of Theodore's
classmates.

Theodore had arrived at Harvard determined to be a naturalist.
He no longer entertained such plans, though his interest in nature

continued as fervent as before. One reason for this change was Alice Lee. In the back of his mind all through courtship of the Sunshine Girl was the determination now and forever to shower her with the best things in life. To do this, it seemed to him, would require far more money than he would make as a naturalist. "I have enough to get bread," he said, meaning the money inherited from his father. "What I have to do if I want butter and jam is to provide the butter and jam." As he saw it, there would be little butter and jam in the existence of a naturalist.

At the beginning, Alice Lee was alarmed at Theodore's insistent wooing. This failed to deter him. "See that girl?" he asked a friend at a party. "I'm going to marry her. She won't have me, but I'm going to have *her*." In addition to a happy disposition, Alice was intelligent and curious. But she found Theodore's enthusiastic talk of birds, animals, fish, and trees at times boring, if not dull. Gradually, though, she gave way before his frontal attack on her emotions and the couple became officially engaged.

This took time and was a not altogether happy period in Theodore's life. His diary called Alice a "wayward, willful darling" and a "laughing, pretty little witch." Sometimes her witchery drove him wild. At one point he bought a pair of imported Italian pistols and threatened to challenge any rivals to a duel. He had occasional tiffs with his Sunshine, and after one hid in the woods, refusing to emerge until a relative tracked him down and forced him to listen to reason. Yet, when things went well with the courtship he sat on top of the world. "By Jove," he wrote in his diary, "it sometimes seems as if I were having too happy a time to last. I enjoy every moment I live—almost."

Despite emotional ups-and-downs, he managed to be a good student, confounding professors with his searching questions. He no longer studied six hours a day, but after finishing his studies compensated by reading one or two books a day. In his lifetime Theodore Roosevelt probably read as many books as any human being could. He read as energetically as he did everything else, appearing to attack a volume rather than peruse it. Clutching a book tightly in both hands, he gave the impression of reading by the page rather than by the sentence. A rapid, greedy devourer of words, he quickly absorbed the gist of a full page.

More than ever his lodgings at 16 Winthrop Street were a menagerie of lizards, turtles, birds, and snakes, together with stuffed owls and antlers on the walls. Theodore still boxed daily; ran instead of walked; exercised strenuously at every opportunity. Despite this, his legs continued spindly. He consulted the college physician about this. "Skip rope like the little girls," the doctor advised. Theodore began skipping rope, and characteristically did so on the front porch of 16 Winthrop in view of passers-by. He also undertook to eat more. "If a man doesn't eat, he can't work," he decided. His appetite was astounding for the rest of his life.

At Harvard Theodore also showed that he thought big. In his senior year he discovered that no history of naval warfare in the War of 1812 existed. "I will write one myself," he stated and immediately undertook the formidable task. With all this amorous and extracurricular activity, he still made Phi Beta Kappa, graduating twenty-first in a class of one hundred seventy-seven.

The next step was marriage. He and Alice set a date in October, 1880, whereupon Theodore left his fiancée alone in Brookline to take a three-month vacation in the West. This was a brave step for a young man whose fevered mind had told him only a few months before that someone might run off with his beloved. Yet more than pleasure was involved. Theodore was accompanied by his brother Elliott, who had been suffering mysterious problems. Handsome Ellie, youngest of the brood, always seemed the best adjusted of the children. But something had happened. He had been sent to St. Paul's School at Concord, New Hampshire, and there suffered a lapse diagnosed as a nervous breakdown. In the company of a doctor he went to a military post in Texas, and in rugged frontier surroundings gradually recovered while hunting and breaking in horses.

Now he and Theodore went for a further hunting trip in Iowa and Minnesota. It was Theodore's first exposure to the wild West and he reveled in it. As always, he sent home a torrent of letters. In one he wrote, "We are traveling on muscle and don't give a hang for any man." Still, he did not lose sight of his coming marriage for which he considered himself eminently prepared. "Thank Heaven, I am at least perfectly pure," he wrote in his diary.

Alice Hathaway Lee and Theodore Roosevelt were married on October 27, 1880. It was a busy marriage month for Roosevelts, since the wedding of James and Sallie Delano had taken place twenty days earlier. The clan converged on Brookline, supplemented by Corinne's friend Edith Kermit Carow, the girl the Knickerbocker Roosevelts had expected Theodore to marry. The wedding day was the groom's twenty-second birthday; the bride had recently turned twenty. The pair took no extended honeymoon, for impatient Theodore had already enrolled in Columbia Law School. Instead, they spent two weeks alone at Tranquility, in Oyster Bay. At last Tranquility was tranquil, and to Theodore the fortnight was a more blissful idyll than anticipated. "My cup of happiness is almost too full," he wrote. "Our intense happiness is too sacred to be written about."

One fine day Theodore took his bride to the top of Sagamore Hill, near O'Connor's Bluff, where a growing Teedie had declaimed poetry into the wind. The crest of Sagamore offered a sweeping view of Oyster Bay, Cold Spring Harbor, and Long Island Sound. Alice enthusiastically approved Sagamore as the site of a future home and Theodore made plans to buy it, together with ninety-five surrounding acres.

After the honeymoon the newlyweds moved into an upper floor of the family house at 6 West Fifty-seventh Street. And now Theodore began to grapple with life's problems. After a few classes at Columbia, he knew the law moved at too slow a pace for him. Even with a degree he would lack the patience to practice. What, then, to do? Money presented no problem, for despite talk of bread, butter, and jam Theodore was financially well off. Of his money affairs, Professor Howard K. Beale writes, "Theodore

Roosevelt talked so constantly of himself as not wealthy that the facts are surprising." The young man had inherited some two hundred thousand dollars from his father. In a day before income or inheritance taxes, with necessities and luxuries cheap, this was tantamount to wealth. Concludes Professor Beale: "To protest, as Theodore always did, that the family was other than very wealthy was to carry modesty to the point of telling less than the whole truth."

Though he had no career, Theodore was not idle. "I think I should go mad if I were not employed," he said once. In a letter to his sister Bamie, he deplored some Harvard classmates who had decided not to work: "fellows of excellent family and faultless breeding, with a fine old country place, four-in-hands, tandems, a yacht, and so on; but oh, the decorous hopelessness of their lives!"

In absence of anything better, he decided to continue his law studies, and vigorously hiked the three miles to the law school every day. He joined the National Guard as a second lieutenant and found military life admirable. He boxed daily with paid sparring partners and galloped on horseback around Central Park. His work on the *Naval War of 1812* was desultory, but he still devoured a book or two a day. At night he and Alice went to parties and balls, with Theodore still the dude who wore colorful, top-fashion attire. Yet all through this first joyous winter of marriage he had the feeling of marking time on the road of life. He should be sprinting ahead.

When in doubt a Roosevelt usually went to Europe, and in the spring Alice and Theodore sailed on a delayed honeymoon. First stop was Liverpool, where Theodore visited his Bulloch uncles and their families. The reminiscences of these two former Confederate navy officers fired him with enthusiasm to finish writing his book, and his mind simmered with excitement as he and Alice began a strenuous tour of Europe. In Switzerland Theodore took one look at the Matterhorn, conquered for the first time only sixteen years before, and announced that he, too, would scale it. Alice begged him not to. The couple had met a Harvard classmate of Theodore's and sweet Alice implored him to add his pleas to hers. The man did his best, but Theodore was adamant. "I shall climb the mountain," he proclaimed. Leaving Alice in a comfortable hotel, he scaled the mighty Matterhorn. Pride in his physical prowess was as great—and as boyish—as ever. "I took a guide, but tired him out," he reported home.

While the Theodore Roosevelts continued honeymooning, the lives of other Knickerbocker Roosevelts were in flux.

William Emlen, son of James Alfred, was following his father's footsteps toward the presidency of Roosevelt and Son. This fine firm, founded by Johannes, was the solid base on which Roosevelt fortunes rested. It completely merited such trust. "In an age where circumstances made it easy to sink in commercial quicksands," writes Carleton Putnam, "it rested upon rock, reflecting in each phase a persistent integrity of management."

Corinne, Theodore's younger sister, had decided to marry Douglas Robinson, an American-born, English-educated broker. Young Corinne had grown up to be the feminine counterpart of Theodore, with the same buoyant energy, insatiable curiosity, and all-around zest for life. "Nothing tired her, nothing bored her," said one of her friends.

Older-sister Bamie was quieter, the diplomat and planner of the family. She still suffered from curvature of the spine and found activity difficult. Bamie was plain of face, but beautiful eyes and hair made this easy to overlook. Of all the children, she had inherited her mother's gift for dispensing Southern hospitality in the North. "She could hold fifty guests in the palm of her hand," says one tribute. Bamie, a rare mixture of charm and homeliness, appeared destined to be the spinster of the family. It did not seem that she would ever marry. Yet in time she did.

Handsome Elliott Roosevelt was still at loose ends. Hunting big game had become his main interest in life. In New York he tried to muster interest in Theodore Sr.'s philanthropies with newsboys and crippled children, but his heart was not in it. He traveled to the jungles of India and Ceylon solely for the hunting, one of the first Westerners to do this. Returning for Corinne's wedding, he acted as godfather for newborn Franklin Delano Roosevelt. As a favorite of Franklin's mother he often visited Hyde Park and Algonac, and in the Hudson Valley met a stunning girl named Anna Eleanor Hall, whose family lived on an estate up the Hudson at Tivoli, north of Hyde Park.

In Anna Eleanor's veins ran the blood of Chancellor Livingston, the formidable personable who had administered the oath of office to President Washington and later bedeviled the inventor Nicholas Roosevelt. In fact, the Halls lived on land originally owned by the Chancellor.

Anna Eleanor's upbringing had been strict. Her father lived on inherited wealth, absorbed in a deep study of theology. Alternately stern and sweet, he treated his wife like a pretty child and his children like mindless infants. His daughters were beauties— Hall women always were!—but under Anna Eleanor's blooming exterior lay hidden problems. The same might be said of dashing Elliott Roosevelt, who proposed marriage to Anna Eleanor during a garden party at Algonac. She accepted, and the two were on the road to matrimony.

The young Theodore Roosevelts returned from the European honeymoon in the fall. They did not remain at 6 West Fiftyseventh Street but moved into an apartment of their own at 55 West Forty-fifth Street. Here two maids took care of them. Theodore was more delighted than ever with married bliss and wrote, "I can imagine nothing more happy in life than an evening spent in my cosy little sitting room, before a bright fire of soft coal, my books all around me, and playing backgammon with my own dainty mistress . . . the prettiest and sweetest of all little wives—my own sunny darling."

He had asked the architectural firm of Lamb and Rich to draw plans for the home at Sagamore Hill. The instructions had been vague. "I wanted a big piazza," he recalled later, "where we could sit in rocking chairs and look at the sunset; a library with a shallow bay window looking south, the parlor or drawing room occupying all the western end of the lower floor, [and] big fireplaces for logs." With only this to go by, the architects produced blueprints for a sprawling, solid, comfortable dwelling with Victorian gables and dormers, porches and fireplaces in abundance. The second floor had ten bedrooms. Theodore's next step was to hire a builder, but there seemed to be no great hurry.

His *Naval War of 1812* was almost finished and he felt pleased with the manuscript. He resumed law studies and drill with the National Guard. Yet he still faced the problem of what to do in life. Just before the European honeymoon he had joined the 21st District Republican Club which had shabby headquarters over a saloon on the later site of the Savoy Plaza Hotel. No thought had been given to joining Uncle Barnwell's Reform Democrats, nor did the fact that his Lee father-in-law was a Democrat influence him. "A young man of my bringing up and convictions could only join the Republican Party," he wrote positively.

Now he decided to try politics as a lifetime career. Several considerations propelled him toward this vital step. The first was negative—he could think of nothing else to do. But there were positive pressures as well. Deep in Theodore's background lay the family image of public service. Closer still was the wish to follow in the humane footsteps of his adored father. But Theodore's thoughts were too big for simple charitable committees. To him, public service meant activity on the scale of his Uncle Barnwell— or even bigger!

On more factor may have influenced his decision. Henry Cabot Lodge had been a young history instructor at Harvard when Theodore was an undergraduate. The two had been friendly and Theodore corresponded with him, as he did with nearly everyone he met. Cabot Lodge had run for the House of Representatives and been elected. In considering young friends who had already found promising careers, Theodore may have been impressed by the Lodge success.

The American public came to consider Theodore Roosevelt one of Destiny's fortunate children. Yet, declares author Julian Street, "Destiny assisted Roosevelt in certain instances, but he himself usually assisted Destiny to assist him." At this early point in his life Theodore already possessed the phenomenal Roosevelt drive, which would make him a standout anywhere. Even more helpful to Destiny was the shrewdness he displayed in his first major adult decision in life.

Theodore was wealthy, a Harvard graduate, a young man of an excellent family. His father had been admired; his uncle a prominent civic figure. Another youth from such a background might have tried to enter politics by use of money or influence. Some unusual intuition—perhaps inherited from shrewd Dutch ancestors—advised Theodore to invade politics at the soggy bottom. Accordingly, he burst through the door of the 21st District Club one night and announced that he was ready to begin as a precinct worker.

Other members of the club were the so-called Men in Derbies—ward heelers, saloon keepers, court clerks, party hacks, and a smattering of corner loafers. Theodore's family—notably his cousin Emlen—was appalled at his fraternizing with such types. Ebullient Theodore nipped such family opposition in the bud. When told politics was beneath him, he answered, "I intend to be one of the governing class."

Having done this much for Destiny, Theodore was prepared to let Destiny do things for him. And it did! The 21st District Republican headquarters was informally known as the Jake Hess Club in honor of its burly leader. Jake Hess himself showed no enthusiasm over his new recruit, who wore nose glasses on a silk cord and sported suits of aristocratic cut. However, one Hess lieutenant was Joe Murray, a renegade Tammanyite who had decided the Republicans offered a broader field for his skills. In the accepted precinct fashion, he was alert for an opportunity to unseat Jake Hess.

Where Hess was indifferent to Theodore, Joe Murray viewed

him as pure gold. An election for state assemblyman was immi-
nent and Murray conceived the idea of making Theodore a candidate. Theodore would campaign among his rich friends while
Murray himself got out the poor vote. He sold a majority of club
members on this idea. When Jake Hess nominated a routine candidate, the club rose in revolt to pick Theodore. New York newspapers were delighted at the prospect of a highborn young man
taking an interest in low politics. The *New York Times* hailed
him as "a public-spirited citizen, not an office seeker." With such
support Theodore Roosevelt, on his twenty-third birthday, was
well on the way to the State Assembly. He arrived there, duly
elected, on the first day of the year.

From the beginning Theodore was an Albany celebrity. He was
still a chap who ran rather than walked, and at the official New
Year's legislative party dashed around pumping hands and intro-
ducing himself. Pretty Alice Lee tried to keep up with him,
perhaps to prevent her eager husband from tactlessly accosting upstate legislators with "You're from the country, aren't you?" For
the occasion, Theodore was strikingly overdressed in a tailor-
made suit with lush accouterments. The fledgling assemblyman
spoke in a Harvard accent which lost the letter *r*, and soon his
shrill "Mr. Speak-ah" came to be familiar in the Assembly. His
English was impeccable, and he seemed to have read every book
ever written. He was sandy-haired and side-whiskered. Over sharp
blue eyes the glass of a precarious pince-nez sent off a steady glint.
Prominent teeth made his wide smile extra easy—or was the full
smile really a big, broad grin? Altogether, the boy-legislator cut a
strange figure. "What on earth will New York send us next?" one
colleague wondered.

In the Assembly Theodore allied himself with a reform minority and began a whirlwind activity that wrecked the slow legislative pace. All through his political life he was surrounded by
people who tried to restrain him from indiscretion. The process
began here, with fellow Republicans desperately trying to hold
him to the party line. "He was the most impulsive guy I ever

met," one recalled. "You kept trying to keep him from rushing into destruction! Half the time I used to sit on his coattails [and] say to him, *What do you want to do that for, you damn fool; you will ruin yourself and everybody!"*

In Assembly debate "he had a way of fixing his underjaw so that it menaced like a six-shooter." The word "reform" was constantly on his lips, where it joined Pluck, Honesty, and Morality in his credo.

His name first hit New York headlines when he called out "Mr. Speak-ah" and rose to accuse financier Jay Gould of corrupting a state Supreme Court justice in a conspiracy to control the Manhattan Elevated Railroad. Gould, he cried, "is part of that most dangerous of all dangerous classes, the wealthy criminal class." As Theodore went on to spell out charges, a hush fell over the august Assembly. Such corruption went on all the time in political-financial circles, but by tacit agreement was never mentioned aloud on the floor of Assembly or Senate. Now that damn New York dude had blasted the sacred rule. On the other hand, the *New York Times* was impressed: "Mr. Roosevelt has a most refreshing habit of calling men and things by their right names, and in these days of subserviency to the robber barons of the Street it needs some little courage in a public man to characterize them and their acts in fitting terms."

As that rarest of anomalies, a conservative reformer, Theodore leaned heavily on his instinctive feelings about right and wrong. Otherwise, his ideas were vague, a social conscience hard to find. "No great reforms burned in Theodore Roosevelt as he began the career he was to follow with few interruptions until he died," says biographer Henry J. Pringle. The youth from the moneyed family still bore the taint of the upper-class snob who believed people got what they deserved in the world. To him, reform largely meant wiping out political graft and dishonesty and substituting right thinking and patriotism.

Theodore showed little sympathy for Labor. He believed that improvement in living conditions of the poor was best left to God

Almighty. While posturing heroically for reform he refused to support a bill making it illegal for streetcar motormen and conductors to work a twelve-hour day. He branded this "purely socialistic" and called the men un-American. Next he was asked to join in abolishing conditions of virtual slavery in state prisons. He thought this "maudlin sympathy for . . . men who have deliberately placed themselves beyond the pale of society."

Despite this, the public doggedly kept seeing young Teddy as a reformer, largely because he kept saying so himself. Newspapers praised him as a crusader and an idealist, while his sister Corinne reverently christened him the "Young Reformer" and allowed herself to think for a brief moment that he might one day be President.

There was some reason for this. Up to now, the nation's best-known politicians had been old-style Olympians like Roscoe Conkling, saluted for his "Apollo-like appearance, noble figure, flashing eyes, and majestic voice." Theodore Roosevelt was the first of a new breed—a man with whom people could identify. Despite his high society manner, he was an ordinary-looking young man, with a friendly face and a mind that seemed interested in everything. He was colorful without seeming too different from the rest of humanity. Already voters he didn't know were stepping up and addressing him as "Teddy," the name he disliked. Newspaper reporters, accustomed to relaying dull political news, seized upon the young legislator and wrote stories extolling his euphoric energy. To use a phrase of the future, Teddy Roosevelt had the gift of showmanship.

During his second term Theodore naïvely expected the Republicans to elect him Speaker of the Assembly. But the party machine thwarted him. This frustration, together with the hard work of the session, brought about a return of his asthma. For perhaps the only time in his adult life Theodore Roosevelt admitted he was tired.

In the summer of 1883 he went on another vacation in the wild

West. He traveled alone, for Alice Lee was pregnant, expecting a child in February. For this trip Theodore chose the Bad Lands of Dakota, stopping off at a tiny town called Little Missouri. By this time, his *Naval History of 1812* had been published and well received by the critics. In buffalo hunting, roping steers, and chasing cattle rustlers around Little Missouri he found fodder for more articles and books.

At the same time he discovered the real wild West. *Get action, do things!* he once urged the world. *Be sane, don't fritter away your time; create, act, take a place wherever you are and be somebody!* Theodore did this in the Bad Lands, to the wonder and admiration of rugged cowboys, who called him "The four-eyed tenderfoot from the East." He enthusiastically invested fourteen thousand dollars in the Maltese Cross cattle ranch; he rode furiously across the plains, with extra pairs of eyeglasses in his pocket in case those he wore bounced off; his sombrero, Western shirt, and chaps outdid the Bad Lands' sunsets in brightness. At one roundup he rallied cowboys by shouting, "Hasten forward quickly!" The tenderfoot phrase swept the West, giving rise to high hilarity.

In the fall he was again elected to the Assembly. The term began in January, 1884, when Alice was eight months pregnant. The young couple had decided to leave the apartment on Forty-fifth Street and move back to Fifty-seventh where Mittie, Bamie, and the maids could watch over the mother-to-be. Theodore established a pattern of going to Albany late on Sunday nights, returning late on Friday evening. His joyous arrival back home was always signalized by a thunderous crash of the front door.

This was his routine at the beginning of the week of February 10. When he left on Sunday, Mittie was slightly indisposed. Alice, her moment practically come, seemed cheerful. Matters in the big household appeared so satisfactory that Corinne and Douglas Robinson felt no hesitation in leaving their own infant son there. They then went off with light hearts on a social visit to Baltimore. Early Wednesday morning the Robinsons received a telegram say-

ing Alice had given birth to a girl the night before, and that
Mittie was still indisposed. In Albany, Theodore received a similar
wire. At the moment the Robinsons were enjoying themselves;
Theodore was busy. Neither saw the need for haste in returning to
New York. Corinne and her husband got there first—late that evening. They were met at the door by an ashen-faced Elliott, who
said, "There is a curse on this house! Mother is dying, and Alice is,
too!"

Theodore arrived an hour later, to find his wife almost unconscious. He sat at the head of the bed, cradling her, through the
long night. Only for a few minutes—at two o'clock—did he leave to
stand at his mother's bedside as she died of typhoid fever. After
that he returned to Alice. She died the next afternoon. The reason
given was Bright's disease. The baby girl was fine.

It was the lowest point in the life of Theodore Roosevelt. His
beloved Sunshine and his darling Little Motherling swept off the
earth in twelve dreadful hours! A friend wrote that at the double
funeral "Theodore was in a dazed, stunned state. He does not
know what he says or does." But four days later he left the baby in
charge of Bamie and returned to Albany, where the Assembly rose
in silent sympathy as he took his seat.

Theodore's quick return to the Assembly was partly a sense of
duty and partly intestinal fortuitde. As an elected official, he did
not feel it right to allow personal grief to interefere with public
duty. Besides, as he wrote to a friend, "I have never believed it did
any good to flinch or yield to any blow, nor does it lighten the
blow to cease from working." Yet he remained stricken. "You
could not talk to him about it," one legislator said of his shattering
loss. "You could see at once that it was a grief too deep. He did
not want anyone to sympathize with him."

Political matters distracted him. Theodore had served three
terms in the Assembly and was weary of it. However, the presidential campaign of 1884 loomed ahead and he joined with Henry
Cabot Lodge in a valiant effort to block the nomination of

James G. Blaine. E. L. Godkin of the New York *Post* accused Blaine of "wallowing in corruption like a rhinoceros in an African pool." Theodore agreed. In ringing words he declared that his reformer's integrity would never allow him to support the Man from Maine.

At the Republican State Convention, in Utica, Theodore was applauded as he took his seat. His fame had spread beyond the confines of the state and at the Republican National Convention in Chicago he was the object of much curiosity. People thought he possessed the color that makes a national figure: he was young, rich, and a picturesque dresser who, on the convention floor, wore a natty straw skimmer and carried a cane.

Yet his effort to halt the Blaine bandwagon was a lamentable failure. Blaine won the nomination and Theodore declared himself "savagely indignant, bitterly angry." At the same time the situation brought a crucial moment in his life. Theodore had vowed never to support Blaine, yet Blaine was now the party candidate. President Eliot of Harvard and other noted Republicans bolted to support the Democrat Grover Cleveland. Many of Theodore's admirers expected him to be a profile in courage and do the same.

But as soon as the convention ended Theodore rushed to the Bad Lands of Dakota. En route he was reported as saying, "I have been called a reformer, but I am a Republican." The implication was that he would support Blaine. This was such a spectacular volte-face that some papers refused to print the story, branding it a hoax. Theodore himself dutifully denied the statement, but a month later endorsed Blaine. In taking this step he had ceased to be the amateur in politics, the "public-spirited citizen, not an office seeker." From then on, he was a professional politician.

Yet, for the moment he tried to forget politics. He remained on his Bad Lands ranch. Baby Alice was in the East, tended by Bamie. Before leaving New York Theodore had given a go-ahead for the house on Sagamore Hill, which he planned to call Leeholm in memory of Alice. At the ranch he wrote a tender memoir of Alice which ended: *And when my heart's dearest died, the light went out of my life forever.* With this, he swore never to speak her name again, and sought forgetfulness in riding the range and writing books.

"I'm a literary feller, not a politician, nowadays," he told Dakota cowpunchers.

12

THE ROUGH RIDER

WHILE THEODORE ROOSEVELT ATTEMPTED TO CLOSE HIS MIND TO the recent past, Franklin Delano Roosevelt opened eyes to the universe into which he had just been born.

It was a pleasant world. "In the long shelf of the biographies of American Presidents," Karl Schriftgiesser writes, "one searches in vain for the story of a childhood more serene and secure." In addition, there was comfort, an almost total absence of life's rough edges. James and Sara Roosevelt were entrenched members of the only society they knew. "They *belonged*," says one account. "They lived in great comfort and with a certain style, but without ostentation." Theirs has been called the life of the Last Patroons, a direct line of Hudson River inheritance from the men who carved out domains with the blessing of the old Dutch West India Company. The Last Patroons showed scant interest in the wide world around them, preferring to remain preoccupied with their own circumscribed existence. "They never fell in love except with cousins," one has recalled, "because they never met anyone outside their own families." A writer likens them to background characters in Edith Wharton novels.

Life at Springwood was timeless. There were servants to do one's bidding, books to be read, horses to ride, walks to take, family and friends to visit. Rosy Roosevelt lived in the Red House next door; James Roosevelt's mother lived at nearby Rosedale; younger brother John Aspinwall was close at hand. Rosy owned a coach which covered the roads with speed and style. A few miles down the Hudson lay Algonac; a few miles up the river was Steen Valetje. There were children galore. Rosy had two; John Aspinwall, two more; the nearby Rogers family, a lively group of boys. There was the constant activity of the farm, for Squire James Roosevelt made sure Springwood paid for itself with milk, corn, garden vegetables, and other crops.

Of Franklin's boyhood, his aunt, Mrs. Delano Forbes, says, "He was brought up in a beautiful frame." In it he was ever the central figure. His parents' lives and the entire household revolved around him. Sallie breast-fed him for a year, then dressed the boy in girlish dresses until he was five.

In the quiet of Springwood, Sallie too was changing. As a Delano daughter, one of a large family, her emotions had been diffused. As Mrs. James Roosevelt they were channeled directly toward husband and son. Thus her capacity for loving took on depth and determination, while her girlish whim of iron began turning into a whim of steel. Her feeling for James Roosevelt was a profound mixture of love and admiration. Yet the focal point of her life was Franklin, or "Baby," as she called him at the beginning. It is hard to call Sara an overprotective mother or even a possessive one, since she was aware of the pitfalls of both. But she was dominant. Adding to Sallie's mother-love was a clan vanity that tied her closer to Franklin. She was proud of her Delano heritage and felt he was one of her line. "My son Franklin is a Delano, not a Roosevelt at all," she often said.

Yet James Roosevelt was by no means negative in the family. Much of Franklin's great respect for his father stemmed from the fact that Sallie so often deferred to him. And if Sallie was dominant in the house, James was in charge out of doors. For, despite his austere appearance and haughty appraisal of life, James Roosevelt had remained young in heart. Though approaching sixty, he was still the sportsman who never stopped being interested in the things boys love. He rode, hunted, swam, and sailed boats in summer; skated, sleighed, and steered iceboats in winter. James might look as if he belonged on a horse, but he also enjoyed walking. When in Hyde Park, he walked to the village daily to pick up the mail. In time, he was always accompanied by his son.

"Franklin laughed a lot as a baby," Sallie recalls, and the laughter continued into boyhood. The boy's attitude toward both parents was friendly and lighthearted. His mother was "Sallie," his father "Pops" or "Popsy." Writes Sallie, "My boy Franklin could do everything well." It was no idle boast. His mother taught him to read at an early age, and he often had his nose deep in a book. In the family tradition he was given a pony at four, his own horse a few years later. He went to dancing school and earned pin money doing chores around the farm. He was also good with his hands, able to carve ship models and to stuff dead animals almost as passionately as Cousin Teddy.

Despite her regal appearance, Sallie could be bright and gay, and she stimulated her son's imagination by a fund of stories about childhood days in China. She could even sing sea chanteys taught her by rough sailors on the square-rigger that took her to the Orient. At times she supervised the preparation of exotic Eastern curries for the family table. At the age of eight Franklin was given a stamp collection for, in Sara's words, "James believed in keeping Franklin's mind on nice things, at a high level, but he did it in such a way that Franklin never realized he was following any bent but his own." Collecting stamps, as the world knows, remained a relaxing joy for the rest of Franklin's life.

The children of Hyde Park locals felt sorry for Franklin because he always seemed to be in his father's company. Yet the growing boy had playmates, albeit aristocratic ones. In fact, there were so many children in the Roosevelt area that a kindergarten was started in the Rogers mansion. Here Franklin got a first taste of school. His favorite playmate was Rosy's daughter Helen, who was such a tomboy that she howled with fury when given dolls for Christmas. Sometimes the offspring of other Roosevelts came to visit. One was Eleanor Roosevelt, aged two when Franklin was four. She was brought by her father Elliott from up-the-river Tivoli. Legend says Franklin crawled around on all fours, allowing little Eleanor to ride on his back.

Among children his own age Franklin was inclined to be dominant. In Sara's words:

Franklin had a great habit of ordering his playmates around, and for reasons which I have never been able to fathom was generally permitted to have his way. I know that I, overhearing him in conversation one day with a little boy on the place with whom he was digging a fort, said to him: "My son, don't give the orders all the time. Let the other boy give them sometimes."

"Mummie," he said to me quite without guile, lifting a soil streaked face, "if I don't give the orders nothing would happen."

With all this, Franklin grew into a self-sufficient youth who, like other Roosevelts, was never bored. When playmates left, he hauled out his stamps or his carvings to amuse himself. Often Sallie read aloud while he worked on his stamp collection at her feet. During one such session the proud mother got the first inkling that her offspring possessed an unusual mind. Franklin was so absorbed in his stamps as she read that Sara stopped and said, "Son, I don't believe you are hearing a word I'm reading."

"Of course, I am, Sallie," he replied. He proved it by repeating word for word the last paragraph. Then he added, "Why, I'd be ashamed if I couldn't do at least two things at once."

Franklin's ability to amuse himself was of assistance when the Roosevelt family traveled. For travel they did!

James and Sallie considered Hyde Park the garden spot of the earth. As he grew up, so did Franklin. "All the good that is in me goes back to the Hudson," he wrote once. At the same time the elder Roosevelts seemed to suffer a compulsion to get away from their beloved home as often as possible. Or was it the duty of the rich to travel? Both Roosevelts appeared to entertain the feeling that it was a responsibility of the Last Patroons to set an example of gracious living for those less splendidly born. Furthermore, Sallie said, "One always meets people one knows when traveling."

Baby Franklin's peregrinations commenced a few weeks after birth, when he was taken to Algonac. A short time later he was in New York. Next, the family passed a few days at Coney Island. Mother and son had been given a near-fatal dose of chloroform at the time of Franklin's birth. This slip-up was blamed for the numerous colds and the sinus trouble that plagued him through life. Possibly the Coney Island sojourn was an initial effort to heal still-inflamed membranes.

James Roosevelt took excellent care of his own health, and believed the waters at Bad Nauheim and Bad Kissingen kept him well. He and Sallie tried to make annual summer visits to these Bavarian spas. At the age of two, Franklin was taken on his first trip to Europe. By the time he went to Groton at fourteen he had been in Europe no less than eight times.

At first, nurses accompanied the family. Then a governess, and finally a tutor. At age four Franklin was left at home for three months while his parents visited Mexico City. James and Sallie left him behind again while they went to Europe. In their absence he contracted scarlet fever and his parents rushed home. The fact that her son was under quarantine in his bedroom did not deter Sallie when she reached Springwood. She ordered a ladder placed up to the window and resolutely climbed it. Thus we have the curious picture of a future President of the United States conversing with his stately mother as she perched on a ladder outside his window!

The Roosevelts also kept a year-round suite at the Hotel Renaissance at 10 West Forty-third Street in New York. They spent much time there. Close by the hotel James rented a stable where he kept a few horses. This allowed him to drive to and from Hyde Park, as well as to canter in Central Park on his own mounts.

The winter of 1887 was spent in Washington, D.C. President Grover Cleveland, an old friend of James's, offered the Hyde Park squire a foreign diplomatic post. James refused, stating that the only public office he desired was in his local township. However, he put in a good word for his son Rosy, who aspired to diplomacy. Rosy was appointed first secretary of the United States legation in Vienna and improved his prospects by a large contribution to the next Cleveland campaign.

Several times young Franklin accompanied his father on visits to the White House. On the final one there occurred an episode that seems almost too pat to be true. Yet it happened. Cleveland, a much-harried Chief Executive, bade father and son farewell by patting the boy on the head and saying, "My little man, I am making a strange wish for you. I hope that you may never be President of the United States!"

The Roosevelts owned a rambling summer home on Campobello, a small island off the coast of New Brunswick, close to Maine. Here James sailed a 45-foot sloop with an auxiliary motor. As soon as Franklin was old enough, he had his own sailboat.

However, the peripatetic family did not stop here. If James Roosevelt was not a capitalist on a large scale, he was at least medium-sized, with the perquisites that went with it. He was president of the Champlain Transportation and Lake George Steamboat Company, and throughout his life Franklin cherished fond memories of trips aboard the paddle-wheel steamers *Vermont, Reindeer,* and *Chateaugay.* As president of the Lousiville, New Albany, and Chicago Railroad, James rated a private car, then a status symbol second only to an oceangoing yacht. The Roosevelt railroad car boasted bedrooms, a sitting room, kitchen, and a Negro steward whose specialty was egg bread. In this private car the family rolled over the rails of the United States.

For a time there were many trips to Superior, Wisconsin, the scene of one of James's attempts to make himself a multimillionaire. When Superior failed to live up to James's hopes, he retreated—without visible sorrow—to serving as New York State commissioner to the Chicago World's Fair of 1893. In the private railroad car the family made several official visits to the fair. On one of these James was astounded when a large man in full coachman's regalia stepped out from the welcoming group. Extending a hand, the man said, "Hello, Cousin Jimmy, I'm your cousin Clinton." With this, he touched his tall silk hat, leaped to the driver's seat of a carriage, cracked his whip, and drove the Roosevelts to a hotel. Along the way he identified himself as Clinton Roosevelt, owner of a large livery stable in St. Louis, and explained that he had secured the concession to drive all official visitors to the fair. Franklin never forgot the episode. He figured out that his coachman-cousin must be the many times grandson of one of the sons of Nicholas I who went west.

When Franklin reached the age of thirteen, in 1895, he was given a bicycle and immediately rode it to Algonac. He was being taught by tutors at this time. One was a Swiss lady named Mlle. Jeanne Sandoz who may have planted seeds of future liberalism in the mind of her pupil. She was succeeded by Arthur Dumpson, who accompanied the family to Europe and took Franklin on a tour of the Black Forest while his father enjoyed the baths.

Sallie kept a doting eye on her young son's development—reading, hobbies, health, manners—every single thing concerning him. She saved everything he ever touched. (Later on, Roosevelt did this himself.) So the question arises: Did Sallie have intuitive feelings that her son would grow up to be a great man or did she merely love him so much that everything he did seemed interesting, important, and valuable?

Family members incline to the latter belief, believing she only wished him to enter the legal or some other honorable profession and continue to make Springwood his home. James seemed to nurse the same notion. As Franklin grew older, the boy concentrated his reading on naval history and stories. One day he announced that he intended to enter Annapolis and become a United States naval officer. James took his son aside and with firmness told him that a nautical life was out of the question. An only child who expected to inherit an estate, James explained, could not choose the navy for it would take him too far from home. Franklin must remain on dry land—if possible, the land of Dutchess County. "Study law as I did," James advised. "It prepares a man for any profession."

Franklin's parents had enrolled him at Groton before he was a year old. Now the boy was fourteen and his entry could no longer be delayed. His mother was sorrowful at sending him into a world "whose boundaries were not limited by the barriers the very intensity of our devotion imposed." Yet Franklin found new barriers at Groton. For one thing, other boys his age had been at the school for two years, making it necessary for him to step into a group where friendships were already cemented. Then, too, Groton boys slept in cell-like cubicles with curtains for doors. Daily they rose at seven to suffer through an ice-cold shower. From then on the daily discipline was rigid. At bedtime the boys lined up in best suits, with stiff collars and evening pumps, to exchange good night handshakes with Dr. Peabody and his wife.

Under this drastic switch of environment, Franklin stood up well, exhibiting the flexibility of his later years. "I am getting along finely both physically and mentally," he wrote home. He was hazed by classmates, who made him dance in a corner while hacking at his shins with hockey sticks. The boy took this with such good grace that thereafter he was let alone. He was, however, under constant fire as the only Democrat in a school of one hundred fifty boys.

"He was nice but colorless," a classmate later recalled. At first his main interest was sports. Failing to make the baseball team, he cheerfully accepted the thankless job of team manager. As a senior he turned to debating, where he was assisted by a voice already pliable, with a touch of his father's aristocratic accent that never left it. In choosing sides for debate, Franklin showed commendable sympathy for underdog peoples in the Philippines and South Africa. At times he also worked in a camp for underprivileged boys established by Dr. Peabody. He graduated in 1900, a tall, patrician-looking youth, headed without question for Harvard.

But Hyde Park remained the focal point of his existence. He wrote frequently to Sara, addressing her as "My Darling Mama" or "My Dearest Mummie."

Franklin was popular at Groton and in one way had celebrity status. For the eighteen years which took him from infancy to young manhood had wrought equally drastic changes in the life of Theodore Roosevelt. By this time, Theodore had become the most famous person in the United States and had started to give the Roosevelt name the Royal Family aura it would enjoy over the next sixty years. It was the beginning of the Theodore Era in the family and the Roosevelt Era in the country. Anyone who bore the name trailed considerable luster. In fact, to the intense indignation of Sara, Groton boys and their families persisted in believing that Franklin was the nephew, or even the son, of the tempestuous chap the world called Teddy.

Back in 1884 Theodore had proclaimed himself a private citizen and literary feller, with politics forever banished from his life. This resolve lasted only as long as his mind remained choked with grief over the loss of Alice and Mittie, his pride lacerated by the humiliating Blaine defeat in Chicago. Theodore triumphed over these misfortunes by the best method known to him—strenuous physical exercise. "I am in the saddle all day," he wrote Bamie from the Bad Lands, either taking part in the roundup of cattle, or else hunting antelope . . . and as I own six or eight horses I have a fresh one every day, and ride and lope all day long." He bought more cattle and spent $26,000 for a large ranch at Elkhorn. The cowboys still called him "Four Eyes" and "Tenderfoot," but the nicknames were spoken with respect. One grizzled foreman paid him the tribute of saying, "He's game to the core."

Theodore was never a man to nurse sorrow. "Black care rarely sits behind the rider whose pace is fast enough," he said. His biographer, Henry Pringle, thinks that "there were qualities in Roosevelt that halted introspection soon after it started. He could surrender momentarily to depression, but it could not prevail against an innate robustness, against his adolescence."

After four months in the saddle Theodore again felt the call of politics and bitterly regretted—as he would several other times in life—the emphatic conviction he had put into the statement announcing his retirement. Those who read Theodore's autobiography get the impression that he passed the next two years galloping the range. Such is not the case. With Theodore, to feel was to act, and with the first tug toward politics he rushed back home to campaign for Blaine. From then on he spent about half his time in the East, shuttling between Dakota and Bamie's Madison Avenue home, where his daughter Alice inhabited the nursery.

Soon he had another interest in the East. Sagamore Hill was completed at a total cost of $45,000. As soon as the Oyster Bay home was ready, Bamie and little Alice moved in. Theodore told his sister that he wished the house to be a lively place and Bamie, ever the happy hostess, began to preside over dinner parties and dances. "Life was gay at Sagamore those first years," Hermann Hagedorn writes. A good bit of the gaiety was contributed by Theodore himself. The most determined of cowboys in the West, he was a gentleman-rider in the East, a genial host to the Meadowbrook Hunt for Sunday breakfasts and red-coat riding to hounds.

The great city of New York had not forgotten the Young Reformer whose bravura career in the Assembly promised so much. From time to time feelers came to Theodore from the Republican organization. One offered him the job of president of the City Board of Health. Theodore did not consider this important enough and resumed commuting between Elkhorn and Oyster Bay.

At this point in life, his chief occupation was writing. He wrote seven books in five years, together with numerous articles on hunting and politics. His first Western book was called *Hunting Trips of a Ranchman: Sketches of Sport on the Northern Cattle Plains*. Photographs of the author distributed with it show Theodore, at twenty-seven, attaining the appearance of his later years. His neck was thickening, jaw fattening. His figure was heavier, despite the furious exercise, and behind the rimless glasses eyes were narrowing into the scowl seen by H. G. Wells as "the friendly peering snarl of his face, like a man with the sun in his eyes."

By his books, Theodore hoped to make the bread-and-jam money to pay for Sagamore Hill. He also needed funds because of his own extravagance. Indeed, it has been said that financial extravagance was Theodore's sole aristocratic trait. He might talk poor mouth about day-to-day expenditures, but he could be rash with large sums. The amounts he invested in Bad Lands cattle ranches were far beyond his means. So was investing $20,000 in a New York publishing firm whose executives innocently expected him to be a silent partner.

Yet Theodore's book writing never made him appreciably richer. He was a popular author but never a best seller, though his books were the type of action literature in vogue at the time. Perhaps the difficulty lay in his style, for Theodore never used one word where a dozen would do. At Harvard a professor had said, "His writing is to the point, but does not have the air of cultivation." This continued true.

Since his engagement to Alice Lee there had been a stiffness between Theodore and Edith Kermit Carow, the playmate and correspondent of his youth. Edith was three years younger, a quiet, contained girl with a distinguished facial structure. She read even more books than a Roosevelt and was still the only female Theodore had ever met who shared his enthusiasm for zoology and natural history. Edith had remained friendly with Corinne and Bamie and was often with them in New York. She asked them both to warn her any time Theodore was scheduled to arrive so that she might leave beforehand. One night in the fall of 1885, however, Edith was late leaving Bamie's, Theodore early in arriving. They bumped into each other at the foot of the stairs. In an instant stiffness vanished and the two were again the good companions of yore.

Theodore had stern Victorian principles that told him to remain a widower the rest of his life, mourning Alice Lee. Edith, no less Victorian, felt as he did. Yet in the new intimacy Victorianism slowly washed away. Theodore's entry in his diary on St. Valentine's Day, 1886, was a heart pierced by an arrow. Still, Alice had died only two years before—in fact, on Valentine's Day. Theodore thought it much too soon to take another wife. It is said that he walked the floor through long nights, banging his fist into an open palm, muttering, "I have no constancy! I have no constancy!" Still undecided, he returned to Dakota while Edith went to live in London.

Yet love brought its measure of good luck, for Theodore was now asked to run for mayor of New York City. He had always desired the office, but this particular offer had drawbacks. Henry George, advocate of the single tax, was running for mayor on an independent ticket. Tammany Hall countered by nominating Abram S. Hewitt, wealthy, respected, conservative—the opposite of reformer George. Republican leaders felt that George might pull enough Democratic votes to make a Republican slide-in possible. What they did not realize—on occasion Theodore did—was that Roosevelt's youth and tidal-wave energy made him more dangerous than Henry George to the average Republican. Theodore aptly called such folk the "timid good." On election day the timid good voted for Hewitt. "I do not believe," one said afterward, "that we were really more afraid of Henry George than we were of Theodore Roosevelt's youth." Hewitt won, with Theodore an unhappy last.

This time, however, he did not run to the Bad Lands for solace. Instead, Theodore crossed the ocean to London, where on December 2 he married Edith Kermit Carow. The second Mrs. Roosevelt probably understood Theodore better than anyone alive. She was aware of his ebullient immaturity and on rare occasions was irked by it. But she loved him deeply and was happy to devote her life to tempering his rashness and making his existence comfortable. For Theodore, the marriage forever settled one of life's Absolutes. "The greatest privilege and duty for any man is to be happily married," he firmly stated.

So again Theodore Roosevelt had the pleasure of a European

honeymoon. But while he enjoyed himself, a severe blizzard and freeze killed the cattle on his Elkhorn ranch, which from now on was used as a hunting lodge. When the newlyweds returned to Sagamore Hill, Theodore devoted himself to writing *The Winning of the West,* generally considered his best book. It was a period of comparative inertia for the active man, though Sagamore Hill had many guests. A first son was born to him in September and christened Theodore Jr. "He exercises more vigorously than anyone I know," the father declared with soaring pride. Already Theodore Sr. had a delightful companion in his daughter Alice, who was growing up to be clever and energetic—as a Roosevelt should.

Continuing in the background were the hushed voices of those who still considered Theodore a man destined for the White House. Foremost among these was his sister Corinne. But a more potent figure was Henry Cabot Lodge, now on the verge of becoming senator from Massachusetts.

Lodge is a peculiar figure in the life of Theodore Roosevelt. Called "the scholar in politics," he was quite as much the proper Bostonian as Theodore was a proper New Yorker. Small and ferretlike, Lodge spoke in a raspy voice likened to the tearing of a bedsheet. Where Theodore was volcanic, Cabot Lodge was controlled and calculating. Carleton Putnam states, "Roosevelt's capacity for work was phenomenal, while Lodge's was only extraordinary."

To some observers the two men represented a Damon-Pythias friendship on a gigantic scale, for the assistance given Theodore by Lodge at strategic moments went far beyond the call of friendship. To others, the senator from Massachusetts performed his generous acts only to fatten up Theodore for the Big Kill. Almost from the beginning Lodge had viewed Roosevelt as a potential Chief Executive and he never wavered during this period of his friend's obscurity. "I do not say you are to be President tomorrow," he wrote. "I do not say it will be—but I am sure it may and can be!"

For the moment no path to the Presidency was visible to the

naked eye. However, in 1888 one materialized with Benjamin Harrison's election. Theodore had campaigned rousingly for Harrison in New York and expected a reward. Strange to say, in Theodore's political career nonelective appointments did as much —if not more—than his victories at the polls to push him toward the Presidency. Yet each appointive post was offered with great reluctance.

Now Senator Lodge pressured Harrison to give the deserving Oyster Bay Republican a post in Washington. The President demurred, at which Lodge applied more pressure. Finally Harrison grudgingly offered the post of civil service commissioner at $3,500 a year. This was not considered much of an appointment. The merit system in filling government jobs was brand new, the spoils system old. Of the spoils system a politician had recently said, "We have to take the boys in out of the cold to warm their toes a little." The job of fighting this entrenched philosophy appeared hopeless.

Nevertheless, Theodore leaped from private life as if propelled by a giant slingshot. He advanced on Washington like a combined Lochinvar and Galahad. As ever, reporters clustered around his bounding figure. To them he vowed to extend the merit system as far as the law would allow. "You can guarantee that I intend to hew to the line and let the chips fall where they will," he vowed.

He was bent on achieving civil service reform in record time, and in striving for results he stepped on sensitive toes. He also made full use of the talent for disparaging invective, which was his greatest verbal and writing gift. His main opponent was the dignified merchant John Wanamaker, who, for campaign contributions to the Republicans, had been named Postmaster General. Theodore characterized the well-meaning Wanamaker as possessing "a very sloppy mind . . . doesn't speak the truth. . . slanderous falsehoods . . . sly intolerance, cruelty, and meanness that would be shocking to a barbarian." His attacks became so personal and his thirst for newspaper publicity so avid that both Lodge and Edith Carow Roosevelt hastily counseled moderation.

But Theodore rampaged on, next giving the President a taste of his tongue. After one frustrating interview with the Chief Executive, he bitterly exclaimed, "Heavens, how I like *positive* men!" Yet the benign Harrison seemed to understand his unruly civil service commissioner. "The only trouble I ever had with managing him," he recalled later, "was that . . . he wanted to put an end to all evil in the world between sunrise and sunset." Again he described Theodore as "impatient for righteousness."

Theodore considered Washington little more than a big village, and while living there from 1888 to 1895 devoted himself to civil service reform, an increasing family, and the rigors of authorship. The larger issues of government failed to interest him. More important, perhaps, was the fact that Washington discovered *him*. Theodore continued to provide colorful copy for reporters and his big teeth and glinting glasses were a godsend to political cartoonists. Though little more than a minor official, he became one of the best-known figures in the capital city.

In off-hours he mingled with the erudite group dominated by Henry Adams and John Hay. Rudyard Kipling, then a Washington resident, liked to sit in the Cosmos Club and watch Teddy in action. "I curled up in the seat opposite," he wrote once, "and listened and wondered until the universe seemed to be spinning around and Theodore was the spinner." The number of books Roosevelt had read astounded even his best-educated companions. Some of them accepted him as an intellectual, but others entertained doubts—Theodore was a man who had called Thomas Paine "a filthy little atheist." Of a novel by Henry James he wrote, "I think it represents the last stage of degradation . . . the book is simply diseased. I turned to a story of Kipling's with the feeling of getting into fresh, healthy, out-of-doors life." Some of his critics felt Theodore never fully digested the huge gobs of words he read and eternally remained an example of education without culture. But he amazed even these carpers by the reckless scope of his reading.

The election of Grover Cleveland, a Democrat, seemed to promise an end to Theodore's lively tenure as civil service commissioner. However, the faithful Lodge again went to bat for him, pointing out that Theodore had done an excellent job, despite the publicity. Cleveland agreed and kept Theodore in the post.

In this period Theodore's moments of greatest delight came during vacations and weekends at Oyster Bay. Here he applied his teeming vigor to hiking, riding, sailing, swimming, hunting, and botany and bird watching. By now he had three sons and two daughters: Alice, Theodore Jr., Kermit, Ethel, and Archie. Quentin was born in 1897. His own boys were not quite old enough for hikes, but the numerous offspring of nearby Roosevelt families joined him and ten-year-old Alice in long, rugged Obstacle Walks. With Teddy striding in the lead, everyone involved went through, over, or under—but never around!—all obstacles such as haymows, barns, or streams.

Another of Theodore's pet games with the children was to plunge down the sandy steepness of Cooper's Bluff, then whirl around and climb back up. He taught boys and girls to swim by tossing them off a dock or a boat into deep water. This was successful in every case except that of Elliott's daughter Eleanor, who had a deathly fear of water. When tossed overboard, she simply sank once, twice, before Uncle Ted pulled her back. "He was very indignant," she recalled later. Eleanor also disliked the wild scrambles up and down Cooper's Bluff and the way the boys teased her with snakes. "But," she says, "I learned to bear with it." Uncle Ted read Norse sagas and poetry to children gathered around campfires, and this she liked. Theodore grew fond of the shy, gangling girl who so plainly felt inadequate. In time she became his favorite niece.

In Washington Theodore continued restless. He and Grover Cleveland got along well personally, but civil service reform had lost its bloom. "Struggle as I will, my life seems to grow more sedentary," he lamented to Bamie. "My chance of doing anything in the future worth doing seems to grow continually smaller."

His gloom at this point highlights the most amazing quirk of

Theodore's character. As long as he talked or moved with his accustomed rapidity he seemed to feel a supreme confidence. But when quiet or alone he was prey to doubts and fears incomprehensible in so fiery a figure. Lodge and other intimates were only too aware of this. At one point the senator told him, "You see things too darkly . . . everyone thinks you are one of the most sanguine of men. I . . . know better." Yet the world knew only the confident, challenging Theodore, and now this dazzling figure was rescued from the boredom of Washington by the city of New York.

There a corrupt police force had been accepting millions of dollars from prostitutes and brothels, gamblers and gambling dens. Mayor Strong fought back by establishing a four-man police board of honorable citizens. He asked Theodore to be one member. On advice of Lodge, Theodore refused until assured of election as president of the commission. This, in effect, made him a police commissioner. He accepted the post in May, 1895.

In a group the four appointees arrived afoot at Headquarters on Mulberry Street. While the other three proceeded at a dignified pace, Theodore ran ahead, waving to reporters and onlookers. Inside the building he took immediate charge. "Where are our offices?" he demanded. "Where is the board room? Now, what do we do?" A more discerning man might have noted that the other commissioners resented his manner of taking control. "Thinks he's the whole board," one member grumbled. It was the beginning of an active animosity.

As a state assemblyman Theodore had known Jacob Riis, reformer and author. Through Riis he now met Lincoln Steffens who, as a reporter, had been in the forefront of graft exposure. One day Riis and Steffens sparked a curious scene. Like many others, they were convinced that Police Commissioner Roosevelt would wind up in the White House and decided to find out if he thought so, too. Riis put the question. Theodore, comfortably seated behind his police commissioner's polished desk, jumped up in a rage. Eyes blazing, teeth bared, fists clenched, he rushed around the desk, ready to throttle his questioner.

"Don't you dare ask me that," he shouted. "Don't you put such ideas in my head. No friend of mine would ever say a thing like that, you . . . you . . ."

Slowly getting a grip on himself, he pulled Steffens close and put an arm around Riis's shoulders. In solemn tones, he said:

Never, never, you must never either of you remind a man at work on a political job that he may be President. It almost always kills him politically. He loses his nerve; he can't do his work; he gives up the very traits that are making him a possibility. I, for instance, am going to do great things here, hard things that require all the courage, ability, work that I am capable of, and I can do them if I think of them alone. But if I get to thinking of what it might lead to . . .

He paused as his face—Steffens remembers—screwed into a knot. As if speaking to himself, he ended, "I must be wanting to be President. Every young man does. But I won't let myself think of it; I must not, because if I do, I will begin to work for it, I'll be careful, calculating, cautious in word and act, and so—I'll beat myself. See?"

Theodore richly enjoyed himself as police commissioner. "I am fighting vile crime and hideous vice," he told Bamie. He had found out in Washington that reform was best accomplished under the white glare of publicity, and now he invited headlines as he dashed into a police cleanup. At age thirty-seven he was still a fancy dresser who wore a gaudy cummerbund sash, the tasseled ends of which swung to his knees. Trailed by reporters, he tore from precinct to precinct, catching policemen who were asleep, drinking beer, or beating prisoners. At night he attended Fifth Avenue dinner parties, then put a coat over his trim evening clothes to roam the streets until dawn. For this whirlwind of activity newspapers dubbed him Haroun-al-Roosevelt while the cartoonists spoofed him.

For a year it was bully—*just bully!*—to use the word that dominated Theodore's vocabulary. Then he made the mistake of taking the police commissioner's job—or himself—too seriously. On the statute books lay a neglected law which ordered saloons closed on Sunday. Conscientious Theodore decided to enforce it, though the action was certain to antagonize the city's poor, to whom the saloon was a treasured Sunday beer-drinking oasis.

Warned on all sides that enforcement would be a highly unpopular move, he stood adamant. "I shall procure the enforcement of the Sunday closing law not by spurts but by steadily increasing vigor," he orated. His fellow commissioners, so long antagonistic, refused to back him up. Even Mayor Strong protested—in Theodore's words, "telling me to let up on the saloons and impliedly threatening to turn me out if I refused." Worst of all, the clergy withheld support. Yet Theodore drove reluctant police to close saloons on Sunday. A volcano of protest erupted, until the situation was resolved by a magistrate who ruled Sunday drinking permissible with meals and called any food a meal. Theodore was indignant. "One pretzel will get a man seventeen beers," he grumbled.

So, after little more than one pleasurable year Theodore Roosevelt was given a strong taste of public disfavor. It was a nasty brew, especially as he remained convinced of his own rightness. Fed up with New York, he was once more saved by Henry Cabot Lodge, who talked the newly elected President William McKinley into offering a Washington post. Theodore wished to be Assistant Secretary of State, but McKinley offered to make him Assistant Secretary of the Navy, for which authorship of *The Naval War of 1812* had served as preparation. The President made his gesture with extreme reluctance.

In recent months Hearst newpapers had begun violently agitating for a war to free persecuted Cubans from the yoke of Spain. Wild atrocity stories had set the public imagination afire. Theodore appeared to approve an attack on Spanish-held Cuba, calling the prospect "a bully war." In part his bellicose attitude stemmed from a wish to enjoy the supreme experience of war himself, but he also envisioned the war as making America stronger and more influential in world affairs.

However, the placid McKinley wished no such talk around him. "There will be no jingo nonsense under my administration," he told Lodge. "I am afraid Roosevelt is too pugnacious." But Lodge extracted from Theodore a promise to behave and he was made Assistant Secretary of the Navy.

Seldom has a sober promise been honored so briefly. For Theodore was unable to curb his reckless utterances. "Great masterful races have been fighting races," he pontificated. To the Naval War College he declared, "No triumph of peace is quite so great as the supreme triumphs of war." He made the undiplomatic remark that President McKinley had a spine like a chocolate éclair. His immediate superior, Secretary of the Navy Long, was afraid to stay away from the Navy Department for fear his jingoistic Assistant Secretary would do something rash. Finally, Long was forced to skip a day and Theodore gleefully cabled Admiral Dewey to prepare the fleet for eventual action. In his diary the patient Long wrote, "It shows how the best fellow in the world—and with splendid capacities—is worse than no use if he lacks a cool head and judgment."

With the declaration of war in April, 1898, it was unthinkable for Theodore Roosevelt to remain behind an executive desk in the Navy Department. It is also easy to imagine that McKinley and Long were anxious to see him go. Congress had authorized recruitment of three dashing cavalry regiments in the West and Southwest. Roosevelt was offered command of the first, with the rank of full colonel. In a fine sporting gesture he gave the colonelcy to Captain Leonard Wood, a jingoist army doctor who had some experience as a commander.

Teddy accepted the rank of second-in-command, and immediately wrote Brooks Brothers for a "blue cravennet regular lieutenant-colonel's uniform without yellow on the collar, and with leggings." Newspaper correspondents dubbed his 1st Volunteer Cavalry the "Rough Riders" and to its banner flocked a motley assortment of polo players from the East, cowboys from the wild West, and skilled horsemen from all over. "It was the society page, financial column, and Wild West Show all wrapped up in one," a reporter wrote.

So began the happiest period in Theodore Roosevelt's life. This was indeed a bully war, the Rough Riders a jim-dandy regiment! At training camp Theodore was euphoric, galloping around giving orders to his men and issuing rousing statements to the press. "Theodore is absolutely radiating," a Rough Rider wrote home. He drank beer with his enlisted men—many of them New York bluebloods—and for this earned the hatred of top army brass. Hatred increased as the Rough Riders arrived in Florida to the accompaniment of fanfare from correspondents like Richard Harding Davis. Colonel Wood was forgotten and the regiment was called "Teddy's Terrors." When Teddy's Terrors landed in Cuba, it seemed to many back home that they were fighting the Spanish-American War single-handed.

It was a Barnum-and-Bailey war for the Rough Riders. Yet the conflict had its seamy side. The Rough Riders and other American troops faced men with guns who were out to kill. For all his exhibitionism, Teddy was on the frontline of fire as were his mounted men, a few of whom were killed. Teddy showed great moral courage in sticking up for the rights of his volunteers against the Regular Army—another black mark against him.

The Rough Rider charge up San Juan Hill became the peak moment of the bully war and a notable moment in American history. "San Juan was the great day of my life," Theodore said after that. Colonel Teddy, in cocked campaign hat, teeth flashing, rimless glasses glinting, came to typify the Spanish-American War. He expected the Congressional Medal of Honor when all was over, but he had earned the everlasting enmity of Regular Army commanders. They saw to it that he never got it.

13

A ROOSEVELT IN THE WHITE HOUSE

AS THE TRANSPORT BEARING THE TRIUMPHANT ROUGH RIDERS reached Montauk Point from Cuba, a reporter spotted the solid figure of Theodore Roosevelt leaning on the rail.

"How are you feeling, Colonel?" he shouted.

"Disgracefully well!" Theodore called back in the voice once described as an "oddly manful squeak."

He had reason to feel well. Even in faraway Cuba, Theodore realized he had become the most popular man in the United States. Nothing had been said openly, but a road to the Presidency seemed miraculously to have opened and on it were few obstacles. Most of these seemed to vanish when an emissary of Boss Tom Platt entered Theodore's tent to dangle the governorship of New York before his glinting specs. Teddy was already hard at work on a book to be called *The Rough Riders*—a pundit later said it should be called *Alone in Cuba*—and he requested time to mull the idea.

There were a few problems still to be adjusted between the Boss and the Colonel. Platt did not like Theodore. At the same time the colorful Rough Rider was so popular that no other candidate could be considered. Still Platt was determined to save face by driving a hard bargain. He insisted that Theodore as governor must "clear" appointments and decisions with him. He also wished Theodore to pay him an immediate visit so that the candidate would appear to be requesting the Republican nomination.

After deliberation, the cocky Rough Rider went to see Boss Platt who held court in a corner of the bar of the old Fifth Avenue Hotel at Madison Square. By doing this Theodore dealt a shattering blow to Reform Republicans who had expected to run him as a candidate and oust Platt from control of the statewide party. At first Reform circles were incredulous. Sputtered the Reverend Charles H. Parkhurst, "I do not believe that Teddy Roosevelt—I call him Teddy because I know him so well—has so far humbled himself as to go to Mr. Platt." But Theodore had, and the two men plotted a campaign almost cynical in its cleverness. Little mention would be made of state politics and none whatsoever of a recent Republican scandal over Erie Canal funds. Instead, patriotism and national issues would serve as the rousing theme.

Theodore's kick-off speech was delivered from a flag-bedecked platform at Carnegie Hall, in a rousing Fourth of July atmosphere. Bands played "There'll Be a Hot Time in the Old Town To-night," then and always Theodore's campaign song. The topic of the speech was "Duties of a Great Nation," and it abounded in such high-flown platitudes as "Our flag is a proud flag, and it stands for liberty and civilization."

After that Theodore boarded a campaign train for a speechmaking swing around New York State. He was accompanied by eight Rough Riders in uniform, and Teddy himself waved a wide-brimmed black hat similar in design to the jaunty khaki chapeau he wore in Cuba. At each stop a Rough Rider bugler stepped to the rear platform to sound a cavalry charge. As he did, the other Rough Riders followed, carrying American and regimental flags. Then Teddy appeared, to begin: "You have heard the trumpet that sounded to bring you here—I have heard it tear the tropic dawn when it summoned us to fight at Santiago!" After this he orated, "The guns of our warships have awakened us to a knowledge of new duties."

The Theodore Roosevelt who campaigned for governor of New York had just reached the age of forty. He stood five-ten, with a solid body on long legs. Despite his reckless expenditure of energy, he was inclined to gain weight. A thick neck pushed his head forward, giving him a pugnacious look. He was never quiet, and put as much emotion into an ordinary conversation as into a major speech. He chopped the air with strong gestures or punched a fisted hand into the palm of the other while changing expressions flipped over his square, squinting face. Above the sensitive mouth of his childhood he had grown a drooping mustache which seemed to vanish completely when his lips spread wide over glistening, protuberant teeth in his famous grin. When excited, Theodore's jaw clamped tight and its muscles writhed. His thick hair showed no sign of receding, while over gray-blue eyes the ever-present nose glasses on the black cord gave a glint to his face.

"Out of his countenance two men were wont to gaze at the world," a correspondent said. "One was primitive, impetuous, imperious, splashing out a reservoir of vigor; the other was sophisticated . . . often feline." It is a curious fact that on the rare occasions when he publicly removed his nose glasses Theodore's face lost its colorful ferocity, to appear mild and ordinary.

This was Theodore's first campaign for office with a full family in the background, and the Oyster Bay Roosevelts gave an initial display of the intense emotional solidarity that characterized them. Despite external health and vigor, the Republican Roosevelts were elemental haters. Though his sons were barely old enough to understand what was going on, they—no less than Edith and Alice —knew that Teddy was absolutely right in everything, his opponent totally wrong.

In this campaign there was much outlet for hatred. Theodore's Democratic rival bore the aristocratic name of Augustus Van Wyck. The Roosevelts hated him, all Democrats and—especially— the Reform Republicans who had decided to support Van Wyck.

In Cuba, Theodore had made disparaging remarks about the fighting worth of the National Guard, and its New York members refused to endorse him. Perhaps the smoldering Guardsmen started the malicious rumor that Theodore did not storm San Juan Hill. Someone did—and it was widely believed.

With all this, the Republican candidate was not the expected shoo-in. Did the disillusioned Reformers count against him or had the people of New York begun to find flaws in tempestuous Teddy? Boss Platt asked himself these questions after Theodore was elected by a disappointing 18,000 majority. The Boss made shrewd note of the fact that the new Governor was more popular outside his state than in it.

On the day following the election a Harvard classmate asked, "Theodore, what kind of governor are you going to be?" The Governor-elect answered, "I am going to be just as good a kind as the politicians will let me be."

His record in Albany reflects this limited aspiration. He pushed through a civil service reform law and a tax on corporate franchises. His attitude toward the workingman was friendlier than it had been in the Assembly; he recognized the need for labor votes. He was well disposed to the eight-hour day and to similar concessions, but any suggestion of labor's right to strike drove him into a fury. In all his record as governor was not exceptional. His tenure has been called remarkable chiefly for the fact that during it he first said, "I have always been fond of the West African proverb: *Walk softly and carry a big stick; you will go far.*"

Teddy's over-all plan was to serve two terms of two years each as governor, then win the presidential nomination in 1904. In this he counted without Boss Platt, who felt the agreed-on promise to "clear" things meant Theodore would allow him to approve or veto Albany decisions. To Teddy it meant merely telling Platt what he planned to do, then charging ahead to do it. He did this so often that Platt lost his temper. "I want to get rid of the bastard," he told a crony. "I don't want him raising hell in my state any longer. I want to bury him!"

Platt could not very well kick Theodore downstairs, but he could hoist him upward. He hatched a plan to get the 1900 vice-presidential nomination for Theodore. When the Governor heard stories linking his name with the Vice-Presidency, he made Platt promise to forbid the New York delegation to vote for him. Aware of Theodore's out-of-state popularity, Platt agreed. Even without the New York vote the convention could be stampeded for rough-and-ready Teddy.

Oddly enough, Henry Cabot Lodge also urged Theodore to try for the Vice-Presidency. It is at this point, Henry Adams and others feel, that Lodge was prepared to slaughter the friend he had so unselfishly fattened over the many years. By getting rid of Theo-dore in the dead-end Vice-Presidency, Lodge's own chances for the Presidency would be improved.

For once, Theodore disregarded the counsel of his tried and true friend. He went to the Republican Convention in Phila-delphia determined to refuse the Vice-Presidency. Yet, as ever, his actions were ambivalent. He stepped dramatically onto the con-vention floor in the wide-brimmed campaign hat with the Rough Rider flourish. (According to one story, he had a bandage over a cut on his scalp and wore the hat only to hide it.) As he strode aggressively down the aisle, delegates went wild. Republicans were weary of the familiar faces of Boss Platt, Mark Hanna, Matt Quay, and Chauncey M. Depew. When Theodore rose to second the nomination of McKinley, cheers boomed like thunder.

Back in his hotel, the peculiar man sat reading a heavy tome called *The History of Josephus* while delegations burst in and out of his room chanting, "We want Teddy!" In hotel lobbies Roose-velt sentiment was a merger of the practical and the emotional. Practical politicians said, "We need a ticket made up of McKinley, a Westerner with Eastern sympathies; and Roosevelt, an East-erner with Western sympathies." The emotional plea was "Give us someone to yell for."

Theodore Roosevelt was overwhelmingly chosen for the Vice-Presidency. Only the New York delegation sat on its hands as directed. Tom Platt grinned like a Cheshire cat, as perhaps did Henry Cabot Lodge. The only dissatisfied person in the hall was Mark Hanna, who had masterminded McKinley into the Presidency four years before. Hanna called Teddy "the mad cowboy." Now he burst out, "Don't any of you realize there's only one life between this madman and the White House?"

In the campaign Theodore did the talking while the amiable McKinley sat comfortably in Washington and Canton, Ohio. Teddy delivered nearly a thousand campaign speeches in twenty-four states, speaking without microphones to large crowds, sometimes above street noises and hecklers. Periodically he lost his voice and doctors ordered him to rest his throat. After one such order he went to the New York home of Corinne and Douglas Robinson. There he talked the night through.

Theodore's speeches pictured a bright new world. "We are a great people and we must play a great part in the world," he said. "On the whole," he told another audience, "we think that the greatest victories are yet to be won, the greatest deeds yet to be done, and that there are yet in store for our peoples and for the cause that we uphold, grander triumphs than have yet been scored." The vote was overwhelmingly Republican, with a plurality of 849,000, the largest in over twenty-five years.

A period of anticlimax followed. Roosevelt had nothing to do but mark time until the inauguration on March 4. He talked of a hunting trip to Colorado, "taking a hack at the bears in the Rockies," he called it. Meantime he went to Sagamore Hill. Friends continued to assure him that he was on the road to the Presidency, but Theodore felt he had made a fatal misstep. Again he suffered one of his periods of gloom. "I see no attractive outlook," he wrote forlornly. "I shall probably end my life as a professor in some small college."

Following the March inauguration he presided over a four-day session of the Senate, which then adjourned. Theodore returned to Sagamore Hill, where with the coming of summer he was a leader in fun and games. "There was something torrential about

[his] nature," recalls Nicholas Roosevelt, a boy at this time, "a great upswelling of interest in people and ideas, and a steady outpouring of love and affection for those close to him." Each of Theodore's own children had an exact contemporary among the cousins in other Roosevelt families. There were many other cousins and friends in addition. In all, about thirty eager children looked up to Cousin Ted—never "Teddy"—as a leader and ever-exciting pal. He took packs of boys on long camping trips; and after one of these, Corinne's son exposed a secret of Theodore's popularity. "My, but Uncle Ted is bully!" the boy told his mother. "He never asked me to wash once!"

As Vice-President, Theodore found one addition to life. He was in great demand to deliver his fist-pounding orations. In the summer of 1901 he made a speaking tour of the West. During this time the ordinarily healthy Roosevelt children were plagued with a series of ailments that kept them in Roosevelt Hospital. When Theodore returned, he, too, developed bronchitis and entered the hospital. In late August Edith took the recuperating children to the Tahawus Club in the Adirondacks for the beneficial mountain air. Theodore was to join them for a week of mountain climbing. Then all would return to Sagamore.

En route to meet his family Theodore detoured to an outing of the Vermont Fish and Game League on the Isle La Motte in Lake Champlain. Here he received the first inkling that Destiny was close. At the Pan-American Exposition in Buffalo the gentle McKinley was shot twice by a young assassin who shouted, "I done my duty!" Roosevelt rushed to Buffalo where—like the rest of the world—he convinced himself that the President was recovering. But in reality Buffalo physicians, more alert to professional courtesy than to medical skill, were slowly killing the martyred man.

Theodore joined his family at the Tahawus Club, and on September 13—a Friday!—he ruggedly set out with a party to climb Mount Marcy. After reaching the summit the party started downward in midafternoon. On the path they met a mountain guide with telegram in hand. "I had had a bully tramp and was looking forward to dinner with the interest only an appetite worked up in the woods gives you," Theodore later wrote. "When I saw the runner I instinctively knew he had bad news, the worst in the world." The telegram said McKinley was sinking.

Even so, Theodore did not depart at once for Buffalo. Instead, he went to bed at nine o'clock. At eleven he was awakened by a second telegram reporting McKinley on the verge of death. A man like Theodore Roosevelt could never attain the Presidency in quiet fashion and now, in wild haste, he began a lurching all-night carriage ride to North Creek where a locomotive panted at the head of a special train. Recent rains had made the twisting mountain roads doubly dangerous as relays of drivers and carriages carried him over the 35-mile journey. "Push ahead!" he rallied the drivers. "If you are not afraid, I'm not. Push ahead!"

At North Creek he was deferentially greeted as "Mr. President." To his wife he dispatched a terse telegram: PRESIDENT MCKINLEY DIED AT 2:15 THIS MORNING. THEODORE ROOSEVELT.

Theodore accompanied the McKinley funeral train to Ohio, then, on September 22, he took possession of the White House. (Edith had returned unescorted from the Adirondacks and was at Sagamore packing for the move to Washington.) For dinner on his first night in the White House, Theodore invited his sisters, Corinne and Bamie, and their husbands. At the end of the meal he said, "Do you realize this is the birthday of our father? I feel it is a good omen that I begin my duties on this day. I feel as if our father's hand were on my shoulder, and as if there were a special blessing on the life I am to live here."

It is stimulating to imagine the hands of the other Roosevelts in his line also resting on the new President's shoulder as he spoke: those of Claes Martenszen, Johannes, Jacobus, Jacobus I, and Grandfather C.V.S.; and those of their wives, Jannetje Thomas, Heyltje Jans Kunst, Heyltje Sjoerts, Annetje Bogard, Maria Van Schaack, Margaret Barnhill, of whose Irish strain Theodore was so proud, and his mother, Martha Bulloch, whose Scotch and Southern bloods were almost equally cherished.

By all the laws of heredity, each in this line of dual ancestors should have contributed to Theodore Roosevelt's personality. Yet such an image is hard to sustain. For the man now occupying the White House was less a Roosevelt than an explosive phenomenon.

Instead of Roosevelt traits, Theodore may have manifested the contemporary characteristics of his native land. His flaws and virtues equated those of the United States of America as it rounded 1900 to enter the century that would make it the most powerful nation on earth. The country was young—Theodore, at forty-three, its youngest President. The country was anxious to flex national muscles—Theodore constantly flexed his. The country was ready to demand a voice in world affairs—Theodore saw himself as a statesman President, one who would talk turkey to Kaiser Wilhelm, the Czar of Russia, the Emperor of Japan, and other potentates. Lastly, the country had progressed from infancy to adolescence—Theodore was a perennial adolescent.

"His exuberance suited the national mood exactly," Walter Lord writes. The country was shifting from the old rural, individualistic life to an industrialized order, just beginning to comprehend its financial and military potential. Mass production had started to make life more comfortable. Recent Presidents had been colorless men, who either failed to recognize this change or made no effort to dramatize it.

Theodore was the opposite—even if he did not precisely understand the changes, he was ready to provide the drama. With him in the White House there was never a dull moment. To many successful men life is a jungle with menace on all sides. To Theodore it was a jim-dandy boxing match, fought by the foursquare rules of the Harvard gym. He attacked problems as he led Obstacle Walks —through, over, and under, *but never around*. He loved life and met it head on, arms flailing.

One newspaper expressed amazement at his daily activities: "the scrapes he gets into, the scrapes he gets out of—the things he attempts, the things he accomplishes—the things he demolishes—his appointments and his disappointments—the rebukes he administers and the rebukes he receives—his assumptions, presumptions, omnisciences, and deficiencies." Much of what he did and said sounds stuffy and pompous today. But Teddy always gave a feeling of gaiety and fun. "To be with him was inevitably to have fun, because of the humor, cheerfulness, and warm affection he radiated," writes Cousin Nicholas. Theodore believed he had been put on this earth to have a bully time, and the feeling rubbed off on the entire country.

Ever propelling him forward was the fabulous energy. It was a nervous, rather than a dynamic, drive—one observer calls it his "berserker blood." Theodore's pounding energy never let him stop. It was accepted by press and public alike as something to be grateful for, but a few of his friends attempted to discover its source. One was his Harvard classmate Bradley Gilman, who writes:

The quality in him which I find most difficult of analysis—both by my own study and his friends—is his astonishing energy, expressed both physically and mentally. I cannot account for it fully, either by known laws of heredity or by the fact that he persistently and intelligently built up and repaired and rebuilt his physical as well as his intellectual equipment all through his life. The fact that he was a very sound sleeper—as he has assured me—will account at least in part for his wonderful resources of nervous strength. But these explanations do not fully explain . . . his tireless vigor.

Gilman remembers that Roosevelt laughed a lot. "I am inclined to see in his free and frequent laughter a partial explanation for his conservation of corporeal nerve tone," he continues.

According to William Allen White, "Roosevelt chuckled, was not above a guffaw, and loved a roaring belly laugh." Yet the subject of laughter brings up more questions. For Theodore does not appear to have been an overly humorous man. The best examples of his wit are biting political phrases. Occasionally he could say such things as "I am only an average man but, by George, I work at it harder than the average man." He called his critics "eligible for the Ananias Club, which already has a long waiting list." Of his ability with the French language he said, "I speak with daring fluency." But rather than an unusual sense of humor, his free and frequent laughter seems to indicate one more method of letting off surplus nervous energy.

With the laughter went an equal quickness to get angry. Stories by Lincoln Steffens abound in such phrases as: "He lost his temper . . ."; "He stopped, glared angrily at me . . ."; "He stood there at his desk looking, as he often looked, as if he had half a mind to beat me up." Of Franklin D. Roosevelt it was often said, "The Boss has his Dutch up." Theodore's anger was not so Dutch, since it came and went as rapidly as his chopping laugh. Theodore himself was aware of his hectic energy and violent changes of mood, and professed to believe himself scatterbrained. Once he said, "I guess I am rather a lurid companion at times."

That most astute of observers, Henry Adams, began by regarding Theodore with dislike, but ended up fond of him. "Roosevelt," he wrote, "more than any other living man, showed the singular primitive quality that belongs to the ultimate in matter— the quality that medieval theology assigned to God—*he was pure act.*"

Theodore's rampaging personality keeps obliterating his deeds, and historians have found difficulty in evaluating this first of the Roosevelts to reach the White House. For years after his death biographers were inclined to treat him as a President whose extravagant posturings far outweighed his sensible actions. A Pulitzer Prize-winning biography more or less followed this theme. Then a more admiring group stepped forward, trying to bolster the lightweight image. With the election of John F. Kennedy in 1960, great efforts were made to find parallels between the nation's two youngest Presidents. But Theodore's exact rung on history's ladder is still beclouded by his personality.

Doubt has even been cast on his success as Teddy, the great Trust Buster, the reformer who tried to walk softly (but never could!) and carry a big stick. According to popular history, the stick was used to clobber the mighty capitalistic combines whose owners Theodore, ever the political phrasemaker, called "malefactors of great wealth."

But few of his reforms really stuck—the trusts refused to stay busted! In fact, the Theodore who wielded the big stick did not actually intend to bust trusts but merely to make them behave. He was still that most paradoxical of types, the conservative reformer. His ideas of reform were based less on sociology and economics than on old-fashioned Right and Wrong, as he judged them. "When I do a thing, I do it so as to do substantial justice," he said once. He saw himself as a moral leader, awakening his countrymen before they dozed into the grip of the malefactors of great wealth. Yet he was able to dramatize even this because he could not stand still and loved a good fight, or at least got great nervous exhilaration out of it.

As a conservative reformer Theodore was necessarily a straddler and, with trusts, his aim was to "Get at the evil in them and uphold the good." A real reformer might ask, "What good?" But Theodore, guided by his sense of Right and Wrong, used the big stick only to clout trusts that grew too big or too greedy. When they behaved, he gave commendation for "real conservatism." Still no one had ever clobbered any trust before, and the public believed it was high time someone did. So again he reflected the national mood.

Inhibiting T.R. as a radical was his ingrained belief that the old days were best. The English historian James Bryce might say, "Theodore Roosevelt is the hope of American politics." But his compatriot Lord Charnwood was closer to the truth when he wrote, "Deeply does he distrust any ideas of progress which are founded in disparagement of older moralities."

As President of the United States, Theodore was an excellent administrator who slashed governmental red tape; he was a Chief Executive who gave full credit to other members of the Administration when such credit was due. He made long strides in land conservation and irrigation, the first President to do so; he did much for public health in reforming meat packing and sponsoring the Pure Food bill; he established a Department of Commerce and a Department of Labor; he resurrected the embalmed Sherman Antitrust Act and used it in his fight against Standard Oil, National Securities, and other trusts. He settled the coal strike of 1902, and in the process became the first President to realize that most malefactors of great wealth were men of small vision, bordering on the stupid. He attacked railroads for discriminatory rates and secured passage of the Hepburn Act. His trust busting restored competition to business; he encouraged a more scientific attitude toward the tariff. He sent the American navy around the world, a major step in making the country a world power; he negotiated the peace in the Russo-Japanese War, with delegates ceremoniously steaming into Oyster Bay to meet with him at Sagamore Hill, and for this he became the first American to win the Nobel Peace Prize.

On a different level, he created the republic of Panama, then seized part of it for the Canal Zone. This was a dubious act of Yankee imperialism in which he never could find a single flaw. "I took the Canal and let Congress debate," he boasted. "And while the debate goes on, the Canal does also."

In all this—and there was much more!—the spotlight was always on Theodore. He was a leader when few Presidents had bothered to lead. "Roosevelt has a knack of doing things, and doing them noisily, clamorously," a contemporary declared. "The public can no more look the other way than the small boy can turn his head from a circus parade." Here, perhaps, is Theodore's great contribution, the virtue by which he should really be judged.

For Theodore vitalized everything he touched. He humanized the American government, and in so doing made citizens feel closer to Washington. Until now only two American Presidents—Jackson and Lincoln—might be called colorful. Theodore was spectacular. He was warm, vivid, friendly, and infuriating. Because of him, a people who had been remote from the Presidency suddenly felt close to it. The nation affectionately called him Teddy and trusted him, for he was obviously not one to dissemble, pull punches, or resort to slick political phrases.

Theodore spoke and acted straight from the shoulder, at the same time displaying his matchless ability for breaking issues down into simple dramatic terms. He was a doer who acted, then went before the public to explain what he had done.

With Teddy in the White House, the nation enjoyed the pleasantest period it has ever known. The young America had a firm image of itself and seemed aware of just where it wanted to go. There was so much to be gained for the middle classes and the poor! Other reformers stepped forward, offering a variety of brand-new paths to progress. But leading the happy procession to the Promised Land was always the toothy, pugnacious, big stick-swinging figure of Theodore, the dervish figure, the one-man vaudeville show in the White House.

"Every faculty, every purpose, every impulse, every physical and spiritual inch of him was over-engined," writes William Allen White. "Yet his qualities were coordinated. He made . . . a well-balanced man in body and mind. If he was a freak, God and the times needed one."

While President, Theodore still boxed a few rounds every day. His favorite sparring partner was Mike Donovan, a scarred veteran of the ring, who informed a delighted world, "Had he come to the prize ring, instead of the political arena, it is my conviction that he would have been successful. . . . He is a born fighter." A political opponent added, "He is just like a punching bag. You hit it and it comes right back at you. The harder you hit him, the quicker he comes back."

Mike Donovan was not the only White House sparring partner. One afternoon Teddy put on the gloves with a young army officer who dealt him a jolting blow on the left eye. For days black spots floated in front of the President's vision. Finally, a specialist was summoned and ordered Theodore to fight no more. The President was indignant: why, he had a bout scheduled this very afternoon, with a jujitsu lesson after that, and jujitsu was such a bully sport! But from then on his sight worsened until he was blind in the left eye. This remained a carefully guarded White House secret.

After cutting down on boxing Teddy developed a passion for tennis—he considered golf a game for sissies. But he diminished his skill on the tennis court by talking while he played. Nonetheless, he hit the ball in characteristic overengined style. His opponents were a group of men his own age or younger with whom he also discussed government problems. This became known as the Tennis Cabinet, as opposed to the older statesmen of the regular Cabinet.

Teddy also continued his beloved Obstacle Walks and at any time might euphorically gather a group of men to begin a furious hike over hill and dale. One of the world's oddest diplomatic dispatches was sent by Jules Jusserand, French ambassador to the United States, who informed his government:

President Roosevelt invited me to take a promenade with him this afternoon at three. I arrived at the White House punctually, in afternoon dress and silk hat, as if we were to stroll in the Tuileries Garden or in the Champs-Elysées. To my surprise, the President soon joined me in a tramping suit, with knickerbockers and thick boots, and soft felt hat, much worn. Two or three other gentlemen came, and we started off at what seemed to me a breakneck pace, which soon brought us out of the city.

On reaching the country, the President went pell-mell over the fields, following neither road nor path, always on, on, straight ahead! I was much winded, but I would not give in, nor ask him to slow up, because I had the honor of *la belle* France in my heart. At last we came to the bank of a stream, rather wide and too deep to be forded. I sighed relief, because I thought that now we had reached our goal and would rest a moment and catch our breath before turning homeward.

But judge of my horror when I saw the President unbutton his clothes and heard him say, "We had better strip, so as not to wet our things in the Creek." Then I, too, for the honor of France, removed my apparel, everything except my lavender kid gloves. The President cast an inquiring look at these as if they, too, must come off, but I quickly forestalled any remark by saying, "With your permission, Mr. President, I will keep these on; otherwise it would be embarrassing if we should meet ladies." And so we jumped into the water and swam across.

Theodore's belief in the strenuous life never faltered. "I preach to you then, my countrymen," he shouted in one speech, "that our country calls not for the life of ease, but for the life of strenuous endeavor." He exhorted army officers to take 50-mile hikes or 100-mile horseback rides. He himself rode the ruggedest hundred miles he could find near Washington to prove it was easy. His love of hunting never abated. At one moment of national financial panic he was on a hunt in Louisiana. While money temples tottered, he emerged to report that "Possum was absolutely the best dish we had, excepting bear liver." Back at the White House he expressed gratification at having bagged a bear.

While urging citizens to join him in physical exercise he also made statements calculated to strengthen the country's moral fiber: "Don't flinch, don't foul, hit the line hard"; "Morality, decency, clean-living, manliness, self-respect—these qualities are more important in the make-up of a people than mental subtlety"; "Of all forms of tyranny, the least attractive and the most vulgar is the tyranny of mere wealth, the tyranny of plutocracy."

To his young military aide, Lieutenant Douglas MacArthur, he gave the secret of his popularity with voters: "I put into words what is in their hearts and minds, but not in their mouths. You must listen to the grass grow." Again, he said, "The most successful politician is he who says what everybody is thinking most often and in the loudest voice." On occasion his ringing generalities were tempered with real wisdom: "We ought not to tolerate wrong. It is a sign of weakness to do so, and in its ultimate effect weakness is often quite as bad as wickedness. But in putting an end to wrong we should, as far as possible, avoid getting into an attitude of vindictiveness toward the wrongdoer."

Close men friends regarded Theodore with affectionate tolerance. Most of them joined British Ambassador Cecil Spring-Rice in considering him an overgrown boy. On the President's forty-sixth birthday, Elihu Root congratulated him: "You have made a very good start in life and your friends have hopes for you when you grow up." Instead of being annoyed, Theodore was "dee-lighted"—another of his pet words.

One afternoon a group of senators cooled heels in the presidential anteroom. When the door opened, Theodore proudly emerged beside the former heavyweight boxing champion, John L. Sullivan. The two talked a few moments more, then Theodore playfully punched Sullivan on a hefty biceps. "Good-bye, John L., old chap," he said, "you are certainly the finest that ever wore mitts."

Once Lincoln Steffens heard a reporter ask the President an abstruse question. Steffens expressed astonishment to Roosevelt, saying, "He put that question to—your—mind!"

"And to what else should he have addressed it to, if not my mind?"

"I—I don't know," Steffens fumbled. "But I have known you a long time, and my impression is that you don't think things out in your mind but that you mull them over somewhere else in your nervous system—and form your conclusion in, say, your hips. If I wanted to get the answer he is after I would talk around indirectly till I got you to thinking out loud about what you were unconsciously concluding in your—hips."

Theodore was surprised but said, "Do you know, that's true. I do think down—down there somewhere."

In the White House, Theodore managed to read two books a day, and he sent frequent demands to the Harvard Library for "Histories or articles on early Mediterranean races . . . or a good translation of Niebuhr and Mommsen or the best modern history of Mesopotamia. Is there a good history of Poland?" He still wrote multitudinous letters to family, friends, and would-be friends, including a picturesque English naturalist and hunter named Frederick Selous, the first man to wear shorts while on safari.

Theodore usually got up at six o'clock and went through half an hour of violent sitting-up exercises. He breakfasted at seven and was at his desk before eight. In the late afternoons he hiked, rode horseback, swam, played rough-and-tumble games with his boys, or did all of these. At lunch and dinner he liked to surround himself with unusual guests. He became the first President to entertain a Negro in the White House by inviting Booker T. Washington for dinner.

Of Roosevelt's lunch and dinner guests, humorist Finley Peter Dunne writes, "He was utterly indifferent as to their political position, their social standing, or their wealth. Everybody who wanted to talked up, about art or politics or poetry or music or war, the President occasionally sending down a booming pleasantry to a friend at the end of the long table." When Corinne Roosevelt's young daughter came to lunch, Theodore placed her at his right. At her other side, he put John Burroughs, the naturalist. Then the two men talked birds and bees across the bewildered girl, who was unable to say a word. A point of contention between the President and Burroughs was whether the song of the chippy sparrow was *twee, twee,* or *twee, twee, twee.*

Corinne and Douglas Robinson were frequent White House visitors, for Robinson had become a conservative financier who reported Wall Street reactions to his brother-in-law. Corinne still resembled her brother. After a trip around the world her husband paid tribute to her as "the strongest and keenest female sightseer alive today. I can think of nothing we have left unclimbed, unseen, unvisited, above or below ground, or by river or by sea."

Douglas Robinson, who had an unusually deep voice, liked to talk. Corinne, as a Roosevelt, was naturally a tireless talker. She also liked to surround herself with other talkers, usually Roosevelts. The Robinsons had two boys, who inherited their father's diapason voice. The result was a species of bedlam in the family home at 422 Madison Avenue in New York. One visitor advised another, "Talk as loudly as you possibly can, and answer your own questions."

Bamie lived in Washington. In 1893 she had crossed family lines by going to London to serve as hostess in the American Embassy for James Roosevelt ("Rosy") Roosevelt, whose Astor wife had died. There she met and married Lieutenant Commander William Sheffield Cowles, USN. Cowles was now a rear admiral and served as Theodore's naval aide.

It was all bully, just bully—and Theodore was dee-lighted! "I have the happiest life of any man I know," he rhapsodized. Yet he continued to suffer the unlikely fits of gloom and uncertainty. He was the most popular man in the United States, perhaps in the entire world. Of this he received almost daily evidence, yet it brought him no confidence. When one friend sought to rally his spirits by citing the crowds clamoring to see him, Theodore muttered, "They come to see the President as they would come to see a circus."

Despite his enormous popularity, he was deeply worried over the election of 1904, the first test for the Presidency on his own merit. "At the moment I am on the crest of a wave," he told Bamie, "but I know that after the crest is a hollow." Theodore's odd lack of true confidence was capsuled by a Washingtonian who said, "No man values public opinion or fears it as much as Theodore Roosevelt. No man seeks popularity as much as he. Mild reproof or criticism of his policy would nearly paralyze him."

Shrewd observers of the Washington scene could also find indication of Teddy's inner insecurities in what Mark Sullivan later dubbed his "balanced sentences"—that is, nearly every one of his strong statements was almost immediately qualified. He was a man who could say, "There have been abuses connected with the accumulation of great fortunes, yet it remains true that [the fortunes] confer . . . immense incidental benefits upon others." Roosevelt reproved big business and in the next breath chided labor for abusing the right to strike: "It should be as much the aim of those who seek for social betterment to rid the business world of crimes of cunning as to rid the entire body politic of crimes of violence." A more obvious example of his balanced sentences came when, as a Rough Rider, he sadly announced the death in battle of a "singularly gallant young Harvard fellow," then instantly added, "An equally gallant young fellow from Yale was also mortally wounded."

Of these balanced sentences, Sullivan writes, "One came to wait for them. It became a little boring in time, to hear him tell of appointing a Catholic to office, and add that he would have appointed a Protestant under similar circumstances."

When occupied by the Roosevelts, the Executive Mansion was flooded by a glare of publicity heretofore unknown in the United States. Indeed, the family provides the first instance of wholesale invasion of privacy by the American press.

For if Teddy was a whirling, provocative figure, his family was the same. Edith Carow Roosevelt was the only one who managed to remain in any kind of shadow—the shadow, of course, being Theodore's. Alice Lee Roosevelt was seventeen when the family entered the White House. She was attractive, intelligent, and independent, with a touch of adolescent defiance appealing to restive women and youngsters of the era. Ten-year-old Ethel was described as a "character," but she behaved much as a growing girl should. However, Kermit, Archie, and Quentin (Theodore Jr. was at Groton) might well have leaped from the mischievous pen of Booth Tarkington. Kermit was twelve; Archie, seven; Quentin, four. They were chips off the old block and the country loved each one.

The sedate White House had never harbored so many children. As soon as moving vans arrived from Oyster Bay with the family possessions, including several menageries of live animals, it became apparent that the living quarters were not large enough. Congress hastily voted an appropriation of $500,000 and the family moved temporarily to more commodious quarters. Two wings were added to the White House, and for the first time the executive offices were separate from presidential living quarters. The size of the state dining room was doubled, while the rooms used for Cabinet meetings and other workaday functions were transformed into bedrooms. Heavy beams and fireplaces installed by President Grant were removed, as was the fancy painted ceiling of the East Room added by Chester A. Arthur. Edith Carow Roosevelt supervised this remodeling, bringing back the eighteenth-century simplicity of the White House. In Theodore's words, the restoration changed the Executive Mansion "from a shabby likeness to the ground floor of the Astor House into a simple and dignified dwelling for the head of a republic."

The three young Roosevelt boys never had as much fun in Washington as they did at Oyster Bay. But they tried! In those harmless days it was possible for them to use the entire city as a playground. They invited cousins and friends to stay overnight at the White House and played games that won them the name White House Gang. At one point they followed the White House lamplighter around the grounds each night. After he lighted a lamp, one of the boys climbed up the pole and blew it out. The White House Gang rode in trolley cars, making faces at people in carriages passing by. One day the boys found themselves making faces at the President, who made a face right back. The boys went unescorted to public school, carrying books like anyone else. An English committee studying American education was astounded to find Quentin Roosevelt sitting in one class. "No better instance could have been afforded of the real meaning of American democracy," its members concluded. A visitor to another school failed to recognize Kermit and inquired what his father did for a living. "Father?" asked Kermit coolly. "Oh, Father's *it*!"

The boys had inherited Theodore's genius for publicity. Quentin soon found a young Negro boy as boon companion and pictures of them filled newspapers. When Archie got measles, Quentin decided the sight of his calico pony Algonquin would cheer the invalid. With the help of a White House coachman he got the pony into an elevator, then proudly walked him into the sickroom.

At White House functions four little figures in nighties—the boys plus Ethel—sat observing everything from a point halfway up the stairs. Whenever possible, Theodore left his official functions for a half-hour pillow fight with his children. After that he read them to sleep.

There was all this, and Alice too! For in her White House years Alice Lee Roosevelt achieved a whirl never equaled by another American girl. Even the motion-picture stars of later years failed to measure up to the adulation given Alice. "If the three young boys and Ethel intrigued the public, Alice fascinated it," says an account. "Her habits of life, her tastes, her clothes, her girl friends and her beaux, her extraordinary physical vitality were the subject of news stories day in, day out, and occasionally of Sunday features outrageous in their sensationalism."

Alice's White House coming-out party in January, 1902, signified the end of official mourning for President McKinley. After it she was dubbed Princess Alice, and princess she was, with none of the drawbacks to which royalty is born. At a moment in history when women were beginning to demand the rights of men, Alice Roosevelt knew she was as good as any male. She had smoked cigarettes before the family moved to Washington, puffing the smoke up Sagamore Hill chimneys. Now she smoked a cigarette in public and the resulting tumult rammed her father's statesmanship off front pages. She slid down a White House banister, landing on her feet in the midst of a group of dignitaries. In her pocketbook she carried a live gartersnake named Emily Spinach —"Emily in honor of a very thin aunt, spinach because it is green."

One evening Theodore's Harvard classmate Owen Wister plaintively asked, "Mr. President, isn't there anything you can do to control Alice?"

Roosevelt thought hard and said, "I can do one of two things. I can be President of the United States or I can control Alice. I cannot possibly do both."

Alice had inherited money from her mother's family and it gave her added independence. In her father's early years as President, she showed a strong partiality for a type he scorned as "Newport cads." Alice was often in high society, and once created a sensation by entering the Newport Casino rakishly carrying a cane. She and her friend Alice Drexel Paul drove a runabout car from Newport to Boston in the record time of six hours. There was much excitement over this, since the girls obviously had broken speed limits. "The trip through the various towns was run at the required speed of eight miles an hour," one paper reported. "But Miss Paul speeded the car to twenty-five miles an hour when they were in the open country."

The public was entranced with Princess Alice and her heedless doings. Babies and styles were named for her. Washington hostesses called her bumptious for responding to invitations with a cheery "That'll be bully!" But Alice probably did more to emancipate women than the grim-lipped activities of thousands of militant suffragettes.

"They are not a polished family," wrote Ellen Maury Slayden, wife of a Texas congressman. But the lady missed the point. The Roosevelts had no need for polish. "I cannot be cheapened," Alice said years later when someone protested that a friend was unworthy of her.

Nor could any Roosevelt be cheapened. They were aristocrats, the first to inhabit the White House since the early days of the nation. To them belonged the aristocratic privilege of behaving exactly as they pleased—even like the Family Next Door.

14

FRANKLIN AND ELEANOR

ON THE DAY PRESIDENT MC KINLEY WAS SHOT, YOUNG FRANKLIN D. Roosevelt and his mother were in Paris after a leisurely summer trip through the Norwegian fiords, Germany, Switzerland, and Italy. Like other Roosevelts and Delanos, nineteen-year-old Franklin kept a diary, though his entries were more erratic and less pithy than those of some relatives. On Saturday, September 7, 1901, he put in his *Line-A-Day*:

Went w. Louis Howland to see the Old Paris, queer old houses Me. de Sevigny's Hotel etc. Most interesting. News came of the attempted assassination of Pres. McKinley.

On Wednesday, September 18, when he and Sara were aboard ship on the voyage home, Franklin left for posterity a matter-of-fact reaction to the news that his Cousin Ted had unexpectedly become President of the United States:

Passed Nantucket Shoals Lightship at 9 a.m. & received news by megaphone Pres. Mckinley died last Saturday. Terrible shock to us all. Arr Sandy Hook 6:30 p.m. but were not allowed to pass quarantine & stayed on board all night.

The following day's entry reads:

Thurs. September 19, 1901. Got to dock N.Y. 9 p.m. & passed Custom-house without trouble. Took 11:30 to Hyde Park. All N.Y. draped for the President. All well at home.

Franklin and his mother were returning to Springwood alone, for James Roosevelt had died in the previous December. The country squire born seventy-two years before in the Presidency of John Quincy Adams had slowly succumbed to heart disease. Dignified to the end, he died quietly in his sleep.

Her husband's death was a stunning blow to Sara. "I wonder how I lived when he left me," she remarked years later. In her fifty years of aristocratic existence there had aways been a man to whose wisdom she deferred. In his will James gave ample testimony to his love, admiration, and trust in Sara. To Franklin he left $100,000 which would bring a lifetime income of $5,000 or $6,000. He bequeathed a like amount to Rosy Roosevelt, even though his older son had married into the Astor millions. He willed Sara the Springwood estate, together with the remainder of his money; and Sara had just inherited a large amount from Warren Delano, who died in 1898 at the age of eighty-nine. But the greatest tribute came when he wrote, "I do hereby appoint my wife sole guardian of my son, Franklin D. Roosevelt, and I want him under the supervision of his mother."

Sara was prepared to act on these words. If her college-student son lacked a father, she would be both father and mother, guiding him serenely toward the place in life to which his background and Hudson River heritage entitled him. Warmed and inspired by her love, he would become a capitalist-squire in the pattern so comfortably established by James.

Sara was much encouraged when Franklin showed signs of wishing to adopt this pattern. He had always been interested in his Roosevelt and Delano ancestors, and now the interest grew to passion. Franklin was a freshman at Harvard when his father died, and entered his sophomore year at the end of the trip to Europe. Soon he wrote Sara that he planned to compile a Roosevelt genealogy as his term paper, ending, "I have been in the library constantly looking up old records, but nothing much is to be found. Do please copy for me all the extracts in our old Dutch Bible and send them to me."

With the aid of Bible entries, his Roosevelt genealogy was completed, and today holds its own with the efforts of professionals in the field. Franklin's genealogy not only detailed the family tree but offered observations on Roosevelt character:

Some of the famous Dutch families in New York have today nothing left but their name—they are few in numbers, they lack progressiveness, and a true democratic spirit. One reason—perhaps the chief—of the virility of the Roosevelts is this very democratic spirit. They have never felt that because they were born in a good position they could put their hands in their pockets and succeed. They have felt, rather, that, being born in a good position, there is no excuse for them if they do not do their duty by the community, and it is because this idea was instilled into them from birth that they have in nearly every case proved good citizens.

At Harvard, Franklin majored in political history and government, which gives support to those who feel that even as a student he nursed vague ideas of a political career. He took American, English, and European history, together with American government, constitutional government, international law, and the economics of transportation, banking, and corporations. Of this last batch of courses he remarked while President, "I took economics courses in college for four years, and everything I was taught was wrong." In addition, he studied English and French literature, Latin, Renaissance art, paleontology, fine arts, and geology. All these, together with a deep interest in America's past, put him on the way to being a better educated man than his political enemies would ever admit.

For the most part his marks were B's and C's—gentleman's marks, Harvard called them. Strange to say, the man who became a master psychologist took no courses in psychology and departed a philosophy class after three weeks. None of his Harvard courses seemed to arouse him intellectually or kindle independence of thought. Franklin was still too young to vote, but he sided with America's conservatives in deploring Theodore's firm settlement of the coal strike as "a tendency to make the executive power stronger than the Houses of Congress." At the same time he was liberal enough to help found a Harvard committee for assistance to the Boers. The students raised $350 which Franklin sent to Cousin Theodore, who in turn dispatched it to sufferers in South Africa.

In college days, Franklin was tall and thin, his weight 146. He wore his hair parted slightly left-center. The young man's brow was high, his face lean, chin pointed. A thin, sensitive mouth was ever-ready to break into the half-moon smile that became so famous later on. Too light for football or rowing, he turned his extracurricular interest to journalism.

After joining the *Harvard Crimson* as a reporter, he wrote Sara that he planned to work hard enough to become an editor. He did this in his junior year, becoming editor in chief, which brought great prestige among his classmates. He won his first election when chosen chairman of his class committee—another honor. Franklin was president of the Political Club and a member of lively Hasty Pudding.

He began George Pierce Baker's class in public speaking but withdrew when Baker advocated an orator's heavy emphasis and gestures. Even in those days Franklin believed a speaker should be forceful, but always natural. Like many well-grounded Groton boys, Franklin earned his bachelor's degree in a fast three years, but decided to return for the fourth year as a graduate student. He did this largely to edit the *Crimson*.

Two personality traits stood out at Cambridge. One was his charm which, in later life, grew so great as to be almost tangible. At Harvard he was anxious to be liked and became a joiner. On nippy Saturday afternoons in autumn he was a cheer leader at football games. Already aware of the potency of his charm, he used it at every opportunity to gain popularity. Inevitably a few classmates thought he used it too much. Embedded in a second characteristic may be the secret of Franklin's lifetime success. In small things and large he could see—or sense—the viewpoints of others. Having done this, he stood ready to consider that point of view. This resulted in a degree of tolerance or liberalism that annoyed some Harvard men.

During two of Franklin's Harvard years Sara lived nearby in Boston. For his mother had found life at Springwood impossible to bear in winter months. During Sara's first year as a widow, a Delano sister had crossed the Hudson to stay with her. At night the two ladies sat before the fire reading aloud *Paradise Lost* and Longfellow's translation of Dante's *Inferno*. The many details of running the farm now fell on Sara's shoulders, and she made efforts to take her husband's place in local affairs. But Sara was accustomed to living close to the focal point of her life. She moved to Boston, where, according to her book *My Boy Franklin,* she leaned over backward never to interfere in her son's social life. By other versions she often entertained him and his friends, providing copious tea and cakes, as well as dinners and after-theater suppers.

Slowly the image of a bearable future took shape in Sara's mind. She could not conceive of Franklin's marrying right after college— not for five years or perhaps ten. Her own dear papa had waited until his mid-thirties to take a bride, and Sallie believed Franklin closely resembled Warren Delano. Her son was sure to study law as his own father had desired. Afterward he would practice in New York or Dutchess County, or both.

To assist this pleasant vision, Sara bought a town house at 200 Madison Avenue. This could serve as Franklin's headquarters as he dipped pleasurably into New York social life. She herself would be much envied by her friends as the mother of so handsome and devoted a son. At the sedate dinner parties in Fifth Avenue mansions he would serve as her escort. He would go alone to the livelier festivities of the Four Hundred, returning to perch on the edge of her bed and tell her about a joyous evening of fun. . . .

But on December 1, 1903, while still a junior at Harvard, Franklin suddenly informed an incredulous Sara that he wished to marry his cousin Eleanor as soon as possible.

The contours of Eleanor Roosevelt's life are well known. She recounted them in her three autobiographies, and in numerous other books of reminiscence and guidance has drawn on her own experience for anecdotal as well as philosophic material. Her books, in turn, are swelled by countless magazine and newspaper articles, together with radio and television interviews. Probably no public figure in history has discoursed as often or as openly on intimate matters.

The marriage of Eleanor's father and mother was not a happy one. Elliott Roosevelt's interests were riding and shooting, while lovely Anna Eleanor Hall relished the gay social whirl. Elliott already had a weakness for drink, and he slowly changed from social to serious drinker. The pair had three children. One died, leaving Eleanor and a younger brother, Hall.

Eleanor was—all the world knows—an unusually shy child. Until her birth Hall girls had been pretty children who developed into beautiful women. Eleanor had the heavy Roosevelt mouth and prominent family teeth. At an early age she knew that her mother was disappointed in her appearance. "She is such a funny child, so old-fashioned," the mother frequently said, and it was apparent that old-fashioned really meant homely. As if aware of what early life held for her, Eleanor was solemn. This further displeased the mother, who called her "Granny." Only her father seemed happy to be with her. He called her "Little Nell," treated her as an equal, and spent every possible moment in her company. He showered her with gifts and on Thanksgiving Day proudly bore her off to dinner at the Newsboys' Home.

As time passed, she saw less of Elliott. When she was five, he broke his leg riding in a horse show. The break was clumsily set. After agonizing months it was broken again, then reset. Pain and confinement shattered Elliott's last resistance to alcohol. A year later the entire family went abroad. Several times on the trip Elliott was placed in a sanitarium. Finally Anna and the children came home alone, leaving Elliott in a Paris institution until Theodore crossed the ocean to get him. At this point Eleanor began to overhear conversations that bewildered her: "Something was wrong with my father and from my point of view nothing could be wrong with him."

When Eleanor was eight, her mother died of diphtheria. With that, the Hall family determined to keep the children from contamination by Elliott or any other Roosevelt. This drove Eleanor into a fantasy world where her father was a constant companion. The Halls lived in a brownstone at 11 West Thirty-seventh Street, and there the child stood for hours at a front window watching for the figure of Elliott to appear. At the age of ten she was told he had died. She was not allowed to attend the funeral, so his death never seemed real. The life of fantasy went on.

The Hall family of grandmother, two aunts, and two uncles treated Eleanor well in their fashion. Grandmother Hall was a Ludlow, and always in the background was her mother, Great-grandmother Ludlow, of whom Eleanor said, "She was *character!*" The girl got no real affection from any of this assortment of relatives and was made to feel like a child among adults.

Grandmother Hall believed in strict discipline and in social behavior stressed outward appearances. She told Eleanor always to mask her true feelings. "Never cry where people are, cry by yourself," was one of her maxims. Subtly Eleanor was taught that because of her homeliness she must make herself an unusually ingratiating person.

One day her grandmother discovered that Eleanor was unable to read. This sparked a succession of French and German governesses, some strict, none sympathetic. Eleanor reacted by telling lies out of fear and eating too many sweets, some of which she stole.

For the most part she had no playmates except her brother Hall to whom she was more mother than sister. The Halls passed summers at Tivoli, north of Hyde Park, in a mansard-roofed mansion with nine master bedrooms and two baths. The only girl of Eleanor's age lived five miles away. At times she was sent to dancing classes at the Archibald Rogers estate near Springwood. Franklin Roosevelt was in the class, while Sara Delano Roosevelt sat on the sidelines.

"I was not a very happy little girl," Eleanor said. The only warmth in her life came from the Oyster Bay Roosevelts during the brief intervals she was permitted to visit them. In New York she was allowed to see Bamie and Anna Bulloch Gracie. In summer she had short vacations at Sagamore Hill. At Christmas she dutifully attended family dances at the home of Corinne Roosevelt Robinson. At these the other growing girls wore fashionable new gowns extending to the calves, but the Halls insisted that Eleanor's dresses be above the knees. Shyness, lack of familiarity with contemporaries, and the knowledge that she was badly dressed turned these Yuletide dances into nights of horror. At them only one boy ever asked the tall, gawky girl to dance. This was her cousin Franklin from Hyde Park. While dancing, the two discussed books. Next day Franklin told his mother, "Cousin Eleanor has a very good mind."

Eleanor was fifteen when the Halls decided the time for school had come. After consultation with Bamie, the girl was sent abroad to Allenswood, a finishing school just outside London run by a Mlle. Souvestre. Here the regime was Spartan, but in Mlle. Souvestre Eleanor discovered a woman with an alert, educated, liberal mind. She had not known such types existed. At vacation time Eleanor toured Europe. Sometimes she was accompanied by Mlle. Souvestre; at other times she traveled alone, for the worldly Frenchwoman considered a girl as plain as her charge safe from predatory males.

In 1902, aged eighteen, Eleanor returned to New York, finding new tensions in the Hall household. Her two uncles had jumped the hurdle from heavy drinking to alcoholism. They were embarrassing drunks, so prone to scenes that the Halls feared to invite guests to Thirty-seventh Street or Tivoli. In both localities, sheltered Eleanor had to spend hours hunting her wayward uncles in saloons.

As a proper debutante Eleanor came out in New York sociey at the Assembly Ball. She went to this in the company of a maid-chaperon who always escorted her to every evening social engagement. At the Assembly, Eleanor suffered further agonies of embarrassment, for the girl had been abroad for three long years. "I did not know a soul," she later recalled. Finally a male contemporary of her mother's recognized her. He seemed old to Eleanor, though he soon married one of her contemporaries. But his recognition was a godsend.

Eleanor Roosevelt came to believe that throughout life she was pushed into the activities that were important to her. At this moment, she was prodded into social work. Before he died her father had taken her to the Orthopedic Hospital as well as to the Newsboys' Home. Like others of the social rich, the Halls had dispensed charity among the Bowery poor at Christmas. Writes Eleanor, "Very early I became conscious of the fact that there were men and women and children around me who suffered in one way or another."

Now she joined the Junior League, then just beginning. With the daughter of Mrs. Whitelaw Reid, she was sent to the slums to teach social dancing and calisthenics to children of the Rivington Street Settlement House. After these afternoons Eleanor, accompanied by the maid, went to dinner parties at the Waldorf and dances at Sherry's.

Eleanor had grown up tall and willowy, with more than her share of the lambent glow of youth. Yet she still thought herself an ugly duckling. One of the crosses she bore was the flaming success of Cousin Alice, now in full swing as Princess of the White House. From childhood Eleanor had stood in awe of Alice, always so outgoing, poised, and fearless. Men hovered around Alice and always had. Because Eleanor was a niece of the President a few men bothered to be polite to her, but little more.

The most dashing young gentleman Eleanor knew was her Hyde Park cousin, Franklin. He was handsome, lighthearted, and confident. Eleanor kept meeting him at odd moments. Once Franklin spied her on a New York Central train as he and Sara traveled to Hyde Park while Eleanor went on to Tivoli. Eleanor was in a coach and Franklin invited her into the Pullman to see his mother.

Later Eleanor was asked to a house party at Springwood, together with a clutch of other Roosevelt cousins. The two young people met again in Washington at the end of 1902, when both visited Theodore and Bamie for the New Year. Franklin's *Line-A-Day* reads:

December 31, 1902. At 11 with Cousin Bammie to call at White House. Saw Cousin Edith. Large lunch at home. To afternoon tea with Alice . . . Eleanor.

January 1, 1903. To the New Year Reception at the White House at 10:30 & stood in inner circle till 1. Lunched with Alice & went to Mrs. Dewey's reception till 4 . . . Dinner at White House & have talk with President. To theatre and sat next to Eleanor. Very interesting day.

Hall Roosevelt was at Groton, and through 1903 Eleanor and her maid took frequent trips to spend weekends with him. Franklin made similar trips down from Harvard to his old school, presumably because Eleanor was going to be there. Eleanor never spoke or wrote much about her courtship, possibly because she did not realize at the time that it was a courtship.

Franklin's proposal of marriage came at Groton in late November, and it was a bombshell to her. Yet the inexperienced girl knew exactly how to cope with it. She said "Yes" to the proposal. On hearing this, Franklin added humbly, "I have only a few bright prospects now." Again Eleanor responded with just the right words, "I have faith in you. I'm sure you will really amount to something someday."

Back in New York, she broke the news to Grandmother Hall,

who inquired if she really loved her cousin Franklin. Eleanor answered that she did, though she later wrote, "I know now that it was years before I understood what being in love or what loving meant."

Grandmother Hall was hardly pleased at the idea of her granddaughter marrying a Roosevelt, but her further reactions are not known. Sara Delano Roosevelt's are, however. She had no reason to disapprove of the daughter of her favorite among the Knickerbocker Roosevelts. In fact, some thought the President's niece lowered herself by falling in love with a Dutchess County Roosevelt.

But Sallie was obviously not happy. Gone were her plans for spending the next few years in the close companionship of her manly son. Then, too, the children were so young: Franklin twenty-one, Eleanor not yet nineteen! It is impossible to accuse so grand a person as Sara of being vain. But she did have a superabundance of pride, and it was cruelly wounded by her son's willingness—even eagerness—to leave her side so soon. Eleanor and Franklin at once tried to win her over. Eleanor wrote:

Dearest Cousin Sally. . . . I know just how you feel and how hard it must be, but I do so want you to learn to love me a little. You must know that I will always try to do what you wish for I have grown to love you very dearly. . . . It is impossible for me to tell you how I feel toward Franklin, I can only say that my one great wish is always to prove worthy of him.

Then Franklin:

Dearest Mama: I know what pain I must have caused you and you know I wouldn't do it if I really could have helped it. . . . I know my mind, have known it for a long time, and know I could never think otherwise. Result: I am the happiest man right now in the world; likewise the luckiest. And for you, dear Mummy, you know that nothing can ever change what we have always been and always will be to each other—only now you have two children to love & to love you— and Eleanor as you know will always be a daughter to you in every true way.

Despite these heartfelt protestations, Sallie felt affronted. As Franklin cheerfully persisted in his plans to wed, the steel-willed mother evolved a stratagem. In February she invited her son and his Harvard roommate on a West Indies cruise, hoping that the trip would make him forget Eleanor. Aboard ship was a charming and stylish Frenchwoman, a few years over Franklin's age, who showed an interest in the good-looking young Harvard man.

In some circles involvement with a mature Frenchwoman is considered part of a liberal education. Not so with Franklin. He delighted in talking to the French lady—all through life he enjoyed the company of women. But on his return he rushed to Eleanor, who had been undergoing her own test of devotion. The girl was visiting in Washington, where, after a stay at the White House, she moved to Aunt Bamie's. With her understanding aunt as mentor, Eleanor had a much better time in Washington than she had ever enjoyed in New York. "The dinners, luncheons, and teas were interesting," she wrote, "and people of importance, with charm and wit and savoir faire, filled my days with unusual and exciting experiences."

Yet she was overjoyed to see Franklin. Returning to New York, she resumed social work at the Rivington Street Settlement House. One afternoon Franklin met her there, traveling by trolley and elevated train to New York slums of whose existence he was blissfully unaware. Eleanor's pupils gathered excitedly around to ask, "Is he your feller?" The girl had to visit a sick child and Franklin went with her, toiling up three odorous flights to the single room where the entire family lived. He glanced around, appalled. On the sidewalk he looked sick. "My God!" he exclaimed. "I didn't know people lived like that!"

Franklin had planned to enter Harvard Law School after graduation from college. But to be near Eleanor he switched to Columbia, living with Sara at 200 Madison Avenue. In the autumn of 1904 formal announcement of the engagement was made. After the New Year presents began arriving. Uncle Ted, just elected President in his own right, was expected to give the bride away, and the date of the wedding depended on his crowded schedule. On March 17, 1905, he would be in New York reviewing the St. Patrick's Day Parade, so that date was chosen.

On March 4 the young couple joined other Roosevelts at Uncle Ted's inauguration. Theodore had campaigned as the Happy Warrior, a phrase taken from a poem by Wordsworth. Now Franklin sat by as the jubilant President bellowed, "All I ask is a Square Deal for every man."

Franklin and Eleanor were married in the twin homes of her relatives, Mrs. Henry Parrish, Jr., and Mrs. E. Livingston Ludlow, at 6-8 East Seventy-sixth Street. Police had a difficulty restraining the large crowd, already excited by the parade and now determined to catch a glimpse of the President of the United States.

Theodore arrived at 3:30. At his side was Princess Alice, maid of honor at the wedding. Theodore had won the election of 1904 by 2,500,000 votes, one of them cast by Franklin who, in his first-in-a-lifetime election, clannishly voted Republican for Uncle Ted. The President's popularity had leaped to greater heights and at the sight of him in an open landau cheers tore the air. Theodore stood up, waving his tall silk hat. Across the street a line of boys on a fence yelled, "Hooray for Teddy. Ain't he the real thing!" Theodore playfully shook his fist at them and one boy tumbled to the ground.

Indoors were Roosevelt, Delano, Hall, and Ludlow relatives, together with numerous Vanderbilts, Sloans, Burdens, Chanlers, Winthrops, Mortimers, Belmonts, and Van Rensselaers. They all clustered around Teddy as he entered. His impish son Quentin once said, "Father always wants to be the bride at every wedding and the corpse at every funeral." Today he was both bride and groom. The Reverend Endicott Peabody of Groton performed the ceremony and at its conclusion Teddy dashed into the library where refreshments waited. The wedding guests followed, leaving bride and groom behind. Soon they followed, standing on the outskirts of the group listening to Theodore's funny stories.

It has been suggested that, at this moment in life, Franklin vowed to outdo his bully cousin in accomplishment. Actually, he did not seem to mind. Nor did Sara Roosevelt, who might well have been annoyed when the spotlight left her darling son. The newlyweds departed in a hail of rice for a week's solitude at Springwood, and following his return Franklin made this mild entry in his *Line-A-Day*: "In town 11 a.m. & Mama gives me a water color of Cous. Theodore."

There were other Roosevelt weddings in the early 1900's, a period which resembled the 1880's in profligacy of family marriages.

One of them crossed family lines to exactly the degree established by Franklin and Eleanor. This occurred when Helen, daughter of James Roosevelt Roosevelt, married Theodore Douglas Robinson, son of Corinne. Family blessings showered on this promising match, but none were audible when Rosy's son James ("Taddy") brought the first smirch of scandal to the Roosevelt escutcheon.

Young James, a sower of wild oats at Harvard, shocked New York society and nonsociety by marrying one Sadie Meisinger, a girl known at the Haymarket Dance Hall as "Dutch Sadie." For half a century the Haymarket had been the city's most notorious sin den, a blatant house of assignation where men bargained outright for the favors of tempting young girls. Possibly Sadie Meisinger was more respectable than her Haymarket sisters, but it is not probable. Otherwise she would not have been allowed on the premises. Newspapers gave the full sensation treatment to this mésalliance, driving James and his bride to Florida under assumed names. The marriage turned out to be as unhappy as the family had predicted. In time James returned to New York and resumed his true identity. The chastened young man then devoted his energies to the Salvation Army.

But the greatest Roosevelt wedding of all time took place in the White House, when Princess Alice became the wife of Nicholas Longworth.

The question of Alice and her suitors had agitated the country since the White House coming-out party in 1902. At first she was reported engaged to an assortment of Yale and Harvard football players, Rough Riders, army and navy junior officers, and young diplomats. As Theodore's activities became global, speculation involved Prince Gustav Adolph of Sweden; Paul Loubet, son of the President of France; Marconi, inventor of the wireless; Grand Duke Nicholas of Russia, and others.

Princess Alice herself paid no heed to rumors but blithely continued having fun. She enjoyed White House life every bit as much as her father and expressed amazement when a reporter asked if the glare of publicity had grown wearisome. "But I love it, I love it!" the girl answered.

Alice danced through so many nights that the public wondered if she got enough sleep. This impelled Theodore to issue a characteristic statement. He was proud, he declared, that his young daughter did not

stay in the house and fold her hands and do nothing. She can walk as far as I can, and often she walks several miles at the pace I set for her. She can ride, drive, ski, shoot—although she does not care much for the shooting. I don't mind that. It is not necessary for her health. She gets plenty of outdoor exercise. That is necessary.

Alice danced more than she walked as she tripped a madcap path from Newport cads to worthwhile Washingtonians. Then Representative from Ohio. To some folk, this was a surprise. Nicholas was thirty-six and bald, though good-looking in a mature, dignified way. But he was no madcap. As Theodore wrote to a curious Edward VII, King of England:

Longworth is a good fellow, one of the younger men who have really done well in Congress; he was from my own college, Harvard, and there belonged to my club, the Porcellian, which is antique as antiquity goes in America, for it was founded in colonial days; he was on the varsity crew and was, and is, the best violinist that ever came from Harvard.

The violin played a part in Nick's courtship, for he was often seen entering the White House carrying it under his arm. Alice had publicly proclaimed the banjo her favorite musical instrument, but when Nick fiddled, she sat enraptured.

In 1905 Roosevelt dispatched William Howard Taft, his Secretary of War, on a tour of the Philippines. Nick and Alice went along as members of the official party. Aboard ship Alice was as irrepressible as ever. On a dare she jumped fully clothed into a swimming pool on the deck below. She so obviously enjoyed Longworth's company that the benign Taft kept asking if the two were engaged. "More or less, Mr. Secretary, more or less," Alice invariably replied.

Another time she regarded Nick speculatively. "Do you see that old, bald-headed man scratching his ear over there?" she asked Lloyd Griscom, American minister to Japan.

"Do you mean Nick Longworth?" Griscom replied.

"Yes. Can you imagine a young girl marrying a fellow like that?"

"Why, Alice, you couldn't find anybody nicer."

"I know, I know, but this is a question of marriage."

Alice quit the party in Manila to tour China and Japan. After her return to Washington, "more or less" turned into "yes." The marriage of Alice and Nick on February 17, 1906, was the first wedding of a White House daughter since Nellie Grant married Algernon Sartoris thirty-two years before, and the first White House wedding since President Cleveland married Frances Folsom in 1886.

Princess Alice was infinitely more popular than these two brides, and her wedding was an international sensation. Gifts came from the King of England, Kaiser Wilhelm, the Czar of Russia, the Dowager Empress of China, the Emperor of Japan, and other reigning monarchs. One gift was a Gobelin tapestry. In Cuba there was talk of giving Princess Alice San Juan Hill as a wedding present. Saner heads prevailed and instead she was sent jewelry worth $25,000.

Franklin Roosevelt attended this White House wedding alone. At it he made himself especially helpful by arranging the bride's train. In photos featuring Alice, Nick, and Teddy, the train sweeps majestically toward the camera.

Eleanor stayed home because she was carrying her first child. The young wife had found many other tribulations in the early years of marriage. Franklin's version of these years has never been intimately told, but Eleanor pictured herself as difficult to live with, an infuriating combination of the helpless, timid, and moody.

The young couple had first lived in the Hotel Webster on West Forty-fifth Street, then moved to 200 Madison Avenue when Sara went to Hyde Park. In neither place was Eleanor required to do more than a little sewing.

With the first summer of marriage had come the traditional European honeymoon. It began in London, where Franklin was mistaken for Theodore and given the royal suite at Brown's Hotel. A photograph taken in Germany shows Eleanor boldly holding a cigarette, but for the most part she remained painfully shy and unsure of herself. For one thing, the girl was ashamed at how little she knew of matters beyond the social sphere of Fifth Avenue. In Scotland she was asked to explain the difference between America's state and federal governments. The niece of the President of the United States was unable to do so.

Back home she encountered new problems. One was Sara Roosevelt, who had made new plans to influence Franklin's life. If I am not wanted, Sara apparently reasoned, I will be needed. She could do this by paying many of the young couple's expenses, though as yet they had no great need of financial help. Eleanor had also inherited one hundred thousand dollars from her father, giving the newlyweds a combined income of $10,000 to $12,000. This was a not inconsiderable sum for young married couples of the time. Still it is always nice to have someone else pay the bills, a fact which Sara understood. Further, Franklin had been brought up with expensive tastes and few curbs on his wishes. Sara's largess would be a means of continuing this. Returning to New York from Europe, the young Roosevelts found that Sara had taken a house for them at 125 East Thirty-sixth Street near 200 Madison. Sara had furnished the house to her own taste and hired three servants.

Here for the first time Eleanor Roosevelt was faced with running a household. Franklin showed her how to keep accounts, but in supervising the servants and providing dinner menus she was a total loss. Years later Eleanor decided she should have discharged the servants and by trial and error made herself learn the subtle art of running a house. At the time the thought never occurred to her.

Matters were not improved by the birth of Anna Eleanor, called Anna, on May 3, 1906. Eleanor had never played with dolls as a child and had no idea how to cope with a real baby. The solution was nursemaids, who not only intimidated the young mother but ordered her about. Eleanor tried to continue her Rivington Street Settlement work, but Sara quickly nipped this bud of independence by warning she might bring germs home to her own child.

One of Sara's annoying habits was to treat the Roosevelt children as her own. Bypassing Eleanor, she bought baby clothes and toys, gave orders to nurses and maids. "I was beginning to become an entirely dependent woman," Eleanor remembered. "I was completely taken care of. My mother-in-law did everything for me." A first son, James, was born in December, 1907. Both Franklin and Eleanor were healthy, yet the first two babies were sickly. A third child, Franklin Jr., born in March, 1909, was robust, but eight months later this infant was dead of influenza.

Next Sara built two handsome, narrow houses at 47-49 East Sixty-fifth Street. Connecting doors linked the residences, while dining and drawing rooms could be thrown together for entertaining. A single entrance served both homes. Sara still believed that children, even when grown up, should defer to their parents as she had deferred to hers. She did all the furnishing and hiring of servants. More than ever Eleanor felt she was losing what little personality she possessed: "I was not developing any individual taste or initiative. I was simply absorbing the personalities of those around me and letting their tastes and interest dominate mine."

At this time Franklin was working as fledgling lawyer in the downtown office of the firm of Carter, Ledyard and Milburn. How well he understood his wife's hurt feelings is a moot question. His lifetime philosophy was to ignore unpleasant matters, for if ignored long enough they usually settled themselves. Soon after the move to Sixty-fifth Street he came upon Eleanor weeping at her dressing table. This bewildered him, because her childhood training in stoicism had never before allowed such a display.

"What on earth is the matter?" he inquired.

Through tears Eleanor answered, "I do not like living in a house that is in no way mine, one which I have done nothing about and does not represent the way I want to live."

Gently Franklin said, "You are quite mad." But after assuring her things would turn out all right, he hastily left the room.

Life seemed to be closing in on twenty-five-year-old Eleanor. In summertime the family went first to Springwood and then on to the big cottage at Campobello, both places owned and dominated by Sara. In these out-of-door months Eleanor felt particularly inadequate, since she was poorly coordinated and bad at games. Highly sensitive and easily offended, she withdrew into hurt silences that she came to call her Griselda moods. Deep within her, Eleanor knew, lay a self, a person in her own right. But something close to a miracle would be needed to draw it out.

In the meantime Uncle Ted had thrashed through his second term as President. "Roosevelt found America in 1901 spiritually mud—he left it marble," wrote William Allen White. He had been in the White House for seven and one half years, since during his first administration he had been President-by-accident, serving out the term of the martyred McKinley. Had Theodore been a bolder man—as bold as the world thought him—he might have demanded a third term, a second election on his own.

Yet on election night, 1904, his exuberance at winning had led him to declare, "Under no circumstances will I be a candidate for or accept another nomination." This was the sort of hair-trigger utterance that both Edith Roosevelt and Henry Cabot Lodge worked to prevent. Why say it? And why, if it must be said, pick the night an election ended, when the words had absolutely no point?

Theodore reversed many of his erratic statements in political life, but in this case his promise not to run became entangled with his innate conservatism and sense of right and wrong. No President had ever run for what amounted to a third term. Theodore's conservatism told him he could not do so; it would be Wrong.

Yet at the same time he cheerfully shattered other precedents. Until him no Chief Executive had ever left the United States, but Theodore went to Panama, where he gleefully operated a steam shovel at work on the Panama Canal. Still he felt duty bound to keep his third-term word, though around him were supporters who hoped he would change his mind.

Was it conservatism, honor, or Dutch stubbornness that made the President cling so doggedly to his impetuous promise? Henry J. Pringle, whose biography of Roosevelt won a Pulitzer Prize, thinks it was the ever-present lack of confidence. He had been afraid of losing in 1904 and could scarcely believe his election. "I am stunned by the overwhelming victory we have won," he wrote to Kermit. "I had no conception such a thing was possible." Having won by a huge majority in 1904, Pringle thinks, Teddy merely moved his unfathomable fears ahead to 1908. He did not believe he would be re-elected again.

Instead, he handpicked a successor, and once again headlong ebullience brought him into strange pastures. Theodore might have given the nod to Charles Evans Hughes or another Republican progressive of his own stripe. But privately he called Hughes "the bearded lady" and passed him by. Instead, he chose William Howard Taft, his Secretary of War.

Taft was a man who stood six-foot-two, and weighed three hundred pounds. He was bighearted, affable. In twenty-five years of public service he had run for office only once, and then for judge of the Superior Court of Ohio. His many other offices, such as collector of internal revenue and solicitor general, had been appointive. Taft had enjoyed being a judge and dreamed of ending his career on the Supreme Court bench. But an ambitious wife and brothers saw him in the White House. Politically Taft was a throwback to McKinley. However, his innate geniality—or astute prompting by his wife—had allowed him to play along with Theodore as a Cabinet member, giving the impression of Republican progressivism.

Men around Theodore saw the situation clearly. "Changing from Roosevelt to Taft is like changing from an automobile back to a horse cab," declared Elihu Root. Yet Theodore saw nothing wrong. He even thought the affable Taft potentially "the greatest President, bar only Washington and Lincoln." One writer thinks that Theodore's adolescent world was always populated by saints or villains, and that Taft was one of the saints.

Having chosen to foist Taft on the American public, T.R. campaigned for him strenuously. Often he had to rally the lethargic candidate by clarion calls to greater action. At the same time Theodore faced the problem of reorganizing his own life. "The days of power had been so pleasant, and so brief," Pringle writes. At the age of fifty Theodore was, in effect, unemployed—an unhappy contingency for which the Founding Fathers made no provision. If Theodore had been president of one of the trusts he castigated he could look forward to twenty additional years on the job and wind up rich. As it was, the man of teeming energy had nothing important to do.

For a time he thought of becoming president of Harvard, a good possibility since Charles W. Eliot had just retired. But one of the Overseers—a relative of Alice Lee!—blasted his chances by gently murmuring, "We need a man of judgment, and is judgment to be

found coupled with such enormous energy?" There were suggestions that he run for senator or for mayor of New York. Theodore
brushed them aside.

Instead, with Taft ensconced in the White House, he went back
to his old life of author, naturalist, and hunter. First he contracted
to do twelve articles a year on political subjects for the *Outlook*.
Each of these magazine pieces would pay him a thousand dollars.
Then he announced a yearlong safari in the African jungle, a
hazardous expedition for a man blind in one eye and poor sight in
the other. But in a letter to his English hunter friend Selous, the
middle-aged former President showed his boyish zest for the adventure:

I fairly dream of this trip. . . . It seems to me too good to be true! I
never expected again to be in good game country; and never at all in
such game country as East Africa must be; I long to see the wild herds,
and to be in the wilderness.

Organizing a big safari turned out to be as complicated as busting a trust, and a further letter to Selous says:

Boston baked beans, canned peaches and canned tomatoes. A few
cases of these would be excellent. . . . You spoke of a special camp chair
of yours with a mosquito net. . . . Is a hair mattress better than a
rubber mattress? I don't see why we want two folding tables and two
sets of folding chairs.

Theodore adventured in the name of the Smithsonian Institution to which he would give the jungle animals he shot. *Collier's*
offered him one hundred thousand dollars for the running story of
his adventures, but he accepted fifty thousand dollars from *Scribner's*, feeling this periodical more dignified for a former President.
A brass band on the dock played "There'll Be a Hot Time in the
Old Town Tonight" as his ship pulled out from New York on
March 23, 1909. In his luggage were nine reserve pairs of eyeglasses.

Theodore stood the eleven-month expedition well, and was sick only five days. "It was a year of pleasant adolescence," says one account. The naturalist in him was ecstatic over the African animals, birds, trees, and mountains. The intrepid hunter shot 296 animals, among them five elephants, thirteen rhinos, and seven hippopotami. The author told of "The joy of wandering through lonely lands; the joy of hunting the mighty and terrible lords of the wilderness, the cunning, the wary and the grim."

At safari's end he met Edith in Khartoum, and the two began a tour of Europe. Theodore had been invited to speak at Oxford, the Sorbonne, and other seats of learning. But it was his personality rather than his speeches that set Europe aglow. Crowds fought to catch a glimpse of the man who typified that new, lusty, and improbable world power known as the United States of America. Everywhere he was greeted by crowned heads, whom he chummily greeted on a first-name basis. Many who saw Teddy were disappointed that he did not carry a Big Stick.

To cap his European tours Theodore represented President Taft at the funeral of King Edward VII. Eight royal monarchs were in London for this occasion, but bully Theodore outshone them all. WHAT WILL TEDDY WEAR? American newspaper headlines wondered. Teddy wondered, too, and finally chose the uniform of an American cavalry colonel, with high-polished boots. At this moment Edith Carow Roosevelt proved herself a woman of sanity, taste, and humor. "Theodore," she said firmly, "if you insist upon doing this, I will have a *vivandière's* costume made and follow you throughout Europe." Theodore rode in the funeral procession attired in black and white evening clothes. Of his European journey he later said, "I felt that if I met another king I should bite him."

While in Europe, Roosevelt learned that President Taft had steered the United States back toward conservatism. At long last the former President realized that he had given his endorsement to a man whose political creed differed from his own. Taft knew he had let his sponsor down and plaintively wrote, "I have had a hard time." To this Theodore replied ominously, "I shall make no speeches or say anything for two months, but I shall keep my mind as open as I keep my mouth shut."

He returned to the United States on June 18, 1910, to find himself still cherished by the American people. For three weeks New York had prepared a tumultuous welcome for its native son. A grandstand stood at the Battery, with seats for 2,500 top-hatted dignitaries. A gold medal had been struck for the occasion, and a navy escort saluted Theodore's ship down the bay. Thousands cheered as Teddy and his wife rode up Broadway to City Hall, and some sang, "When Teddy came sailing home, Hooray! Hooray!" Thousands of others shouted a welcome home during his further progress through the city. It was the greatest reception in the country's history, and not until Charles A. Lindbergh's return in 1927 was it excelled.

More people lined the Long Island roads to Oyster Bay. At home on Sagamore Hill, Theodore and Edith paused to express pleasure at being "in our own home, with our books and pictures and bronzes and big wood fires, and horses to ride, and the knowledge that our children are doing well."

The New York reception was another peak moment in the life of Theodore Roosevelt, a man whose life contained numerous peaks. Perhaps this was the topmost of all, since not a single voice of discord or dissent was heard. "You are certainly the first citizen of the country," his former military aide Archie Butt admiringly told the returned traveler. To this Theodore gave one of his mournful replies. "I think the American people feel a little tired of me, a feeling with which I cordially sympathize," he said.

15

END OF AN ERA

HARDLY LESS THAN HIS COUSIN THEODORE, FRANKLIN DELANO Roosevelt was assisted by Destiny in setting foot on the high road to the Presidency.

Later, reminiscing about his political beginnings, Franklin liked to say that his career began on the day he was "kidnapped" off the streets of Poughkeepsie by John Mack and other Democratic leaders. These local politicos persuaded him to make a speech at a policemen's picnic, and he did so well that they decided to run him for the state legislature.

But opposed to Franklin's fond recollection is a Dutchess County story more compatible with human nature and the curious involutions of politics. According to it, Franklin was first considered by the politicians Thomas Jefferson Newbold and Ed Perkins as they sat discussing candidates for country supervisor. "There's that young Roosevelt of James's," Newbold said. "Why don't we run him?"

Franklin was passed over on this occasion, but his name hung suspended in the political atmosphere. In 1910 Assemblyman Lewis Stuyvesant Chanler decided not to run for re-election, and

Franklin's name came up again. This time Perkins chugged out to Springwood in a red Maxwell roadster. Franklin had been out of Harvard for six years and was still a junior New York corporation lawyer who spent weekends in Hyde Park. Bored by the law and dissatisfied with city life, he responded immediately to Perkins' suggestion that he run for office. "But," he added, "I'd like to talk to my mother about it first."

Perkins clenched his jaw. "Frank," he said sternly, "there are men back in Poughkeepsie waiting for your answer. They won't like to hear you had to ask your mother."

Franklin gulped and said, "I'll do it."

When the experienced Assemblyman Chanler heard that a callow young lawyer had been picked to succeed him he flew into a rage and announced plans to run again. Now it was Franklin's turn to get mad. The Dutchess County group had never seen the young patrician angry before, but now he burst into headquarters in a Dutch fury. "I've got to run!" he roared. "I've told everybody I'm going to!" Perkins waved a reassuring hand. "Calm down," he said. "We'll run you for state senator in a bigger district than Chanler's."

According to Dr. Frank Freidel, F.D.R.'s first biographer, the Democratic politicans in Republican Dutchess County "made cynical use of gentlemen for halfhearted sorties." But there was nothing halfhearted about Franklin's campaign. No Democratic state senator had been elected from his district since 1888. Even so, the young man was determined to win. Indeed, the ambition displayed at this and other early moments of his career refutes those who like to call him an amiable lightweight until matured by the rigors of his polio attack. Where other gentlemen-Democrats might be nonchalant about campaigning, Franklin was in dead earnest. At Washington Hollow one Indian summer afternoon a practical joker plucked his speech from his pocket. There was much hearty laughter at this, but the candidate was not amused. "Campaigning was not a lark to him as it was to the Dutchess County veterans," says one neighbor.

When he caught on to political maneuvers, Franklin added tricks of his own. He hired the red Maxwell roadster and festooned it with posters, slogans, and flags. In this showy vehicle he barnstormed the countryside, traveling from one town to another at speeds as daring as twenty miles an hour. This alone attracted voter attention, for the newfangled automobile had never before been used in Dutchess campaigning. Even at this early date Franklin began speeches with a warm "My friends." At other times he delighted crowds by announcing straight-faced, "I'm not Teddy." Eleanor went along on at least one afternoon of this early campaigning, and later recalled that his delivery was halting. But a new set to his long jaw showed strength and Dutch determination.

In his speeches Franklin attacked bosses and bossism in Albany. Promising the farmers helpful legislation, he ignored national issues. He drove himself and others. "I think I worked harder with him than I ever have in my life," said one campaign ally. To farmers, artisans, and assorted voters the confident, smiling young man extended a firm right hand and said, "Call me Franklin." As in every campaign of his life, he made his last speech at Hyde Park. Hard work, determination, and novel electioneering paid off. He was elected by 1,140 votes.

Franklin had promised voters that the major part of his time would be devoted to his legislative career. This called for a family move to Albany and, after renting the New York house, the Roosevelts took a three-story home on State Street close to the State Capitol. Franklin and Eleanor, three children, two nurses, a wet nurse, and three housemaids, all moved in before the New Year. Sara Roosevelt, who had greeted Franklin's entry into politics with tight-lipped disapproval, went along to supervise the moving and placement of furniture. Sara was now really needed by the young couple, for Franklin's salary as state senator was only $1,500 a year, bringing the total family income to an annual $13,000. His mother's financial assistance was necessary to keep the large ménage afloat, particularly when it came to maids and governesses.

Imperious Sara was much in evidence on New Year's Day, when Franklin gave a catered Open House for constituents and fellow legislators. Among those invited were State Senator Robert F. Wagner, Assemblyman Alfred E. Smith, and a gnomelike correspondent of the New York *Herald* named Louis McHenry Howe.

When Sara reluctantly returned to Springwood, Eleanor was left to manage the household. For the timid young wife and mother it was much like being tossed off the dock into deep water by Uncle Ted. But this time Eleanor contrived to stay afloat. One thing buoying her was the knowledge that at last she was running her own home.

On the first day of the 1911 legislative session, Big Tim Sullivan, Tammany leader, noted Franklin striding confidently down a corridor. "Who's that?" he demanded. When told, he muttered, "So we've got another Roosevelt! This one looks young. Wouldn't it be better to drown him before he grows up?"

Others noticed the young senator, for at twenty-nine Franklin was strikingly handsome. "A Greek god," an Albany veteran recalls. He seemed to glory in the splendid health and height of his fine body, to which the word "supple" was often applied.

Franklin's only physical drawback was nearsightedness, and for this he wore a pince-nez perched on his nose. It did nothing to dampen his sex appeal. The first published newspaper story about him read: "Roosevelt is tall and lithe. With his handsome face and his form of supple strength, he could make a fortune on the stage and set the matinee girls' hearts throbbing."

In the state Senate Franklin immediately began to twist the Tammany Tiger's tail. Joining a group of young insurgent Democrats, he opposed the Tammany-dictated appointment of William F. ("Blue-eyed Billy") Sheehan as United States senator. Shortly Franklin was heading up the Insurgents, demonstrating leadership, courage, and an unusual instinct for timing. At this point he was first quoted as saying, "There is nothing I love so much as a good fight!" His house on State Street became headquarters for the Insurgents, with so much cigar smoke seeping up through the ceiling that Eleanor was forced to move the children's bedroom to the third floor.

Franklin and his cohorts succeeded in blocking the nomination of Blue-eyed Billy but were forced to accept a man no better qualified. It was a dubious victory, with the Insurgents hissed and booed by other legislators. Yet to the public it seemed a triumph of youthful idealism, and for the first time the name Franklin D. Roosevelt won praise in the land.

As the sessions continued, Franklin mastered with amazing speed both parliamentary procedure and rough politics. He also showed an urge to solve problems by action. Indeed, the desire to *do* something about all troublesome matters may be the keynote to his character. In it he much resembled Theodore, though Franklin's type of action was far less bombastic than his cousin's.

As a young legislator he was intensely serious and seemed momentarily to have lost the family ability to laugh. In addition, he had a way of aristocratically tossing his head which some found annoying. One who disliked this mannerism was Frances Perkins, then a young social worker. At the time she thought him "arrogant . . . very active and alert, artificially serious of face, rarely smiling."

Franklin himself later decided he must have been a somewhat stuffy and self-satisfied junior senator. To Miss Perkins he said, "You know, I was an awfully mean cuss when I first went into politics." But against this harsh judgment is the recollection of a friend who found him "alert, cheerful and tremendously ambitious. He had few opinions himself, but he sucked people dry with questions."

As his political education increased, Franklin's hatred of Tammany and its bosses tempered, but he never became a completely dependable party man. For one thing, he was too eager to experiment. "His record as a State Senator," writes James MacGregor

Burns, "was compounded in parts of insurgency, orthodoxy and trial and error." The same would be said of him twenty-three years in the future.

In late 1911 Franklin made a trip to Trenton, where he visited Woodrow Wilson, elected Governor of New Jersey the year before. The state senator was impressed by the Governor and promptly became an original Wilson-for-President man. Wilson, in turn, was charmed by Franklin. He mentioned him to several associates, one of whom said, "I thought all Roosevelts were Republicans." "No," Wilson answered, "this one comes from the Democratic branch of the family, and he is the handsomest young giant I have ever seen."

Full to the brim of Wilson sentiment, Franklin journeyed to the Democratic Convention of 1912 at Baltimore. This was his debut in national politics and it may be said that he made the most of it. His good looks, vibrant body, and buoyant personality won the attention of such seasoned Democrats as William Gibbs McAdoo, Joseph P. Davies, Cordell Hull, and Josephus Daniels. Of his first meeting with Franklin, the easygoing Southerner Daniels later said, "It was love at first sight!" Another man impressed by Franklin was Van Lear Black, publisher of the Baltimore *Sun* and a man of many business interests. After being introduced to Franklin, he exclaimed, "This is the most attractive man I have ever met!"

To these people Franklin appeared to possess the Roosevelt energy in a far more civilized form than Theodore—if Teddy loved life, Franklin loved living. The state senator spent much time with younger convention delegates, using his bright charm and persuasiveness to win Wilson votes. Eleanor had accompanied him, leaving the children with Sara at Hyde Park. However, Franklin was so busy that she returned home, thinking, "My husband would hardly miss me, since I rarely laid eyes on him."

In the end Franklin's vigor and determination helped swing the

New York delegation to Wilson on the forty-sixth ballot. At this high moment of victory, Franklin thought of his wife. He wired: WILSON NOMINATED THIS AFTERNOON ALL MY PLANS VAGUE SPLENDID TRIUMPH.

Franklin had to wage his own campaign for re-elction as state senator in 1912. After a vacation with Eleanor and the children at Campobello, where Sara had purchased them a smaller home on the Bay of Fundy side, he returned to New York to map strategy. Almost at once, he was laid low by typhoid fever, the first of a series of serious illnesses that plagued the healthy-looking man over the next decade. For a few dreadful days it seemed that Franklin's political career might end with defeat while immobilized in a sickbed. But into this breach stepped the mighty-mite figure of the newspaperman Louis McHenry Howe, who in early Albany days decided that Franklin would someday be President. Howe was a gnarled little man, with asthma and an acne-pitted face, whose guile and wisdom perfectly balanced Franklin's energy and enthusiasm. The two men quickly became friends and now Howe left Albany for Hyde Park, where he waged a skillful campaign by poster, newspaper advertisement, and "personal" circular letter. He was also adept at stirring up dissension in Republican ranks.

Howe's entrance into the Springwood household brought tensions, for neither Eleanor nor Sara Roosevelt liked him. Eleanor objected to his appearance and the cascade of cigarette ashes on his vest. Possibly she was jealous of his close mental rapport with Franklin.

Yet Howe liked Eleanor and made efforts to draw her into Franklin's brave new life. "I was as determined that I would not like him as he was that I should," Eleanor recalled. "He kept coming to my desk and talking to me, day after day, until I became interested in spite of myself, and eventually I realized how much he had to offer and was glad to have his advice and companionship."

As election day approached, Howe spurred campaign workers by passing out small checks among them. This depleted the candidate's bank account, but all was forgiven when the still-ailing Franklin was elected by 1,701 votes.

In Washington, six months later, Josephus Daniels was chosen Secretary of the Navy in the new Wilson Cabinet. This was a surprise, for Daniels had understood that he would be Postmaster General. As a landlubber and pacifist, the mellow man had need of a strong, active Assistant Secretary. Suddenly he thought of the right one—that handsome Roosevelt boy, the state senator from New York who had impressed everyone at Baltimore! Roosevelt had told Daniels about his boyish dream of being a navy officer and had lovingly described his collection of ship models, nautical books, and autographs.

Franklin was queried and responded enthusiastically. Why, he would be the youngest Assistant Secretary in the nation's history and the second in his family to hold the post within fifteen years! Woodrow Wilson heartily approved the choice. The only sour note came from Elihu Root, who cocked a quizzical eyebrow and asked Daniels, "You know the Roosevelts, don't you? Whenever a Roosevelt rides, he wishes to ride in front."

So the family moved to Washington, leaving Albany to Theodore Douglas Robinson, recently elected a Republican assemblyman. Like Eleanor, his wife Helen, Rosy's daughter, had switched political coloration to match her husband. Family ties were still binding in Washington, though, for the young Roosevelts rented Bamie's house on N Street still known locally as the Little White House, since Teddy had spent so much time there as President. Theodore himself sent congratulations, saying, "It is interesting that you are in another place which I myself had. I am sure you will enjoy yourself to the fullest as Assistant Secretary of the Navy and that you will do capital work." Sara also wrote a note of motherly counsel, characteristically urging, "Try not to write your signature too small, as it gets cramped-looking and is not distinctive. So many public men have such awful signatures and so unreadable."

Eventually Franklin developed a deep affection for Josephus Daniels, but for a long time he was visibly impatient with his superior. In this he duplicated Theodore, who had been unhappy with Navy Secretary Long. Shortly after entering the department, Franklin described Daniels as "the funniest looking hillbilly I have every seen."

It was Daniels' responsibility to deal with Congress and the President, as well as with myriad contractors, lobbyists, and job seekers. This left Franklin more or less in charge of the Navy Department. He was indeed riding in front! He had brought Louis McHenry Howe to Washington as an assistant, and the two found the work stimulating. In Franklin's own words, "I get my fingers into everything—there's no law against it." He was a proponent of a big navy, and as a result the admirals preferred him to Daniels. "I am *running* the real work," he wrote Eleanor, "although Josephus is here. He is bewildered by it all but very sweet and sad." Franklin's irritation was quite apparent to Daniels, who accepted it with fatherly tolerance. One reason may have been that the young Assistant Secretary was doing an excellent job.

Balancing the peevishness with Daniels was Franklin's enjoyment of naval panoply. As Assistant Secretary he rated a seventeen-gun salute, and improved on this by personally designing a flag to be flown when he was aboard ship. He had the use of a small yacht, and sometimes availed himself of a destroyer to get to Campobello. On such occasions he took the wheel to steer through the treacherous shoals between island and mainland.

He also made ceremonial inspections of the fleet and tours of naval installations on land. Further, he contributed suggestions about over-all ship design. "He was a great trial-and-error guy, but he did have some good ideas," recalls one admiral. Among his many other duties was supervision of navy yards and purchase of supplies. Young Roosevelt found even this nonglamorous work instructive. "The great lesson he learned during these years," writes James MacGregor Burns, "was that bureaucrats, workers, and sailors were human beings with human problems and failings."

As life expanded for the Roosevelt family, Eleanor's forward progress resembled one of Uncle Ted's Obstacle Walks. Doggedly she proceeded through, over, and under—*but never around!*—the new challenges that life placed in her path. The first step toward becoming the remarkable person of her middle and older years was the afternoon of Dutchess County campaigning with Franklin. Next came Albany, where she encountered salty characters like Alfred E. Smith. "I was beginning to get interested in human beings," she said, "and I found that almost everyone had something interesting to contribute to my education."

As the wife of an Assistant Secretary of the Navy, she was forced to pay endless social calls and to entertain at home, as well as stand at Franklin's side during official ceremonies. By forcing herself to survive these ordeals she buried, but never lost, the excruciating self-consciousness that she called shyness.

A continuing problem was Sara Roosevelt, who still expected to be treated with the deference due her age and background. "She was very sure that she knew what was right, that her pattern was the right one," Eleanor recalled. Sara had come along when the family moved to Washington, remaining until they were settled. When she returned to Hyde Park she began to send potatoes and garden vegetables from the farm.

The dowager's main hold on her son's family was that she paid for the many nurses, governesses, and maids of whom Eleanor still stood in awe. Some of them might have come straight from a horror tale. James Roosevelt remembers one nanny who forced him to eat a bowl of hot English mustard as punishment and blames his life-long stomach trouble on her. Eleanor and Franklin were aware of these crude chastisements, but apparently dared not interfere. Only when whiskey bottles were found in Nanny's room did Eleanor grow angry enough to fire her.

Of her first ten years of marriage Eleanor wrote: "I was always just getting over having a baby, or about to have one." With the births of Elliott in 1910, the second Franklin Jr. in 1914, and John Aspinwall in 1916 her days of childbearing ended. Still, this brought no real relaxation. The family had to move to larger quarters at 2131 R Street, and simultaneously Eleanor had become deeply enmeshed in society. "We lived the kind of social life I had never before known, dining out night after night and having people to dine with us about once a week." But socializing brought her further confidence and enough experience at last so that she no longer feared maids and nurses.

Both Eleanor and Franklin inherited the family talent for parenthood. Franklin was a special favorite of the children, who, if they loved him as a father, adored him as a companion. Every night he dashed up four flights to the nursery to embrace the younger ones, saying, "I hope you are snug as a bug in a rug." One child has said, "He was the handsomest, strongest, most glamorous father in the world."

Yet the children had an unmistakable feeling of sharing beloved parents with nameless outside obligations. James writes of Franklin, "When he was around, which wasn't nearly often enough for us, he inundated us with fun and activity, and with love too—but in his special way, which was both detached and overpowering. Sometimes we felt we didn't have him at all, but when we did have him, life was as lively and exciting as any kid could want it to be."

Eleanor realized that the children believed their parents spent too much time away from home, but the social obligations remained. "I had always put my children first in that their lives were planned in a manner which I felt was right for them," she wrote of life in Washington. "But I think for the good of our own relationship and my husband's career we did far more of the social round than was either necessary or wise . . . but at the time I simply never thought I could do anything else."

To the annoyance of the children, parents and doting grandmother persisted in calling them "chicks" or "precious chicks."

Eleanor and Franklin felt they themselves had been bossed too much as children and refused to guide their own offspring, preferring to let them learn things themselves. Franklin, particularly, was loath to discipline any infractions of household rules. Instead, he leaned on sweet reason, which usually worked.

Though preoccupied, busy, and often away from home on long official trips, he always managed to make the children feel he understood their problems. To Eleanor he once wrote, "I am *too* sorry about the bunny's demise—and only hope the funeral and making of the tombstone will console the chicks. I wonder if it was the lopsided one?"

Franklin's annual salary as Assistant Secretary was $5,000, making it necessary for the household to struggle along on $15,000 a year. The sum was hardly sufficient for a family that continued to live in the manner of American nobility, with four servants, nurses and governess, car and chauffeur. Eleanor tried to use her own $5,000 on clothing for the children and herself, or for other household expenses.

Franklin was paid by the navy every two weeks, and at first took the money in cash, blithely stuffing it in his pocket to be spent as he wished. Soon a deluge of unpaid bills drove him to open a checking account and budget his expenses. He also got rid of the Marmon car and chauffeur, buying instead a rakish Stutz of which he was enormously proud. Further economy was necessary, so he began leaving the car at home to walk to the Navy Department. As he strode along, government girls stopped to watch admiringly.

At the same time Eleanor decided her social duties required a part-time social secretary. For this she hired a very pretty young girl of excellent social background. Washington tongues wagged as Eleanor and the children went to Campobello, leaving the girl to do chores for the summer bachelor. Yet at this point letters between husband and wife are at their most devoted. Eleanor addressed Franklin as "Dearest Honey" while he called her "Dearest Babs."

In the end all efforts at economy were defeated by Franklin's zeal as a collector. He never stopped wearing old suits and would not take his family to restaurants because of the expense. Yet he was constantly tempted by stamps, ship models, navy prints, books, autographs, and curiosa.

His extravagance let Sara keep a hold on Franklin. Mother and son were often together, and in 1915 they spent time planning and supervising the addition of two wings to Springwood. But Sara's great hold was financial, as this heartfelt letter from Franklin shows:

Dearest Mama—You are not only an angel, which I always knew, but the kind which comes at the critical moment in life! For the question was not one of paying Dr. Mitchell for removing James' insides, the Dr. can wait, I know he is or must be rich, but of paying the gas man and butcher lest the infants starve to death, and your cheque which is too much of a Birthday present will do that. It is so dear of you . . .

With America's entry into the war in 1917, Franklin's Navy Department duties multiplied, while Eleanor took on canteen and hospital work. Thirty-six-year-old Franklin really wanted to get into uniform. Theodore's four sons had gone overseas, as had Corinne's two. Hall Roosevelt was in uniform, as was James A. of Oyster Bay. Uncle Fred Delano was a colonel in army transport. But when Franklin's resignation was broached to President Wilson, he sent back word, "Tell the young man his only and best war service is to stay where he is."

Franklin continued restive. As the war progressed, he evolved a plan to shut the English Channel to German submarines by a mine barrage. When at last this was put into effect, it aided in precipitating the revolt of German sailors that led to the Armistice.

In 1918, Franklin went overseas on a convoy-destroyer to make an Assistant Secretary's tour of the war zone. On his return he planned to resign and become a lieutenant commander attached to a front-line naval railroad battery. But by the time he got back Washington had received peace overtures. In January, 1919,

Franklin and Eleanor crossed the ocean on an official tour that included observing the Versailles Conference for the Navy Department. As top-ranking navy official on the Continent, Franklin had to choose the ship for President Wilson's return to the United States. He picked the transport *George Washington*, and he and Eleanor sailed back with the President.

Theodore Roosevelt's return in 1910 from his African safari and the tour among Europe's crowned heads marked a turning point in the strenuous life of the former President.

He was fifty-two years old in 1910, with mental and physical energies unimpaired, though his robust body showed signs of wear. Once again he was forced to turn to writing, contributing an article a month to the *Outlook* and polishing his *Scribner's* series into a book called *African Game Trails*. He was also busy on the monograph *Revealing and Concealing Coloration in Birds and Mammals*. Aside from this, he was again virtually unemployed. He professed to relish it. "All I want now is privacy," he told reporters. "I want to close up like a native oyster."

In Oyster Bay Theodore was once again surrounded by a loyal family, and there was much activity around Sagamore Hill. Two days after the rousing New York welcome, Theodore Jr. married Eleanor Alexander, and a year later Theodore became a grandfather for the first time. Kermit returned to Harvard after his exciting year of safari. Archie was ready for Harvard; Quentin had reached Groton age.

Alice Roosevelt Longworth, happily occupied in Washington, had begun to pursue a lifetime of behind-the-scenes political maneuvering. Ethel Roosevelt, young and attractive, was being courted by Dr. Richard Derby of Boston, ten years her senior.

Theodore's larger capacities were hardly called upon by any of this, and from the vacuum of his life emerged another facet of his mercurial character. The former President, it turned out, was a hater. In previous years he may have been too busy meeting the exciting tests of each new day to become noted for this. Up to now he had allowed his family to hate for him, but with time on his hands Theodore proved himself capable of man-sized fury. If nothing else, this exposes another difference between Theodore and his Roosevelt forebears. In two hundred fifty years none of them had given vent to long-time hatred. Instead, the Roosevelts were objective and philosophical about the frustrations of life.

Yet over the next decade Theodore let hatred run his life. In fairness it must be said that this never shriveled his spirit. To friends, family, and public he remained ebullient and good-humored. But his impulses were no longer spontaneous and healthy. Rather, he was driven by a desire to harm and destroy politically two other men. Theodore, who always liked to say he felt strong as a bull moose, now began to resemble a wounded one.

Inevitably the first object of his hatred was William Howard Taft. In Theodore's opinion, the President had betrayed a sacred trust by undermining reforms imperative to the welfare of the nation. Yet it is questionable that Taft was as black as Theodore came to see him. For one thing, the portly President had continued Theodore's trust busting, even prosecuting the powerful United States Steel. The real trouble with Taft may have been less what he did than the way he did it. The most galling thing, perhaps, was that Taft dared to be himself rather than a carbon-copy Theodore.

"Taft means well, but means well feebly," said T.R. in a celebrated utterance. The key word may be *feebly*. From that it was a short step to saying "Taft is hopeless." With this the two friends of twenty years—the two most prominent figures in the land!—engaged in a quarrel that has been called "ugly, venomous, and vindictive." In August, 1910, Taft got a glimmering of Roosevelt's real plans.

The former President began a series of speeches promoting himself as a "new" political personality who advocated New Nationalism in place of the Square Deal. It dawned on Taft that Theodore intended to wrest the 1912 nomination from him. Friends begged Roosevelt to let Taft go down to defeat in 1912 and himself look forward to 1916. T.R. refused. He wanted to boot Taft out of the White House personally.

Public suspense mounted through 1911 as Theodore cagily withheld announcement of his candidacy. At one point a headline in the New York *American* asked TR: RU OR RU NOT? On Washington's Birthday, 1912, Teddy finally spoke in characteristic words: "My hat is in the ring, the fight is on, and I am stripped to the buff."

The statement aroused the lethargic Taft. "Every man who has blood in his body," he said, "and has been misrepresented as I have . . . is forced to fight. I don't want to fight, but when I do fight, I want to hit hard. Even a rat in a corner will fight." Theodore replied with his skilled invective. To some he appeared almost rabid. Said the Louisville *Courier-Journal*: "Unless he breaks down under the strain and is taken to a lunatic asylum, there can be in his name and person but one issue—life tenure in executive office."

Teddy traveled to the Chicago convention armed with volumes by Ferrero and Herodotus to read at odd moments. He was easily the convention favorite but top Republicans—among them Henry Cabot Lodge and Elihu Root—stuck with the party and Taft. As convention chairman, Root ruled against seating pro-Roosevelt delegates. Theodore had expected his great popularity to turn into a steamroller that would flatten all opposition. But the steamroller ran the other way as he sought to stampede the convention for his progressive principles. "We stand at Armageddon and we battle for the Lord," his thin voice exhorted. The steamroller flattened him. Taft, nominated by Warren G. Harding of Ohio, was the Republican candidate.

However, Theodore remained the favorite of liberal Republicans. Chief among them were insurgents known as the National Progressive League, who met after the convention and announced themselves ready to support Theodore for President. Six weeks later he was formally nominated at a third-party Progressive Convention, with Hiram Johnson of California as running mate. Political observers knew that Taft and Roosevelt would split the Republican vote, opening the way to a Wilson victory. "The only question now," quipped Chauncey M. Depew, "is which corpse gets the most flowers."

Once more the cry of "Happy Warrior" was heard in the land, as Theodore added pepper and salt to the pot of a dull campaign. Again he pronounced himself strong as a bull moose, and because of this his supporters were called Bull Moosers. Yet the Bull Moose warrior was not altogether happy in his new role. By espousing the Progressive cause Theodore, always an uncertain liberal, found himself advocating a near-socialist program of federal welfare legislation, farm relief, workmen's compensation, health insurance in industry, heavier taxes on wealth, and limited injunction in labor disputes: "federal interference with every form of human industry or activity," charged the New York *World*. Theodore's uneasiness was apparent in his acceptance speech, of which publisher Frank Munsey said, "While splendidly progressive, it is, at the same time, amply conservative and sound."

One summer night Theodore sat rocking on the porch of Sagamore Hill with his two young cousins, Nicholas and George Emlen Roosevelt. George wryly remarked that up to 1912 Theodore had been the progressive leader of the conservatives, while now he was the conservative leader of the progressives. Theodore mulled this paradox, then exclaimed, "Yes, yes, that's it! I have to hold them in check all the time. I have to restrain them!"

In some ways campaigning was a letdown. His supporters were wildly enthusiastic, with William Allen White later exposing their state of mind by writing, "Roosevelt bit me and I went mad!"

But Theodore was enough of a political realist to know that, although he might beat Taft, he could not defeat Wilson. Yet he pressed on. To make matters worse, his throat really bothered him, and the beginnings of rheumatoid arthritis inhibited his celebrated gymnastic displays.

Taft was a bumbling speaker, Wilson eloquent but pedantic. Only Theodore, with a slight assist from the Socialist candidate Eugene V. Debs, brought color. Then Fate provided a moment of high drama. On the night of October 14, 1912, outside the Hotel Gilpatrick in Milwaukee, Theodore was shot in the right chest by a fanatic named John Schrank—aptly spelled Crank by a few excited newspapers. The would-be assassin fired a Colt revolver at six-foot range, and Theodore felt as if he had been kicked by a mule.

It threw him flat on his back, but he quickly leaped up. The bullet had gone through his crowded inside breast pocket which held a steel case for his spectacles and the folded fifty-page manuscript of his speech. Slowed by steel and wadded paper, the bullet stopped four inches within his chest, fracturing a rib. Showing great presence of mind, Theodore placed fingers to lips and coughed. No blood came, and he knew the shot had failed to reach his lungs.

From then on he acted in accord with his image of bravery and rugged individualism. First he ordered the crowd to stop pummeling Schrank. Faced by the man who had just tried to murder him, he magnanimously said, "You poor creature!" Next, he told those preparing to rush him to a hospital, "I will make this speech or die! It is one thing or the other!" En route to the auditorium he said, "It takes more than that to kill a Bull Moose. I do not care a rap about being shot, not a rap." On the platform he reached into his pocket for the bullet-pierced manuscript. The bloodstained shirt was exposed, rousing the audience into a frenzy of acclaim. Still unsure of the seriousness of the wound, he commenced in a dramatic whisper:

I am going to ask you to be very quiet and please excuse me from making a long speech. I'll do the best I can, but there is a bullet in my body. . . . I have a message to deliver and will deliver it as long as there is life in my body.

I have had an A-1 time with life and I am having it now. (It is) a very natural thing that weak and vicious minds should be influenced to acts of violence by the kinds of awful mendacity and abuse that have been heaped upon me . . . by the newspapers . . . Mr. Debs . . . Mr. Wilson . . . Mr. Taft. . . .

Then, throwing away the prepared speech, he spoke in rambling fashion for fifty minutes, while friends stood next to the podium to catch him if he fainted. Exhausted at the end, he was rushed to a hospital, where at last doctors examined the wound. One medical man emerged to pay tribute to Theodore's physical strength. In a business suit he may have looked pudgy, but actually years of strenuous exercise had made him a mass of meat and muscle. Stated the doctor: "He is one of the most powerful men I have ever seen on an operating table. The bullet lodged in the massive muscles of the chest instead of penetrating the lung." Because of Theodore's fine physical shape, the bullet was left where it was.

Taft, Wilson, and Debs wired sympathy and all three courteously stopped campaigning until Theodore was ready to resume. From his bed Theodore instructed, "Tell the people not to worry about me, for if I go down another will take my place. For always the army is true! Always the cause is there!"

The rest aided his throat and in two weeks he was on the campaign trail once more. At his wind-up speech in Madison Square Garden he looked strong, confident, and cheerful to the 12,000 in the crowd. His cheerfulness seemed unimpaired after the election gave Wilson 6,293,019 votes; Roosevelt, 4,119,507; and Taft, who carried only Utah and Vermont, 3,484,956.

"I accept the result with entire good humor," said Theodore like a bully loser. But had he really lost? He may have lost the election, but he had got the hated Taft out of the White House. Losing the war, he had won the battle. That he had torn the Republican party asunder did not appear to bother him.

In the wake of the Bull Moose campaign another score remained to be settled. All through public life Theodore had been hounded by stories that he was a drunkard, for apparently many

Americans could find no other explanation for his endless energy and picturesque verbiage. Some were aware that his brother had died an alcoholic, and this added fuel to gossip.

For a long time Theodore brushed the matter aside, but at last he was fed up. Usually the stories spread in whispers, but during the 1912 campaign, the Michigan paper *Iron Ore* said, "Roosevelt lies and curses in a most disgusting way; he gets drunk, too, and that not infrequently, and all his intimates know about it." An angry Theodore sued for libel, he would "deal with these slanders, so that never again will they be repeated."

The case was tried in Marquette, and for five days in May, 1913, the foremost men in the land testified that Theodore never stoked his energy with alcohol. Theodore swore, "I don't smoke. . . and I dislike the taste of beer. I have never drunk whiskey or brandy except when a doctor prescribed it." The editor of *Iron Ore* could not produce a single witness. Theodore's suit asked only vindication, and a token verdict of six cents was awarded him.

With this victory he again reverted to writer-explorer, journeying with son Kermit into the deepest jungle of Brazil. This was a more perilous trip than the African safari, since it led up the Amazon in search of the tributary River of Doubt, whose origin and course had never been charted. Jungle fever, tropical rains, malaria, rapids, and whirlpools were constant hazards. An expedition expected to take six weeks lasted eight months.

It ended when Theodore jumped into the rapids to save two canoes from smashing against rocks. Hurled against a sharp stone, he suffered a deep gash on the thigh. It became infected, and once more Theodore was heroic. To Kermit he gasped, "I want you to go ahead. We have reached a point where some of us must stop. I feel I am only a burden to the party." Kermit refused and floated his suffering parent downstream under a blazing sun. Back in civilization, the party learned they had been given up for lost.

In May, 1914, Theodore reached New York, leaning on a cane and supported by two men. "It was such a shock to friends to whom his unusual physical vigor had always been a source of wonder," a newspaper story said. Yet after two weeks at Sagamore Hill, he was off to Madrid, where Kermit married Belle Willard, daughter of the American ambassador to Spain. Theodore thoroughly approved the match. "Belle is a perfect trump," he opined.

At Sagamore Hill again, he began his autobiography, together with a *History of African Game Animals*. From time to time he paused to lament the high cost of putting sons through Harvard and Groton. His lamentations may have been justified, for the number of children produced by most Roosevelts had a way of spreading the family fortune thin.

It was another period of comparative quiet in Theodore's life. With Taft gone from the White House, he had no target for his newfound capacity to hate. However, politics provided one when he learned that Woodrow Wilson was negotiating a treaty with Colombia. In effect, the treaty apologized for Teddy's Yankee-imperialist seizure of Panama and offered indemnity of $25,000,000. Of all Theodore's acts in the White House, he remained most sensitive over this highhanded move. Vigorously he continued to defend it, gloating, "I took the Isthmus, started the Canal, and then left Congress, not to debate the Canal, but to debate me."

T.R. and Wilson had abused each other soundly in the 1912 campaign, though Teddy's sharpest verbal shafts had been saved for Taft. By the end of the campaign Wilson detested Theodore, while Teddy only disliked him. But with the Colombia treaty, dislike rose to hatred.

Wilson's vacillation over American entry into the European war increased it. At first Theodore's youthful admiration for Germany let him take an impartial view of this conflict. Of Germany's ruthless invasion of Belgium he wrote, "When giants are engaged in a death wrestle, as they reel to and fro, they are certain to trample

on whomever gets in the way of the huge, straining combatants."
He also saluted the Germans as "a stern, virile and masterful people."

But his volatile emotions soon swung to the Allies and became
entwined in his hatred of Wilson. Theodore was every bit as impatient of the government as he had been in 1898. Two years before
the country entered the war he was beating the drum for American involvement, accusing Wilson of "weasel words," of being "a
pacifist . . . an utterly cold-blooded politician always . . . without a
single scruple."

Theodore had hopes of receiving the Republican nomination
for President in 1916. At the same time he was so bent on involvement that he said, "It would be a mistake to nominate me
unless the country has in its mood something of the heroic"—by
which he meant war. The Republicans picked Charles Evans
Hughes as candidate, while the declining Progressives again chose
Teddy. He refused the nomination, knowing it would mean another Bull Moose split and certain victory for Wilson. "I shall
strongly campaign for Mr. Hughes," he promised. Relishing this
extra opportunity to revile Wilson, he shouted in his last speech of
the campaign, "There should be shadows at Shadow Lawn [Wil-
son's Princeton home], the shadows of men, women, and children
who have risen from the ooze of the ocean bottom and from the
graves in foreign fields; the shadows of the helpless whom Mr.
Wilson did not dare to protect lest he might have to face danger."

One of Theodore's inspirations was a Rough Rider regiment of
cavalry riflemen which he would lead overseas, with the French
government footing the bill. With America in the war, he saw his
Rough Riders as a vital part of the American army. He insisted on
presenting this idea to Wilson in person. Assistant Secretary of the
Navy Franklin D. Roosevelt arranged the meeting. During the
hourlong talk Theodore was on his best behavior, and Wilson remarked to his secretary, "He is a great big boy. I was . . . charmed
by his personality. There is a sweetness about him that I found
very compelling. You can't resist the man!"

Yet he could. Wilson took no action in the matter of Theodore's rugged regiment until at last he became annoyed at the many questions put to him about it. Even in anger Wilson was lucid, and now he said, "Colonel Roosevelt is a splendid man and a patriotic citizen . . . but he is not a military leader. His experience in military life has been extremely short. He and many of the men with him are too old to render effective service, and . . . he as well as others have shown intolerance of discipline."

Theodore's record during the war years was both good and bad. On the good side, his bellicose war speeches did more to prepare the nation for the sacrifices of war than the reasoned words of Wilson. Soldiers landing overseas realized this and one wrote home to say so. Teddy answered in a characteristic letter which hangs today at Sagamore Hill:

That is a mighty nice letter of yours. You are the kind of American who is doing the work in which I believe more than any other at this time. Of course, we ought to have been in the war two years before we entered it, and if we had done so Russia would never have broken and the war would be over now and Germany crushed.

On the debit side, his turndown in the matter of the regiment further increased his hatred of Wilson. At the same time it soured his jingoism, making him the kind of speaker who ranted, "The only way to make a Hun feel friendly is to knock him out." Wilson's Fourteen Points, he declared, were "fourteen scraps of paper." His last wartime speeches, one writer says, "fed the spirit that expressed itself in lynchings, amateur witch hunts, intolerance of every kind. . . . He mixed his hateful talk with his awful cult of purging society by sacrifices in war."

Meanwhile, his four sons were in the thick of battle. Ted Jr. was wounded twice and cited for gallantry. Kermit won the British Military Cross. Archie was wounded and won the Croix de Guerre. Quentin had bad eyesight, but, along with Hall Roosevelt memorized the oculist chart and became a combat aviator. "The first thing you know," Finley Peter Dunne told Theodore, "your four sons will put the name Roosevelt on the map."

Then, in July, 1918, came word that Quentin had been killed in aerial combat behind German lines. Quentin was probably Theodore's favorite and the news shattered him. Hermann Hagedorn, with Roosevelt at the time, writes, "With Quentin's death, the boy in Theodore died."

Deep grief for Quentin seemed to aggravate growing physical weaknesses. Five months earlier Theodore's chronic throat condition had spread to the middle ear. At the same time he suffered a bad attack of inflammatory rheumatism, together with an abscess on the injured thigh. The accepted treatment for middle-ear infection was a mastoid operation, but doctors did not operate, possibly because Theodore's heart was weak. Discharged from Roosevelt Hospital, he was deaf in one ear as well as blind in one eye. His balance was impaired and he had to learn to walk all over again.

In the fall he was back in the hospital with acute pains in lower back and legs. His mind was unimpaired, but he faced the prospect of spending the rest of his life in a wheelchair. His spirits alternated between confidence and despair. He was sixty years old on October 27, 1918, and on that day proclaimed, "I am ahead of the game. Nobody ever packed more varieties of fun and interest in the sixty years." At other times he said, "I feel as though I were a hundred years old and had never been young."

He was released from the hospital at Christmas, and Edith wrote the boys that "he watched the dancing flames and spoke of the happiness of being home." One night he turned to her suddenly and said, "I wonder if you will ever know how much I love Sagamore Hill."

Even in spite of bad health and grief over Quentin, he still had energy for politics. Henry Cabot Lodge paid bedside visits and the two crafty warriors made plans to harpoon the League of Nations, less because it was a league of nations than because it was the brainchild of Wilson. At this time, the pair apparently conceived the effective stratagem of luring a few Democratic senators to their side, giving the impression of bipartisanship.

Theodore was by now several times a grandfather, and he passed much time in the company of lively, fascinating children, one of them named Theodore IV. He was also able to write articles and editorials. He spent January 5, 1919, in his wheelchair, correcting proofs. As night approached, the inflammation in his joints grew more painful. A doctor was called, and Theodore told him, "I feel as though my heart were going to stop beating."

Treatment reduced the pain and at eleven o'clock he went to sleep in the bedroom he loved. At four in the morning an attendant who slept in the next room heard deep breathing. He called the day nurse, but when she arrived breathing had ceased. Doctors diagnosed a coronary occlusion by blood clot.

Later that day Henry Cabot Lodge rose on the Senate floor to intone, "Greatheart is dead!"

But Vice-President Marshall's tribute may have been better. "Death had to take him sleeping," he said, "for if Roosevelt had been awake, there would have been a fight."

16

FROM POLIO TO THE WHITE HOUSE

WITH THE DEATH OF THEODORE, THE ROOSEVELT FAMILY AGAIN became the sprawling group it had been before the Rough Rider's rise to heights of national fame in the faraway days of 1898.

Now the most prominent Roosevelt was Franklin, who still served as Assistant Secretary of the Navy. But the American public anticipated much from Colonel Theodore Roosevelt, Jr., and his brothers, Kermit and Archie. When these young heroes returned from overseas they were expected to enter politics, relighting the bonfire image of their explosive father.

Already the Senate fight for United States membership in the League of Nations had been joined and was moving slowly toward defeat of American entry. This was exactly as the late Theodore had wished. If Teddy had still been alive and in good health he would probably have been the Republican candidate for President in 1920. Considering the mood of a war-weary nation, he might well have won the election.

In view of this, the Oyster Bay Roosevelts still considered themselves supreme. Among other things, they permitted Henry Cabot Lodge to express the family feeling toward Franklin when he said,

"He is a well-meaning, nice young man—but light." Secretary of the Interior Franklin K. Lane also made a belittling remark about Franklin, but his contained a kernel of wisdom. "Young Roosevelt knows nothing about finance," Lane said, "but he does not know that he does not know."

Yet those who viewed Franklin as a charming lightweight failed to realize how the war years had matured him. The triumphs of his later life have caused his early accomplishments to diminish, but at the age of thirty-eight, which he reached in 1920, Franklin was already a remarkably successful man.

After serving in the New York State Senate, he had been Assistant Secretary of the Navy during a world war in which the navy played a vital part. During his seven years in the department he had aggressively pushed, fought, and shouted for action. In the words of James MacGregor Burns: "Long hours, tough decisions, endless conferences, exhausting trips, hard bargaining with powerful officials in Washington and abroad, had turned him into a seasoned political administrator."

At the same time he looked so handsome that it was easy to notice only the surface charm. Franklin had aged somewhat in appearance, but newspapers still compared him to a matinee idol. "Roosevelt has a bearing that William Faversham might envy," declared the New York *Herald*. "His face is long, finely shaped, and set with marks of confidence. . . . A firm, thin mouth breaks into a laugh, openly and freely."

But the Franklin Roosevelt who performed such prodigies of endeavor for his country in wartime was not the big-shouldered figure of his later years. He stood a slender six-foot-two, weighing only 170 pounds. It has been said that the Franklin of those years was a taut man rather than a solid one. Even with the buoyant Roosevelt energy he still gave an impression of mercurial vitality— a man who could burn himself out.

At this moment the really rugged Roosevelt appeared to be Alice Roosevelt Longworth. With the death of her adored father, the onetime Princess Alice had seized the flaming torch of his hatred for Woodrow Wilson. Alice was now a woman in her late thirties, who bounded up flights of stairs two, even three, at a time. She had inherited her father's love of reading, and seemed to devour books rather than sleep through Washington nights. She was a voluble and erudite talker, and any who failed to recognize her familiar face would know her by the huge handbags she carried.

As the wife of an important congressman from Ohio—a man destined, it was said, for the House Speakership—and herself an important Washington figure, Alice Longworth was well equipped to battle the League proposal. By day she occupied a favored seat in the Senate gallery and waved encouragement to her cohorts. By night she did yeoman service by turning her Washington townhouse into a headquarters for the Battalion of Death, a name given to the anti-League forces headed by Henry Cabot Lodge and Democratic Senator James Reed of Missouri.

At home Alice employed her great prestige, magnetic personality, and trenchant sarcasm to win new recruits for the Death Battalion and to keep old members in line. At last the forces of Death won the fight, and as much as anyone Alice Roosevelt Longworth, her father's daughter, deserves credit for this doubtful victory.

Defeat of the League forces, together with the country's desire for a return to what Warren Harding soon called "normalcy," foreshadowed a Republican victory in the election of 1920. This, of course, would mark the end of prominence for Franklin D. Roosevelt. Yet for a brief moment the coming campaign raised his prestige.

Franklin traveled to the San Francisco convention as a member of the New York delegation, and again his good looks and personality commanded immediate attention. He made himself more conspicuous on the opening day of the convention when, to begin the proceedings, a huge oil painting of Woodrow Wilson was unveiled behind the platform. Delegates rose and began a cheering snake-dance through the hall. Only the Tammany-dominated New York delegation sat mute, while the marchers exhorted, "Come on, New York!" It was more than delegate Franklin could bear.

Leaping from his seat, he wrenched the New York standard from the hands of a Tammany stalwart. Holding it high, he joined the milling throng.

Franklin favored Alfred E. Smith of New York as the Democratic candidate, and was given the job of seconding his nomination. Smith lost and James M. Cox of Ohio was picked as the nominee. Cox was a middle-of-the-roader, closely associated with neither Wilson, nor the League. Like his opponent, Warren G. Harding, he came from Ohio, where he was a newspaper publisher and governor of the state (the handsome Harding, also a newspaper publisher, was senator). Governor Cox now had to pick his Vice-President and was advised to take Roosevelt who would neatly balance the ticket: Franklin had been closely associated with Wilson and the League, he was a liberal Democrat, he bore a vote-getting name.

Cox approved but ordered, "Clear it with Tammany."

Boss Murphy of Tammany had little love for Franklin, but he was pleased by the gesture. "This is the first time a Democratic candidate for the Presidency has shown me courtesy," he declared. "I don't like Roosevelt, but now I'd vote for the devil himself if Cox asked me." Next day Franklin was nominated by acclamation.

Said Franklin, "The action in San Francisco was the greatest possible surprise to me, and has entirely upset my plans for a peaceful summer." At Campobello, Eleanor was equally astonished when an emotional telegram from Josephus Daniels brought the news. Franklin quickly recovered from his surprise and began to concoct ambitious plans. "If things go through on November second," he vowed, "I am going to make an effort to put the job of Vice-President on the map for the first time in history." Among other things he planned to ask Cox for permission to sit in on Cabinet meetings. For the moment he concentrated on persuading the candidate to wage a vigorous campaign. Then he hastened back to Hyde Park for the notification ceremonies. On that afternoon 5,000 people trampled the gracious grounds of Springwood, which up to now had never been host to more than a lawn party.

In the 1920 campaign Franklin made nearly a thousand speeches and in every possible way exerted himself for the Democratic cause. Though a far more colorful man than Cox, he managed to make himself conspicuous without overshadowing the presidential candidate. From a campaign-special railroad car, he delivered speeches in cities, towns, and whistle stops. Everywhere women crowded around him and praised his good looks and charm. Franklin made a special point of getting to know the lowly campaign workers and from them learned for the first time, so Frances Perkins believes, that the average voter cared less about exalted issues than about jobs, family security, and a comfortable future.

Leaving each crowd, he grinned his confident grin and urged, "Come and see me some time!" This was the first election in which women were permitted to vote, and Eleanor rode with him in the private car trying hard not to notice the fuss other women made over her husband. Once again Louis McHenry Howe prodded her to take greater interest in politics. While the men on the train—among them Stephen Early, on leave from the AP, and Marvin McIntyre—sat together planning strategy, Howe carried speeches to Eleanor and asked her opinion. Gradually her voice was heard in campaign councils.

Franklin was often mistaken for Theodore's son by old Bull Moosers, who shouted, "I voted for your old man and I'll vote for you!" Or, "You're just like your old man!"

This bothered Republicans, who put Colonel Theodore Roosevelt, Jr., on the campaign trail to set matters straight. After a speech at Sheridan, Wyoming, Theodore Jr. was asked to explain the presence of a Roosevelt on the opposing ticket. "Franklin is a maverick," snapped Theodore. "He does not have the brand of our family."

This constitutes the first recorded breach of any kind between the two families. Eleanor, so closely connected with both, seems to have resented it most. According to some sources, she refused to speak to Theodore Jr. for years. In a short time the breach widened when Nicholas Longworth called Franklin a "denatured Roosevelt"—a remark that sounds more like viperish Alice than gentle Nick.

Eventually the score was evened by that peerless lady, Sara Delano Roosevelt. One day a friend asked her why the Oyster Bay branch seemed to hate her family. Sara gave a charitable sigh. "Perhaps," she murmured, "it is because we are so much better looking than they are."

In campaigning for the Vice-Presidency, Franklin radiated buoyant optimism. But when Marvin McIntyre asked him if he had any real illusions about winning, the candidate replied, "Nary an illusion." So defeat by the Harding-Coolidge ticket may not have been too great a blow to him, though it was a shattering defeat, giving the Republicans a plurality of 7,000,000 votes. "It wasn't a landslide, it was an earthquake," lamented Joseph P. Tumulty, secretary to Woodrow Wilson.

When the victorious Harding unveiled the list of his appointments, Theodore Roosevelt, Jr., proudly occupied the post of Assistant Secretary of the Navy. It seemed a proper choice to everyone but an admiral who groaned, "I have had to stand two Roosevelts—I cannot stand another!" Theodore Jr., the new golden boy of the clan, confided to intimates that his next step was to run for governor of New York.

For Franklin it marked the end of an eleven-year road. Whether he thought of some day returning to politics is an interesting question. To Stephen Early, about to go back to newspaper work, he made the cryptic remark, "Thank God, we are both comparatively youthful!" On the surface, though, politics appeared to vanish from his mind. Having paralleled the career of Cousin Theodore for eleven years, he now moved into the pattern set by his own father.

During his days as state senator he had helped organize the law firm of Marvin, Hooker and Roosevelt. This was reactivated as Emmet, Marvin and Roosevelt, with Franklin a working partner. His friend Van Lear Black had also appointed him vice-president and Eastern district manager of the Fidelity and Deposit Company of Maryland, a large bonding and insurance firm. For this position alone Franklin's salary was $25,000 a year. With his inheritance and law practice he was in a position to command some $50,000 a year, with excellent opportunities for investment on the side.

So the role of medium-sized capitalist so gracefully enacted by James appeared ready for him. Franklin and his family would spend weekdays in New York, weekends at Hyde Park, summer vacations at Campobello. His children were growing, with young James already at Groton. Springwood had been enlarged in 1915, and Sara still owned the two houses on Sixty-fifth Street.

Though Franklin and Eleanor had often gone through long periods away from each other while he served in Washington, they were still close. He affectionately addressed her as "Babs," and wrote to her as "Dearest Honey." She had joined the children in calling him "Pa." Indeed, Franklin may have viewed his wife through rose-colored glasses. One day he showed Frances Perkins a pastel portrait of Eleanor that made her look young and vapidly sweet. "It's very pretty," Miss Perkins commented politely. "Yes," he responded. "I always liked it. It's just the way Eleanor looks—lovely hair, pretty eyes."

Sara Roosevelt's pleasure at having her son return to the Hyde Park-New York orbit may well be imagined. James's widow still believed that mother knows best and regarded her thirty-nine-year-old offspring as a mere boy. She never failed to ask if he was warmly dressed when he left the house. There was a strong bond of love and admiration between mother and son, but the two strong-willed people were often at odds. Eleanor soon learned the peril of leaving them alone together during differences of opinion. Before long voices would be raised in heated argument.

It is doubtful that Franklin Roosevelt was ever bored by life, and the existence opening before him seemed both stimulating and a relaxing shift from the rigidities of government. He did not intend to neglect public life and had already accepted several honorary posts, among them chairman of the Boy Scouts of

Greater New York and Overseer of Harvard. He plunged into this new world with his usual vigor, working at the insurance office in the morning and at the law office in the afternoon.

But to Eleanor, if not to Franklin, all this was anticlimactic. "I had long ceased to be dependent on my mother-in-law," she wrote. "I was thinking things out for myself and becoming an individual." To occupy her time, she took a course in shorthand and typing, another in cooking. She joined the League of Women Voters and as in Junior League days was immediately pushed into work that immensely broadened her life. Since Eleanor had been the wife of an important government official, the League ladies considered her an ideal person to keep track of Washington legislation as wheels began turning under the Republicans. Eleanor was still politically naïve, but two experienced women were assigned to instruct her.

Thus Eleanor watched as forces gathered to deal her husband an underhand blow. Indeed, this shapes into one of the curious and portentous episodes in Franklin's life. During his tenure as Assistant Navy Secretary, liquor and drugs had been found in the possession of personnel at the Newport, Rhode Island, navy base. More, young sailors were being tempted down paths of homosexuality. Roosevelt appointed an investigation board to clean up conditions at Newport. Without telling him, the board used sailors as decoys to trap the homosexuals. The story leaked to the press and Republicans accused Franklin of direct responsibility for the tactic. He denied it and ordered the board to stop.

With Republicans back in office, a Senate Investigation Committee had reopened the old scandal in an effort to discredit the previous administration. LAY NAVY SCANDAL TO F. D. ROOSEVELT —DETAILS UNPRINTABLE, the *New York Times* headlined. The Senate Committee promised a public hearing during which Franklin could present his side of the case.

In June, 1921, he sent his family to Campobello as usual, then waited in New York through July for a summons to testify in

Washington. On July 31 he learned that the committee planned to release its report without hearing him. "He was galled and infuriated," says one account, but the words seem mild. Franklin was furiously angry—his Dutch was indeed up! Still the committee was adamant and there was nothing he could do but fume helplessly.

He visited Washington, then returned to New York for a few more days. Before starting the trip to join the family at Campobello, he spent a day on a chairman's visit to the Boy Scout camp at Bear Mountain. Then he took a train for Boston, where he boarded Van Lear Black's yacht for the trip to Campobello.

The polio attack that hit Franklin Roosevelt a few days later had the knell of deepest tragedy.

Possibly the first factor contributing to it had been Franklin's failure to associate with rough-and-tumble children as a boy. By keeping to his aristocratic playmates he had been sheltered from the barrage of disease germs which immunizes most children. Then, although Franklin seemed outwardly healthy, he had suffered an unusual number of serious illnesses as a man. Following his five-week attack of typhoid in 1912 he had had acute appendicitis, lumbago, tonsillitis, pneumonia, double pneumonia, and influenza, together with frequent sinus attacks and head colds which may have been caused by the overdose of chloroform at birth. In December, 1919, his tonsils had been removed, and after that he seemed less prone to sickness.

Other factors may also have contributed to the polio attack. For one, the pre-polio Franklin was a fellow who worked off anger by furious activity. "When Father was mad," writes his son James, "his way of working off steam was through an outpouring of physical vigor." Seething fury over the Washington vice charges drove him to new and tiring extremes. In the midst of this he made the visit to the Bear Mountain Boy Scout camp, and a strong possibility exists that he picked up the actual polio germ from a Boy Scout.

Arriving at Campobello, he was still angrily driving himself. On the afternoon of August 9, roughhousing with his boys on the deck of the Black yacht, he toppled off into the freezing Bay of Fundy. He laughed this off as a great joke, but the icy waters dealt his body a severe shock.

The next afternoon he took Anna, James, and Elliott out in his small sailboat *Vireo*. On an island close to Campobello they spied a forest fire. The four landed, cut evergreen boughs, and spent several hours vigorously fighting it. Back on Campobello, a hot, weary Franklin suggested a refreshing dip in Lake Glen Severn, a mile and a half away. With the children after him, he ran at dogtrot to the lake. The swim failed to invigorate him—the only time in his life this had happened, he told Eleanor on his return to the cottage. So he suggested another dip into the colder waters of the bay. In wet bathing suits, the four finally jogged back to the house.

Here Franklin found his daily mail and newspapers. Out of doors, still wearing the damp bathing suit in air turning chill, he sat and read for thirty minutes. All at once a shattering chill and sharp pains shot through him. He went to bed. Next morning he was feverish and still in pain. He also complained that his right leg was weak. When he tried to get up, the right knee buckled. Next, both legs became affected. By the third day the paralysis had spread to nearly every muscle from the chest down.

The knell of tragedy continued as doctors examined him. This was an era alert to the presence of infantile paralysis, and Franklin himself had been terrified that one of his own children might catch the disease. During the infantile paralysis epidemic of 1919 he sent a navy destroyer to Campobello to bring his family home, to avoid the exposure of a long railroad journey. Yet the first doctor, a local man, summoned to his bedside diagnosed the illness as a deep cold and chill.

When the pain and paralysis spread, an eminent physician vacationing at Bar Harbor was called. He concluded that "a clot of blood from a sudden congestion had settled in the lower spinal cord, removing the power to move." He recommended deep massage of the affected regions, and the difficult chore was diligently performed by Eleanor and Louis Howe. It has been called a tragic mistake. Eleanor herself suspected polio and relayed her fears to Uncle Fred Delano, who was in Newport. He persuaded a Boston specialist to make the trip to Campobello. At last, ten days after the initial attack, Franklin's illness was correctly diagnosed.

He was suffering hideous pain, the nerves of his body and legs so sensitive that weight of a sheet was excruciating. The doctor put wire hoops between body and bedclothes and ordered a regime of hot baths. But even in his worst moments Franklin realized that the illness was a terrible shock to his young children, and he tried to grin as they fearfully peered in through the doorway of his bedroom at Campobello. By words and attitude he attempted to give the impression of confidence in a quick recovery. "Terrible as it was for him," recalls James, "he had the mental depth and compassion to realize how overwhelmingly frightening it was for his children, and he tried to lighten *our* fears."

In mid-September four strong men carried Franklin by stretcher to a motor boat for the two-mile chug across water to the mainland. Here the stretcher was passed through the window of a private car sent by faithful Uncle Fred.

Franklin was as helpless as a baby. Yet his favorite hat was cocked on his head, a cigarette in a holder jutted from his tight-clenched teeth, and he cradled his pet Scottie in his arms. He put up a brave front, smiling and waving to his silent children. From outside the railroad car only his head was visible, and for the moment he looked like the debonair F.D.R. of old.

At Presbyterian Hospital in New York his sickness was diagnosed as acute anterior poliomyelitis. The pain increased as his legs started to jackknife and casts were placed on them to arrest the process. For weeks it seemed that his back, arms, and hands would be paralyzed, but slowly they improved. The legs, however, stayed limp and useless. Through it all Franklin showed amazing fortitude, but later he confessed that waves of despair had engulfed him and he had decided that God had forgotten his existence.

By Christmas, 1921, Franklin was well enough to be taken by ambulance to the Sixty-fifth Street house, where his bedroom had been equipped with a trapeze and exercise rings over the bed. As rapidly as possible he began to crawl and Indian wrestle with his boys. It was a moment of triumph when at last he was able to get upstairs on hands and knees.

While laboring to restore life to his dead legs Franklin was the focal figure in what John Gunther calls "a battle to the finish between two remarkable women for Franklin's soul." Sara Roosevelt had never ceased her efforts to dominate her son's life, and now she saw one more opportunity to pin him under her maternal thumb. Sara had been in Europe when Franklin was stricken, but on her return she made up her mind that he was a helpless invalid. She determined that he must lead the life of a crippled Hyde Park squire, forever removed from politics and the world.

Opposing her with deep determination was Eleanor, ably seconded by Louis Howe. From the start Eleanor's role in this family tragedy had been no less heroic than her husband's. She had, indeed, nursed the patient so well that doctors urged her to continue as head nurse. Eleanor had made up her mind that Franklin must be treated as a healthy man, never a sick one. Like him, she considered polio a purely physical matter—a bodily short circuit in no way affecting the brain. As fast as possible she got rid of nurses and banished signs of invalidism from the house.

Louis Howe had been on the verge of taking a well-paying job with an oil company. Now he spurned it, to devote the rest of his life to the man he called "the Boss." At Eleanor's suggestion Howe moved into a room of the Sixty-fifth Street house. Eleanor also faced the problem of bringing up five energetic children in a home where the once dominant father lay helpless.

With this went the clashes with Sara, of whom Eleanor wrote, "Her anxiety for his general health was such that she dreaded his making any effort whatsoever." Only once did Eleanor break down, and then she sobbed uncontrollably for hours. She recovered quickly, to face more battles with Sara. These became increasingly intense as Eleanor and Howe began bringing stimulating people home to see Franklin and so keep alive his interest in the outside world.

Over the next seven years Franklin Roosevelt progressed to the point where, legs locked in steel braces, he could first walk on crutches, then with a cane while leaning on a friendly arm. Indoors he was usually pushed in a wheelchair that was particularly small because of the narrow halls and doors at Springwood and Sixty-fifth Street. He could not stand or walk without the heavy, painful braces—and never did as long as he lived. Nor could he be left alone except to sleep. His slightest need required help from someone nearby.

Years later Eleanor was asked if she thought her husband would have achieved the Presidency without the polio attack. "Yes," she answered, "but he would have been a different kind of President."

One way to evaluate the change in Roosevelt is to say that before polio life had been a splendid game. Afterward it was a serious matter. In Eleanor's opinion, recovery from the attack brought her husband a strength and courage he had never demonstrated before, "for he had to think out the fundamentals of living and learn the greatest of all lessons: infinite patience and never-ending persistence." Frances Perkins sees the battle with polio as a "spiritual transformation."

Opposed to these two views is that of James Roosevelt, who thinks his father had his great courage before being stricken. "I believe that it was not the polio that forged Father's character," he writes, "but that it was Father's character that enabled him to rise above the affliction." James also thinks his father was headed for the Presidency and would have achieved the White House no matter what happened.

The fact remains, however, that Franklin truimphed mentally

and spiritually, if not physically, over his affliction—so much so that Robert E. Sherwood later called him the healthiest man he had ever known. Inability to use crippled legs did not change or inhibit his personality, though he was constantly reminded of restrictive handicaps. Franklin had been a restless type who liked to jump up and stride around. In the Navy Department he had loved to roam from office to office. Now he could not do this. It brought him an awesome patience, but at the same time he never ceased to be vexed when someone near him got up to pace.

One way Roosevelt worked off excess energy was by talking. In his days as President visitors to his office often found themselves inundated by an unexpected verbal barrage of Roosevelt reminiscence, humor, and opinion. Some were uneasy to find themselves taking up so much of the Chief Executive's time. John Gunther was one. He made repeated efforts to end his interview, but the President refused to let him go.

Roosevelt was never a bore—Gunther calls his talk "bright, sharp, chatty, and discursive." But in the early days of invalidism his immobility placed him at the mercy of boring talkers. In later years, with a large staff at his disposal, he devised stratagems for escaping the long-winded. But at first he spent many hours listening to them. In the process he discovered many curious crevices of human character, and again learned that people care most about their jobs, security, and personal happiness.

Roosevelt tried to swim himself back to health, for in water he was able to move his legs. He blamed the icy Bay of Fundy for his polio attack, and when swimming in a warm pool he would call out, "The water put me where I am and the water will bring me back!"

He first swam in the pool of his Dutchess County neighbor, Vincent Astor. Then a pool was built at Springwood. In the winters of 1922 and 1923, Franklin cruised with a Harvard classmate on a 71-foot houseboat off the Florida coast. Finally, in 1924, he learned of Warm Springs, Georgia, where the waters remain a constant 88 degrees the year round and have exceptional buoyancy. Until a short time before, Warm Springs had been called Bullochville in honor of the family of Theodore Roosevelt's mother. In fact, a few Bullochs still lived in the area.

At Warm Springs, Franklin found a dilapidated resort with the faded charm of prebellum days. In the years that followed, many experts assured him that the Warm Springs waters contained no special therapeutic properties. Roosevelt never believed them.

While swimming or playing water polo at Warm Springs, Franklin felt certain that he could regain use of his legs. As a result, he began to spend long winter months there. Eleanor did not like Warm Springs, despite her Bulloch blood. Nor, amazingly, did Sara Roosevelt avail herself of this opportunity to be close to her son. Usually Franklin was accompanied to Warm Springs by Marguerite ("Missy") LeHand who had become his personal secretary shortly after the 1920 campaign. With the help of Miss LeHand he worked on a history of *Old Ironsides* which, when completed, he vainly tried to sell to a Hollywood studio. In time the story of *Old Ironsides* was made into a film, and Franklin always felt that some parts of the scenario had been stolen from him.

The arrival of a onetime vice-presidential candidate at an obscure Georgia resort was the stuff of newspaper stories, and to visiting reporters Franklin described his high hopes for recovery. This attracted other polio victims, young and old. To them all Franklin became "Dr." Roosevelt as he zestfully taught new arrivals the restorative exercises he had learned or devised himself. He also supervised the installation of manual controls in a Model T Ford and drove briskly over country roads.

As time passed he and the other polio sufferers grew annoyed by the guests at the resort hotel, most of whom looked down on the "polios" and thought the disease contagious. To rid the place of these unsympathetic folk, Franklin drew $200,000—nearly all his money—out of the bank and purchased the 1,200 Warm Springs acres to serve as a hydrotherapeutic resort. It was incorporated as a nonprofit enterprise known as the Georgia Warm Springs Foundation.

Ever in the background was politics. . . .

From his headquarters in the Roosevelt household, Louis McHenry Howe strove mightily to keep the name of the Boss alive in the public consciousness. As early as November, 1921, with Franklin at his sickest in Presbyterian Hospital, Democratic winners of the New York State election received what appeared to be personal letters of congratulations from the stricken man. In the next few years Howe and Roosevelt sent thousands of letters to every part of the country, congratulating winners or commiserating with losers. The two kept in close touch with both state chairmen and lowly precinct leaders, asking advice and making inquiries in Franklin's name. As he traveled to and from Warm Springs, Franklin never failed to stop off in Washington, seeking out Democratic congressmen. In Georgia he kept in friendly touch with local politicos.

Guiding him in this was Howe, who simultaneously pushed Eleanor deeper into the fray. She had now joined the staff of the Todhunter School, where she instructed girls from top-drawer families in literature, history, and current events. Howe urged her to become an active member of the State Democratic Committee and to begin making speeches. For days he worked with her to eliminate a nervous giggle which vitiated her first efforts as a public speaker.

In 1924 Roosevelt was functioning (always with the shadowy Howe) as head of New York's Al Smith-for-President forces. The Democratic National Convention would be held at Madison Square Garden during the summer and he determined to make his first public appearance since his illness by personally nominating Smith. He was a delegate, making daily appearances at what turned out to be the longest political convention in American history. Three years had passed since the polio attack and he could walk slowly and awkwardly by propping a crutch under his right arm while gripping another person's arm with his left hand. As he did this, his legs were locked rigidly in steel braces. Forward movement was accomplished by pivoting with arms and torso and throwing his body ahead by brute strength.

For the speech nominating Smith, Franklin insisted on taking the ten steps to the speaker's stand alone on two crutches—the first time he had ever attempted such a feat. He practiced for weeks walking with braces and crutches and holding tight to a lectern for long periods.

On the day of the speech sixteen-year-old James assisted him to the rear of the platform. "Outwardly," James recalls, "he was beaming, seemingly confident and unconcerned, but I could sense his inner tenseness. His fingers dug into my arms like pincers." The strain became apparent as Roosevelt brusquely ordered a man on the platform to test the lectern to make sure it would support his weight. Then he seized the second crutch and swung forward. As he propelled himself, Franklin looked pale and drawn. But on reaching the lectern his face broke into a wide, flashing grin and his head tossed back in the proud old gesture that once annoyed people but now seemed full of gallantry and courage.

Roosevelt had been the party's vice-presidential candidate four years earlier—a handsome, vibrant figure. Now, addressing the Garden throng, he looked brave and tragic. Even so, his effect on the crowd was amazing. He had been cheered daily on making a labored entry into the hall on the arm of son James. As a speaker, he was given a three-minute ovation. His voice, always warm and pleasant, had gained new resonance and vigor from the massive musculature exercise and swimming had developed in his chest, where all his bodily energy seemed centered. "You could always waltz to anything Roosevelt said," a musician remarked later. It was true on this humid day in 1924.

Roosevelt spoke for thirty-four minutes and ended by rousingly calling Smith "the Happy Warrior of the political battlefield." The crowd yelled for one hour and thirteen minutes, stopping only when Franklin reappeared to hold up a hand for silence. Through the rest of a dull convention he remained a shining figure. Said the New York *World*: "Adversity has lifted him above the bickering, the religious bigotry, conflicting personal ambitions, and petty sectional prejudices. . . . It has made him the one leader commanding the respect and admiration of delegations from all sections of the land."

As such a man, Franklin might have claimed the 1924 presidential nomination for himself, but he quickly nipped such talk by stating flatly, "I will not run for political office until I am able to walk without crutches." But his huge popularity was not enough to win the nomination for Al Smith, and John W. Davis was finally chosen as the Democratic candidate.

This left Smith free to run again for the New York governorship. Opposing him was Theodore Roosevelt, Jr., who had resigned as Assistant Secretary of the Navy to be succeeded by his first cousin, Theodore Douglas Robinson. It had been the ill-fortune of Theodore Jr. to be Assistant Secretary during the Teapot Dome oil scandal. He had not been directly involved, but in politics such subtleties never count. Eleanor was a member of the Democratic State Committee and with her approval a huge, steaming teapot was put on a truck and labeled TEAPOT DOME. This followed Theodore all around the state. He lost the election and not until much later did Eleanor decide that in approving the traveling teapot she had been guilty of poor sportsmanship.

Over the next four years Franklin lived in New York City, Warm Springs, and Hyde Park. (Not until 1933 could he bring himself to go back to Campobello.) In New York he managed to work a full day. Arising at 8:00 or 8:30, he exercised and ate breakfast, then met with Louis Howe or others until 10:30. After this a chauffeur drove him downtown to the Van Lear Black insurance office. Grace Tully, the second of his personal secretaries, was introduced to him at this point and recalls: "The vitality of his face contrasted sharply with the helplessness of his legs. . . . The first time I saw him lifted out of his wheelchair and carried by valet and chauffeur to a place in his automobile, I turned away and cried."

Roosevelt had wearied of the sedate trust and estate cases handled by the firm of Emmet, Marvin and Roosevelt and had joined with Basil O'Connor in a livelier practice. The firm was known as Roosevelt and O'Connor. At this point Franklin engaged in the private business ventures that later drew such ridicule from Republicans.

As a businessman no less than as a politician he was inclined to take risks, and some of his investments have a surrealist tinge. One was a company organized to carry freight between cities by dirigible. He wildcatted in Wyoming oil, speculated in German marks, backed resort hotels, and lost $25,000 in a venture to freeze Maine lobsters for a rise in the market. His proneness to plunge financially has been attributed to the fact that he could always fall back on Sallie's money. But in such ventures Franklin at least thought big, if a trifle unrealistically. And some of his projects—such as automatic vending machines and advertising in taxicabs—were well ahead of the times.

Franklin's main aim in life was still to regain use of his legs. By 1928 he had discarded crutches to walk with a cane and braces, holding onto another person. One day at Warm Springs he managed a few lurching steps without cane or supporting arm, though with the ever-present braces. It encouraged him enormously. Franklin truly believed that two more years of exercise in the Warm Springs waters would rebuild his muscles enough to make walking possible. Apparently Eleanor did not share this optimism, perhaps on the private advice of medical men.

Nineteen-twenty-eight was another political summer, and Franklin again determined to nominate Al Smith at the convention in Houston. He went there with his son Elliott. Once more the White Knight of the assemblage, he was described by journalist Will Durant:

Here on the stage is Franklin Roosevelt, beyond comparison the finest man that has appeared at either convention. . . . A figure tall and proud even in suffering; a face of classic profile; pale with years of struggle against paralysis; a frame nervous and yet self-controlled with that tense, taut unity of spirit which lifts the complex soul above those whose calmness is only a stolidity. . . . A man softened and cleansed and illumined with pain . . .

Franklin's speech nominating Smith was written with the radio audience in mind, showing an early awareness of the medium so important to him later on. This time the Happy Warrior was nominated on the first ballot.

Al Smith was a controversial figure, a far cry from the usual presidential candidate. He was a Roman Catholic; a steadfast Wet in a Dry era; a man whose sidewalks-of-New-York voice grated out "raddio" for radio; a snappy dresser who wore a brown derby. He had been an excellent governor of New York, and a pioneer in social reform. Still, with so many personality-strikes against him, it was doubtful that he would even carry his home state.

As time passed, Smith and his advisers could think of no man but Franklin who might be elected New York's Governor and also continue Smith's enlightened legislation. Knowing this, Franklin sent Eleanor to represent him at the state convention in Rochester. He went to Warm Springs, hoping to escape all pressure. He even stayed away from his cottage—prophetically named the Little White House—for fear Smith would reach him by telephone.

At Rochester, Roosevelt-for-Governor talk persisted. One who listened was F.D.R's daughter, Anna. Now Mrs. Curtis Dall, she had just made Franklin a grandfather for the first time. GO AHEAD AND TAKE IT! Anna wired Warm Springs. YOU OUGHT TO BE SPANKED! Franklin wired back. But eventually Al Smith got him on the telephone.

There are at least three wildly diverging versions of the phone call and its aftermath. One says Smith refused to leave the long-distance line until Roosevelt personally took his call. Franklin kept the presidential nominee waiting an hour at the end of a dead line, then accepted the call. Eleanor's story is that she put in the call to her husband and got him on the wire. Then she handed the phone to Smith and rushed from the hotel room. By far the most dramatic account comes from Frances Perkins, who remembers three calls placed by Eleanor at a rate of one a day. They clearly expose Franklin's thinking.

In the first call he said, "I'm not well enough to run. It's out of the question."

In the second, "I need another year of treatment and then I'll be as good as ever, ready to do whatever they ask me. But if I leave now I'll not get my health or strength back. It means just that. My health depends on it. It's now or never!"

In the third, Eleanor let Smith speak. "Frank, it's your duty," the Governor said in effect. He then told Roosevelt that the millionaire John J. Raskob stood ready to assist in further financing of the Warm Springs Foundation and thus relieve him of worries involved. Franklin asked to talk to Eleanor. "Do you think carrying New York depends on my running for Governor?" he asked.

"I'm afraid it does."

"It appears that they think I have an obligation to run. What do you think?"

Eleanor sidestepped. "I know it's hard, but that's what they believe," she replied. With this, Franklin agreed.

The decision ended his seven-year struggle to walk again, and he knew it. Yet no one ever learned how he felt about abandoning the fight. "I never heard him say later whether he regretted it or not," wrote Eleanor. "Having decided, he put any other possibility out of his mind."

At Warm Springs the other polios were miserable at losing the cheering presence of Dr. Roosevelt. In New York State, Republican newspapers charged that desperate Democrats had been driven to nominating a "sick" man. The experienced Al Smith snorted, "The Governor does not have to be an acrobat. We do not elect him for his ability to do double back-flips or a handspring. Ninety-nine percent of the work is accomplished at his desk."

Even the Democrats expected Franklin to wage an easy campaign. Yet he roared delightedly into full-time combat. All the old love of politics was there in greater measure. Much of his campaigning was done from the open back seat of a touring car. He spoke warmly, departing crowds with his old words, "Come and see me some time!" After the campaign many did. On only a few occasions in life did Roosevelt ever refer to his invalidism. But as Republicans continued to hammer at it, he greeted a crowd at Syracuse by saying, "Well, here's that helpless, hopeless invalid my opponents have been talking about. I have made fifteen speeches today. This will be the sixteenth."

On the national level, intrepid Al Smith was in trouble. Not only did his religion and urban personality work against him, but his opponents added libels which said he planned to invite the Pope to Washington.

On election night, Roosevelt and Smith sat watching returns which added up to a Democratic defeat. Smith had lost the nation and New York State as well. Roosevelt, too, appeared to be a loser, and before rural returns were in he returned to Sixty-fifth Street. A few intimates believe Franklin gave up so readily because he wished to lose and be free to continue his efforts at walking. Missy LeHand was among those who believed this and she herself hoped for a Roosevelt defeat.

Frances Perkins left with the family but, after bidding them good night, listened to an inner voice which told her to return to Democratic headquarters at the Hotel Biltmore. There—in an incredible scene—she found Sara Delano Roosevelt, seated alone, unwilling to admit until the last vote was tallied that her darling boy had lost the election. A look at the board told Miss Perkins that the dowager Sara might be right, for rural returns were showing a slow trend toward Franklin. By early dawn Roosevelt was a victor by 25,000 votes, and his mother and Miss Perkins were among the very few who knew it.

With Franklin in the Governor's chair, Roosevelt life went on much as before. Eleanor still taught at the Todhunter School, while the family wrestled with the kind of problems that beset other American families. In 1929 Franklin wrote a friend:

This family is going through the usual tribulations. James is getting over pneumonia; Elliott is about to have an operation; Franklin Jr.

has a doubly broken nose and John has just had a cartilage taken out
of his knee! Anna and her husband . . . are taking a short holiday in
Europe and their baby is parked with us at the Executive Mansion.
Eleanor is teaching school two and a half days a week in New York,
and I am in one continuous glorious fight with Republican legislative
leaders. So you see that it is a somewhat hectic life.

In Washington Alice Roosevelt Longworth was making a career
of enlivening the capital city. Princess Alice, now wife of the
Speaker of the House of Representatives, chafed at the boredom of
Washington under phlegmatic Herbert Hoover. An opportunity
to brighten her world was soon furnished by Vice-President
Charles Curtis. An unmarried man, Curtis needed a hostess for
his own dinner parties and a partner for others. He named his
sister, Mrs. Dolly Gann, his official hostess. This gave Mrs. Gann
the privilege of sitting at President Hoover's right at any functions
not attended by Mrs. Hoover.

Alice, who had been steeped in Washington protocol from the
age of seventeen, insisted this could not be. Why, there was no such
thing as an *appointed* official hostess! As the wife of the Speaker of
the House, *she* should be seated at the President's side in his wife's
absence. It was also her privilege to precede Mrs. Gann at all
times. Alice raised such an uproar over this matter of protocol
that it landed in the lap of the President, who hastily consulted
the diplomatic corps. The corps lived up to its name by creating a
rule permitting the appointment of a political hostess. With this,
irate Princess Alice played her trump card. She refused to attend
any dinners at which Mrs. Gann would be present. This proved
catastrophic, for a successful Washington dinner without acidulous Alice was unthinkable.

Having made her point and perhaps enjoyed a loud laugh,
Alice resumed attendance at Washington dinner parties. But in
the boom days of 1929 the Alice Longworth-Dolly Gann feud was
a sensation.

Life was closer to the real and earnest in another Oyster Bay
branch. Theodore Roosevelt, Jr., had been named Governor of
Puerto Rico by President Hoover. After successfully handling this

post, he was dispatched to the Philippines to be Governor General there. From both faraway places Theodore received an unusual amount of publicity in the American press. He was often seen in photographs showing him in white tropical attire, his friendly features creased by a grin. Apparently Theodore's Republican relatives nursed hopes that he would succeed President Hoover in 1936.

The Wall Street collapse of 1929 and the emergence of Franklin as a national figure ended such dreams. Franklin was elected for a second term in 1930, and with this his eyes were clearly beamed on the Presidency. Louis McHenry Howe had been joined in the inner circle of advisers by Judge Samuel I. Rosenman; James A. Farley, former state boxing commissioner; and Edward J. Flynn, boss of the Bronx.

Their efforts reached an exciting climax in 1932, in a country ravaged by depression. There were 14,000,00 Americans unemployed. "Brother, Can You Spare a Dime?" was the doleful song of the moment, and the nation had become only too familiar with breadlines, soup kitchens, apple selling on street corners, and shanty towns where the unemployed slept in packing cases and discarded cars. The shanty towns were called Hoovervilles, in honor of the unhappy President trying to stem the gradual economic collapse. Hoover had created a Reconstruction Finance Corporation and supported federal aid to states. But nothing the President did seemed to work. The national mood was one of quiet desperation, yet there were no cries for violence. "The American people seemed benumbed," writes James MacGregor Burns.

On the night of July 1, Roosevelt sat comfortably in a leather chair in the Executive Mansion at Albany. By his side was a radio tuned to the Democratic National Convention in Chicago. Within easy reach stood a telephone connected directly to Chicago, where a loudspeaker amplified his voice to rally those working to help him win the presidential nomination. In his files were several speeches already written for him to deliver during the campaign.

However, there were a few anxious moments to be lived

through. Nineteen-thirty-two looked like a year in which any Democrat might win, and Al Smith, Newton D. Baker, Governor Ritchie of Maryland, John Nance Garner of Texas, and others were hungry for the nomination. The New York delegation was steadfastly pro-Smith, a considerable blow to Roosevelt prestige. A two-thirds majority was needed, and for a moment the Roosevelt forces appeared to reach peak strength. Then slowly it began to recede. Behind the scenes a frantic deal offered Garner the Vice-Presidency. The Texan accepted, giving Roosevelt his majority. The convention band played "Happy Days Are Here Again," which would now be F.D.R.'s campaign song, and in Albany the Governor sank blissfully back in his leather chair. Around him the assembled family and secretaries hugged one another and tossed paper into the air. Finally Eleanor said, "I'm going to make some ham and eggs."

Instead of accepting the nomination at home, as was traditional, F.D.R. chartered a two-motor plane and set off with family and staff on a hazardous three-stop flight to Chicago. At the convention he stood before the crowd and promised, "I pledge you, I pledge myself, to a new deal for the American people." Not until the next day, when newspapers seized on these two words, did new deal become New Deal.

To prepare for the rigors of the coming campaign, Roosevelt rented a 40-foot yawl and took a weeklong cruise with three of his sons as crew. As the campaign progressed, he added a group of idealistic college professors like Raymond Moley, Rexford G. Tugwell, and A. A. Berle, Jr., to his staff—later they were to be called the Brain Trust. Historians have remarked that in campaign speeches he did not spell out the more revolutionary features of the New Deal. Yet Roosevelt was determined to win the election and trimmed his speeches accordingly. In New York he had already established a Temporary Emergency Relief Administration which channeled $20,000,000 to despairing citizens. Other aspects of the New Deal were forecast in a speech at the Commonwealth Club in San Francisco.

Political reporters noted that crowds listened almost silently, without giving vent to the usual campaign hullabaloo. For once, it seemed, the country wanted to hear every syllable a candidate uttered. Though his own life was comfortable from a financial standpoint—it had been made more so when brother Rosy died in 1927, leaving him another hundred thousand dollars—Franklin still seemed to understand the plight of the average American, whom he now called "the forgotten man." In him voters seemed to see not only a potential leader but a friend.

His nomination aroused the full venom of the Oyster Bay Roosevelts, and from Washington Alice Roosevelt Longworth hurled fiery barbs at her two cousins. But for the moment she was topped by quiet Edith Carow Roosevelt, who was quoted as saying, "Franklin is nine-tenths mush and one-tenth Eleanor." Two members of the Oyster Bay clan remained friendly, however. They were Corinne Roosevelt Robinson and Teddy's son Kermit, who after writing several adventure books, had settled in the shipping business.

But for the most part Oyster Bay reactions were expressed by Mary Willis Roosevelt, widow of the financier James. Dipping her pen deep in scorn, she wrote a letter to the relative she addressed as "Dear Franklyn":

I shall not sail under any false colors, but tell you that, because of your running mate, your silly attitude about that "forgotten man" and all the rest, that you have said about the President, in your very bad political strategy, in attacking him, a thing that has always been considered bad form in politics, I am unreservedly against you.

James, who saw hundreds of men a week in his work said, there were no "forgotten men" but plenty who thought they were owed something for *nothing*, was dead against such ideas of socialistic patting them on the back, as you were handing out. You have only belittled yourself by talking like this, and I know many people who, because of it, have decided they will *not* vote for you.

In his rejoinder Franklin first evened matters by addressing "Dear Marye." Then he wrote:

Thank you very much for writing to me. It is good to hear from you. I am sorry that you feel as you do, but I must tell you quite frankly that it never really occurred to me that you would vote for me.

In November Franklin carried forty-two states and won 472 electoral votes. His strenuous experience in the Navy Department, his courage during the polio attack, his instinctive love of trial and error, his native-born confidence—these had combined to bring him to the point of believing that there was a solution for any problems, even a depression. "If you have spent two years in bed trying to wiggle your big toe, everything else seems easy," he said once.

With such feelings, he had to wait four months, until March 4, while the country sank lower and lower into the economic mire. As Inauguration Day neared, the number of unemployed swelled to 17,000,00 and—most alarming of all—the nation's banks were failing.

One of Franklin's last acts as a civilian was to attend the funeral of Corinne Roosevelt Robinson. Then he boarded the train for Washington, to become the thirty-second President of the United States. As he did so, Franklin Roosevelt was completely himself. For reasons since forgotten, his Dutch was up against the Pennsylvania Railroad and he insisted on crossing the Hudson by ferry, to ride in a private train on the tracks of the Baltimore and Ohio.

During the train trip he sought solitude. "I have always thought my husband's religion had something to do with his confidence in himself," Eleanor wrote later. "He believed in God and His guidance." As the train clacked toward Washington and the heaviest problems ever faced by an American President, Franklin was discovered by James A. Farley seated alone in the rear of the observation car. "He started to talk along spiritual lines," Farley recalls, "his faith in God, the necessity of Divine guidance. He spoke very spiritually. It made a great impression on me."

17

THE SECOND PRESIDENT

FRANKLIN DELANO ROOSEVELT took the oath of office as President of the United States with one hand resting on his family's old Dutch Bible. Between its covers lay entries of births and deaths in the handwriting of Isaac Roosevelt and others of the line. The Bible was open to First Corinthians: "faith, hope, and charity, these three; but the greatest of these is charity."

It was six minutes after one o'clock, March 4, 1933, a gray Saturday when the country seemed—like New Amsterdam before the arrival of Peter Stuyvesant in 1647—to have reached its nadir. For now in a multitude of crises, a thousand farms were being foreclosed each day and the majority of the country's banks were shut. Time seemed to be running out for the United States, with only Franklin D. Roosevelt—seven generations removed from sturdy Claes Martenszen van Rosenvelt—in a position to stem the decline.

The country's economic plight at the time has been compared to a Gordian knot which an unhappy Herbert Hoover had desperately been attempting to untie. In his inauguration speech, Roosevelt indicated that he planned to slice the Gordian knot rather than untie it. He opened with ringing phrases: "This great nation will endure, as it has endured, will survive and will prosper. So first of all let me assert my belief that the only thing we have to fear is fear itself." He viewed the nation's problem mainly as a breakdown of material matters: "Plenty is at our doorstep, but a generous use of it languishes in the very sight of supply." He spoke with uplifting confidence and actually seemed eager to shoulder the enormous burdens of a Depression Presidency. Of the mandate that had put him in office he declared, "In the spirit of the gift, I take it!"

The ceremonies over, he vanished into the White House, where members of his own staff and stay-over Republicans labored night and day through the weekend to stem the tide of economic disaster. One of Roosevelt's first acts was to order that a member of the Roosevelt family or the presidential staff remain close to the White House telephone every night. Thus when a desperate citizen put in a call to the President, he would speak to a responsible member of the Administration.

Roosevelt knew the American people demanded action—any action—and his first forward step was to declare a bank holiday, which closed all the nation's banks. "This is the happiest day in three years," quipped humorist Will Rogers. "We have no jobs, we have no money, we have no banks; and if he had burned down the Capitol, we would have said, 'Thank God, he started a fire under something!'"

Most historians who have scrutinized the family that produced two Presidents in a little over thirty years have concluded that Franklin Roosevelt, no less than Theodore, was a phenomenon of nature, an inexplicable figure in a sedate family line. As one writer says, "In the seventh generation this dynasty of the mediocre suddenly blazed up with not one, but two, of the most remarkable men in American history."

But is this true of Franklin? Without belittling the Theodore branch of the family it seems possible to say that Franklin's ancestors provided him with a heritage that should make an American President. In Theodore's case, a demon energy caused him to burst loose from a pattern of Roosevelts who for the most part remained comfortably within their orbit of wealth. Franklin, too, broke loose from orbit. But energy was not the primary reason for his doing so. Rather, Franklin's advance to the Presidency seems the inevitable progress of a wellborn, strong, clever man.

Indeed, it may be asked: *If Franklin Roosevelt was not a type to be President, who was?* Nearly all his ancestors from Nicholas on had contributed time and talent to serving the city of New York, Dutchess County, or the nation. On Theodore's side, this ideal of public service had been channeled into hospitals and personal good works. Franklin's ancestors, though they had charities, were more sensitive to the world. From Isaac on, each male of the line had been intelligent in his fashion, several cuts indeed above a dynasty of the mediocre. To this, both Franklin's mother and grandmother brought the rousing blood of Yankee traders.

From the males and females of his line, he inherited a buoyant, optimistic temperament, a resourceful mind, and unusual charm. The family wealth added a background of comfort which brought personal confidence and freedom to think independently. From his forebears—the Roosevelts especially—he also got the deep religious strain that never failed to nourish his spirit in times of stress. With this went the moral fiber to lead a moral life. Finally, the existence he himself had chosen gave him an apprenticeship in politics unusual for a man his age.

Still there is one aspect of Franklin that cannot be explained on a basis of heredity. It is, in fact, as mystifying as Theodore's torrent of energy. This is Franklin's comprehension of, and interest in, the struggles of the average citizen. If in Theodore the family energy turned inside out, Franklin upset the Roosevelt pattern by understanding the rest of humanity. Few Roosevelts, Aspinwalls, or Delanos before him had shown more than a token concern about their fellow men. As fortunate folk, these families took an interest in community affairs and distributed charity and largess to the local families around them. Yet this always remained an aristocrat's interest.

In Franklin's case it became a real concern about other people.

He had always responded to his fellow human beings and derived many of his best ideas from contact with the more intelligent among them. At the same time he was sympathetic toward the people as a whole. As Eleanor wrote, "Throughout Franklin's life there never was any deviation from his original objective—to help make life better for the average man, woman, and child. A thousand and one means were used, difficulties arose, changes took place, but this objective was always the motive for whatever had to be done."

Where did this instinct come from—how did a born aristocrat possess such humane feelings? A few biographers credit his boyhood tutor, Mlle. Sandoz, with planting seeds of liberalism. But if this had been the case, the young man should have gone through a period of liberalism, or even radicalism, in college. Franklin did not. On the other hand, Theodore may deserve much of the credit, for when Frances Perkins first met Franklin he was a young man who shared her excitement over Theodore's brand of Progressivism. Contact with navy yard workers during World War I may have alerted young F.D.R. to the common man's struggle to survive.

But however the thoughts started, they had certainly taken root by the time he served as Assistant Secretary of the Navy. During one Hyde Park weekend in 1917 Sara Roosevelt undertook to lecture her son and daughter-in-law on the responsibilities of the American aristocrat. Surprisingly, Eleanor and Franklin talked back to her, declaring that the days of the aristocracy were numbered. This so upset the dowager that she was unable to go to bed after Franklin and Eleanor left for Washington. Instead she sat up writing her son a long letter deploring his acceptance of what she called "the trend to shirt sleeves." In conclusion she wrote, "I do not feel that my precious Franklin really feels as he expressed himself."

No doubt Roosevelt's polio attack further sharpened his compassion toward humanity, and afterward he fraternized more often with his earthy Hyde Park farm neighbors. He was never the type of reader who might have attained greater depth from the books of deep thinkers, but during the long days of recuperation he undoubtedly pondered many matters that might not otherwise have occupied him.

Still it is impossible to point to the moment when Franklin dramatically became aware of his fellow man. Apparently he was just born that way. "He responded to people," Frances Perkins thinks. "His principal social talent lay in making people feel at ease in his society and getting them to talk about things they knew." It was, moreover, an ability that allowed him to get along famously with all kinds of men and women. During the New Deal days of legislation aimed at economic royalists, the President cruised contentedly with a group of capitalists on Vincent Astor's yacht *Nourmahal*. Many Americans marveled at the incongruity of this, but it failed to bother F.D.R.

Roosevelt also had a rare gift for inspiring the mass of the people, and an up-to-the-minute instinct told him how best to do it. The President had been in the White House only eight days when he delivered his first Fireside Chat. It was delivered on Sunday, March 12, when the nation's banks had been closed for a week, with no citizen able to cash a check or withdraw money from a savings account. The next day the banks were to open again, and Roosevelt decided to go on the radio to explain the meaning of the moratorium and how the banks were able to resume operation. These Fireside Chats became his closest tie with the people, and of them Gerald Johnson has said:

The supreme achievement of Franklin D. Roosevelt was not the United Nations, nor the victory in a double war, nor the Atlantic Charter, but the Fireside Chat . . . it was the Fireside Chat which gave him the power to accomplish all his other works.

For all their ultimate success, the Fireside Chats were at first an example of Franklin's favored trial-and-error technique. He knew that he wanted to speak to the people, but not how. Secretary Marvin McIntyre sent word to both NBC and CBS in Washington that the President would make an airwaves talk on Sunday night, but was not sure of the tenor of the talk. In view of this, he wished to see two possible network introductions. One must be formal, the other informal. At the Washington office of CBS, Harry Butcher and Robert Trout worked on these. The formal one began "Ladies and Gentlemen." The other cosily said that the President wished to speak to the people as if he were seated beside them in the living room around the fireplace. Into this introduction Butcher inserted the phrase "fireside chat." When the President read it, he exclaimed, "That's it!"

The world was simpler in those days and Robert Trout, then functioning as CBS presidential announcer, remembers walking informally across the White House lawn on the night of March 12. Inside he was told to proceed upstairs to the Lincoln Study in the family living quarters. Here the President sat chatting on a sofa with Louis McHenry Howe. Mrs. Roosevelt was not present, though later she often brought her knitting to Fireside Chats. Newspapermen were never allowed; only family and friends. The Roosevelts were still moving and in the hall Trout walked past trunks and packing cases marked: FROM HYDE PARK—TO THE WHITE HOUSE.

Near the microphones in the Lincoln Study, F.D.R. had placed one of his favorite ship models. As the hour of ten approached, the President was lifted from the sofa and placed in a small steel wheelchair. He looked relaxed and cheerful. The legend atop one microphone had just been changed from Columbia to CBS, and he asked, "What does that mean?" Then he established himself behind the microphones and—consternation! The edited copy of his talk could not be found, and never was. Quickly Roosevelt was given one of the smudged, stapled, mimeographed copies intended for distribution to the press. With this in hand, he began, "My Friends, I want to talk to the people of the United States for a few minutes . . . about banking . . ."

The limelight that bathed the Teddy Roosevelt family in the White House had been a warm, effulgent glow. With the Franklin

Roosevelts, it was too often a vicious, merciless illumination. A few people had muttered that Theodore was a traitor to his class. Under Franklin the mutterings made a clamorous crescendo.

Indeed, the seething hatred F.D.R. aroused in some quarters is difficult to envision today. He was a man who had practically saved the country during the first hundred days of his administration. He had done it by means that were bold but not radical. Action not reform, had been the line of his thinking, and in so doing he preserved American capitalism. Yet vilification from the Right was perhaps his most visible reward. Writes historian Richard Hofstadter: "Nothing that Roosevelt had done warranted the vituperation he soon got in the conservative press or the obscenities that the hate-Roosevelt maniacs were bruiting about their clubs and dining rooms."

Hardly less than Franklin, Eleanor surprised the nation. The first person to be jolted by her was chief White House usher Ike Hoover. He was taken aback when Eleanor began to operate the White House elevator herself rather than wait for a doorman to arrive and propel her upward. Then the country was astounded as she became her husband's eyes, ears, and, particularly, his legs. The First Lady seemed to be everywhere: in slums, on breadlines, in migrant camps, coal mines, and Negro schools. One of the few hearty laughs in deep depression days came from a *New Yorker* cartoon by Robert Day picturing two men at work in the murky depths of a mine. "For gosh sakes," says one to the other, "here comes Mrs. Roosevelt!" Over the radio comedians quipped that Admiral Richard E. Byrd, in the solitude of his Antarctica shack, had set two places for dinner one night, "just in case Eleanor drops in."

To her enemies the First Lady was only gadding about, making a damned nuisance of herself. Yet Eleanor knew exactly what she was doing, as did Franklin. Many tributes have been paid to the former First Lady, but perhaps not enough has been said about her ability as an accurate reporter. Eleanor Roosevelt saw things clearly and recounted them lucidly. In the early days of his illness

Franklin had found that his wife could be trusted to give a graphic account of anything she saw or heard. More, she had a special gift for generating interest in whatever her husband or Louis Howe asked her to investigate.

When Eleanor returned to the White House after a junket into some unlikely area, she reported in detail to her husband. In her widespread travels she also displayed the Roosevelt energy at its most indefatigable and integrated. Never did she seem to grow weary or to forget anything. The First Lady was endlessly patient, unfailingly polite. It was inconceivable that she had once been shy and self-conscious, but by now Eleanor had decided that life must be lived. To a group of girls graduating from the Todhunter School she said, "Most people die of boredom. I wish for you the ability to be curious and the unselfishness to think of others, which will in the end bring greater interest to your own lives. I wish for you always the ability to feel the flow of new ideas, so that you will never be old, never be bored."

Still, hatred of the Roosevelts continued unabated. On her trips Eleanor flatly refused to be burdened by the company of a Secret Service man. Bowing to the inevitable, the Service appointed her a full-fledged agent and gave her a revolver. The Roosevelt family was hugely amused by this, for Eleanor was not one who would ever pull a trigger. For a time her sons called her "Annie Oakley." But Roosevelt-hatred had reached such a pitch that the mayor of one midwest town threatened to have the First Lady arrested for carrying a concealed weapon if she entered his bailiwick.

With such hysteria went scurrilous stories, one of which said that Eleanor stayed away from the White House so much because the Roosevelts were unhappily married. Next, the hatred grew to include the Roosevelt boys. All of them possessed the family energy, together with a rootlessness that drove them from scrape to scrape and, as time passed, from wife to wife.

With the passage of years it has become easy to look back on Franklin Roosevelt as a Chief Executive confident, eager, and inspiring, riding roughshod over opposition and governing the country with poise and authority.

Such, however, was not the case. F.D.R. faced many obstacles and much opposition, even in his early years in office. Wall Street and the business community were opposed to him, as were eighty percent of the nation's newspapers. The moneyed classes hated him and called his policies "Soak the rich." Conservatives accused him of spending too much. His old friends Al Smith and John Raskob formed the critical Liberty League and attacked him. Men like Huey Long and Father Coughlin stirred the discontent left over from the depths of the depression.

Roosevelt's victory in 1936 was the greatest in American history, with Alf Landon carrying only Maine and Vermont. Yet the President and those around him took the contest with the utmost seriousness. Some pundits even predicted his defeat. The esteemed Mark Sullivan called him a "one-term President," while historian Charles A. Beard wrote, "Roosevelt's spell of leadership has been definitely broken."

New problems arose following the election. The Supreme Court, most of its members in their seventies, was hamstringing New Deal legislation. Now it declared the National Recovery Act unconstitutional. Roosevelt tried to pack the Supreme Court and to purge Democratic congressmen who opposed him. History labels both these acts blunders.

They were, in any case, moments of setback and loss of prestige. Yet Franklin's enthusiasm for office never wavered. "He went at the job of the Presidency as if he had been Chief Executive all his life," writes John Gunther. "He loved the job and throve on it." Another correspondent recalls "That big, beaming smile of his!" It was visible in nearly every public appearance he made.

Roosevelt, it has been said, was a President who "presidented." Where, in pre-polio days, his tall body was so frequently called supple, his mind now rated that description. His was an intellect that waxed, rather than waned, on an abundance of advice, much of it conflicting. "His flypaper mind," one associate called it. For his Cabinet he chose such rugged individualists as Harold Ickes, and to them no less than to his staff he was always the Boss. He put together teams of advisers, running from idealistic Brain Trusters to hardboiled politicians.

Roosevelt likened himself to the quarterback of a football team, calling out the signals. On all near him he lavished his full charm, leading many to believe he agreed with them when he did not. Yet Norman Thomas, for one, doubts that President Roosevelt was ever much influenced by what he read, or by advice from anyone. "To him government was a great big give-and-take between himself and the public," Thomas believes. "And he expected the people he helped to be grateful."

One of Franklin's first acts as President was to visit the ailing Justice Oliver Wendell Holmes. When the President left, Holmes rendered an opinion. "A second-class intellect, but a first-class temperament," he said. Richard Hofstadter echoes this: "At the heart of the New Deal was not a philosophy but a temperament. The essence of this temperament was Roosevelt's confidence that even when operating in unfamiliar territory he could do no wrong, commit no mistakes." Deep in this temperament lay an eagerness that made him view each new problem in life as fresh and stimulating. It was this buoyant quality of optimism which made some people feel that Roosevelt matured slowly and even remained a bit of an adolescent all his life. "Till the end of his days, he was eager as a boy," John Gunther writes. In this, of course, he resembled Cousin Theodore. But despite traces of adolescence, Franklin was mature in other ways. Theodore was not.

In Roosevelt eagerness and optimism merged with an inner strength to create one of those exceptional men who enjoy making decisions. Grace Tully, his secretary for seventeen years, states, "The trait I believe Roosevelt possessed in more generous degree than most people—it was a trait the country was to sense on Inauguration Day—was a *will* to assume primary responsibility for events." Miss Tully recollects many occasions on which the President, learning that a branch of government was wrestling with a knotty problem, said, "All right, send it over here. My shoulders are broad. I can carry the load!"

Also ever-visible was Roosevelt's profound love of politics. "What he really cared about was high politics," Arthur Schlesinger thinks, "not politics as intrigue, but politics as education. Nothing government could do mattered much, he deeply believed, until it was firmly grasped by the public mind." Yet politics is politics and the President equally enjoyed its labyrinthine ways as he maneuvered legislation through Congress. With political opponents he liked to test his charm and supple intellect. "He could take a man ninety-five percent against him, and win him around to being fifty-five percent for him—and be very grateful for the fifty-five percent," recalls Thomas Corcoran.

In a definitive appraisal of her husband, Eleanor concluded that mixed with Franklin's desire to make life happier for the masses was a liking for the mechanics of politics as both a science and a game. This involved understanding the reactions of people and gambling on the understanding. She also felt that Franklin viewed himself as an instrument chosen by the people and felt that, as such, he had an obligation to enlighten and lead. In her opinion there was no problem he did not think human beings could solve. "I never knew him to face life, or any problem that came up, with fear," she wrote. High on her list of his virtues she placed a sense of humor which, at the right moment, allowed him to turn the most serious subject into an object of fun.

Though Franklin was widely accused of leaning to the Left, he was not as radical as most people thought. On Inauguration Day he might have led the country to dictatorship or socialism. Among his advisers were some who expected him to nationalize the banks as a first step toward a socialized country. Others anticipated an immediate repeal of Prohibition. Instead, the President allowed the banks to open as before and advocated only 3.2 percent beer.

With his second term, the great reforms like Social Security began. They, too, divided the country and made his years in office a continuing series of crises. Indeed, from the Bank Holiday to the invasion of Normandy and the Yalta Conference the President lived in the midst of tension and turmoil. He was engulfed by it, Eleanor said. Yet she recalled that, no matter how severe the strain, he never lost a night's sleep.

When faced with a particularly difficult problem, Franklin liked to banish his staff and reach into a bottom desk drawer for his beloved stamp collection. On this he worked silently for hours. Seemingly wrapped up in his hobby, he actually was mulling his decision. Before 1932 he had decided for reasons of economy to concentrate on Central and South American stamps. But as President the entire world of stamps lay at his fingertips. Learning that the State Department tossed out foreign envelopes, he ordered the stamps snipped off and brought to him every Saturday in a sack. He thoroughly enjoyed mounting stamps and on his travels carried a wooden box of stamp paraphernalia. He was always disappointed when visiting dignitaries ceremoniously presented him with albums in which the stamps were already mounted.

Eleanor, whenever she was in Washington, tried to invite unusual and stimulating people to the White House for dinner, thus varying the President's monotonous round of conferences with Cabinet members, diplomats, politicians, and visiting firemen. Daughter Anna and son James lived in the presidential mansion for long periods, and there were always grandchildren chasing through the corridors. Roosevelt's own lively sense of humor lightened his burdens; it has been said that the only respect in which Eleanor let her husband down was in her inability to join in the fun, frolic, and foolishness he so richly enjoyed.

Roosevelt was bothered by frequent head colds and sinus attacks, and on awakening in the morning often announced he felt "rotten" or "like hell." By the time he reached his desk, however, no one could tell how he felt. "The Boss full of wisecracks when he signed his mail this morning," noted one secretary. "It's hard to tell how he feels sometimes because he never betrays it in ill temper." F.D.R. liked to tell jokes, tossing his head back in the famous laugh at the punch line. He was capable of quick wit.

Once a young naval aide pushing his wheelchair bumped him into a filing cabinet. Roosevelt asked, "Young man, are you trying to file me?"

Roosevelt smoked two packs of cigarettes a day (quite a lot for a sinus sufferer) and liked to clamp the ivory holder tight between his teeth. "Have a cig," he would say, informally offering his case to those near him. He called his girl secretaries "Child" and liked to keep track of their social activities. He enjoyed playing practical jokes, but most of all he liked to tease. By far the favorite object of his teasing was Sara Delano Roosevelt, in whose presence he told outrageously untrue yarns about the bibulous and amorous activities of Delanos and Roosevelts. But his favorite way of teasing Sara was to tell what was a true story.

To her dismay, he would launch—cigarette holder happily atilt—into the saga of James Roosevelt Bayley, born in 1814, a grandson of Jacobus Roosevelt and Catharina Hardenbroeck. James Roosevelt Bayley grew up to become rector of the Episcopal church in Harlem. Elizabeth Ann Bayley, one of his aunts, was a devout member of the Catholic Church and founded the Sisters of Charity. In time, she became known as Mother Seton. Inspired by her example, James Roosevelt Bayley also embraced Catholicism, to become first the Bishop of Newark, then Bishop of Baltimore. Winding up this curious family saga, Franklin delivered a final dig to his mother with an offhand reference to "my aunt, Mother Seton."

Roosevelt family tradition reached its peak at Christmas. Never, in fact, have White House Christmases risen to such heights of warmth and spirit as they did in the Yuletides the Franklin Roosevelts spent on Pennsylvania Avenue. Sara journeyed down from Hyde Park, while children and grandchildren converged from all directions. Nor was a White House Christmas for the family only. It became a three-day ceremony which included party (and presents) for both the office and domestic staffs, a dance for the young fry (in the manner of Corinne Robinson's dances of yesteryear), a romp with the toddlers, the lighting of the community tree, a big family dinner, and open house for political cronies. Roosevelt took Christmas customs with old-fashioned seriousness and, to the horror of Secret Service men, insisted on using lighted wax tapers on the family tree. On Christmas Eve adults as well as children hung stockings in the presidential bedroom, where Eleanor stuffed them with practical gifts. Highlight of the holiday was the President's traditional rendering of Dickens' *Christmas Carol*, in which he portrayed all the characters in his best actor-voice. Almost as dramatic was the manner in which he set about carving the family turkey. Yet, in all the frenzied festivity Roosevelt never forgot that this was a religious holiday. On Christmas morning the family attended church.

Roosevelt's background was frequently in his mind. On a morning in 1940 he suddenly said to Grace Tully, "This is the anniversary of my father's birth." "Really, Mr. President?" Miss Tully replied "How old would he be?" Without hesitation Franklin answered, "He would be one hundred and twelve today." The President kissed his sons on arrival or departure, or his sons kissed him. This surprised some friends. When Grace Tully commented on it, the President said he had always kissed his own father and considered it an excellent custom.

On rare occasions chinks in his towering confidence exposed a surprising inner man. He was terrified of fire, a fear which apparently predated polio. The physical helplessness of polio naturally intensified this and, on bedding down in strange surroundings, he always asked, "How do we get out of here?"—meaning in case of fire. At other times he briefly showed a Theodore-like lack of confidence in his ultimate destiny. On the night of the Chicago nomination, Grace Tully's mother referred to him as the next President of the United States. Roosevelt chided her, saying, "We still have an election, you know." Miss Tully herself attributes such lapses to "caution and superstition." But they scarcely fit the popular image of the man of overwhelming confidence. Nor does his extreme caution in leading the nation into World War II.

With all this, Franklin Roosevelt remained lonely. Even his

family admits that he never unburdened himself of inner thoughts. Eleanor believed that an upbringing with an elderly father and an inflexible mother drove Franklin to keep personal feelings locked tight within. In any event, Roosevelt always believed his inner emotions were his own exclusive business, and he resolutely protected what has been called the privacy of his nature. "Of what was inside him, what really drove him, Father talked with no one," James writes.

"Everything was a campaign with him," thinks CBS correspondent Robert Trout, who recalls that as the presidential train swung through the Midwest and West on campaign trips the President's clothes became more rumpled, his voice took on an easy drawl, his hat looked more battered. At one stop Eleanor stood beside him in neatly darned stockings.

In truth, politics seldom strayed from his mind. In April, 1937, the President was cruising on the Gulf of Mexico when he learned that a young Texas named Lyndon Johnson had been elected to the House of Representatives in a runoff election. The President invited Johnson to board the presidential train at Austin and ride with him to Washington. On this trip the worshipful young man began to adopt Roosevelt mannerisms. "He was just like a daddy to me always," President Johnson has said.

At times Roosevelt seemed over his mental depth in New Deal economics and by 1939 appeared to have run out of stimulating political ideas. Yet his belief in himself, together with the excitements of office, kept him in top fettle. In 1940 his decision to run for a third term became his strongest break with tradition. Apparently the idea had first occurred to him a few years before, when eastern conservatives and southern Dixiecrats posed a threat that might shift the party from his type of liberalism. As a result, he contemplated a Theodore-like third party, with himself as its candidate in 1940. A grass-roots check showed no third party necessary. Franklin proved so enormously popular that he would be able to shatter the third-term precedent as Democratic candidate.

The idea simmered on, though publicly the President protested that he had no intention of running a third time. By 1940 Europe was locked in a second world war, and Roosevelt had reason to believe himself an indispensable man. Domestic pros and cons also helped his decision. One of Franklin's flaws may have been that he dominated those around him, so that none of his associates ever reached the stature of presidential possibility. When Eleanor called this to his attention, Franklin declared that the right man ought to be able to rise no matter what competition lay in his path. Nor did he feel that he really overwhelmed those around him.

Other pressures drove him to a third term. Having sacrificed for the Democrats what—in his own mind, at least—was the chance to walk again, he wanted the party to win in 1940. Without him Democratic victory was doubtful. Also there was the fact that he enjoyed the Presidency. A final factor may have been his awareness of the pitfalls in handpicking a successor. He had seen this go wrong with Teddy Roosevelt and Taft. In his own experience, Al Smith had become embittered when Franklin refused to heed his advice in Albany.

Sara Delano Roosevelt died in 1941, at the age of eighty-six. Now, at long last, Franklin and Eleanor owned a home of their own, and that home was Springwood. Franklin sincerely mourned his mother, but ownership of the mansion seemed to intensify his love of it. After 1942, with the country at war, he began to find his chief relaxation in trips to Hyde Park. During war years he made nearly forty weekend "blackout visits" to Springwood, traveling by special car from Silver Spring, Maryland, to a spur on the Hudson River tracks in front of the house. These were top-security journeys of which the nation remained unaware. Newspaper correspondents, left behind in Washington, were forbidden to mention them. "The President began to put off and take on security like winter underwear," UPI correspondent Merriman Smith says.

Roosevelt was accompanied to Springwood by a small staff, and at this point in life he was fortunate in having William Hassett as press secretary. Hassett was an easygoing, knowledgeable Vermonter. Like the President, he was a raconteur whose best stories were derived from the American past. The relationship between the two men was close. At Springwood, Hassett usually showed up with the morning mail while the President was in the bathroom shaving. "Park yourself on the can, but don't forget your pants are up," Roosevelt used to tell him. With Hassett, the President fondly recounted stories of his Delano, Aspinwall, and Roosevelt ancestors. Nor did he neglect his own boyhood. "Bill, did I ever tell you about the time . . ." was his familiar opening.

During informal Springwood weekends the President renewed himself physically and mentally. He knew the value of sleep, and liked to get a full ten hours by sleeping late into the morning, with his Scottie, Fala, dozing nearby. Yet one Sunday morning in May he rose before dawn to go bird watching at nearby Thompson's Pond. Returning from this expedition, he reported glimpsing a marsh wren, a red-wing blackbird, and a bittern. He had also heard the songs of twenty-two other birds.

As always, he cast his election vote at Hyde Park, delightedly proclaiming his occupation as "farmer" or "tree grower." He began to design a hideaway cottage which, to his annoyance, newspapers called a Dream House. He also supervised construction of a library to contain his state and personal papers.

Many of Roosevelt's close friends were dead. Louis McHenry Howe, for one, died in 1936 and his intimate role had gradually been taken over by Harry Hopkins. Other friends were deeply involved in the war effort. Roosevelt's four sons were in the fighting forces, while Eleanor's wartime trips had turned global.

So it becomes a curious fact that during war years Roosevelt's chief friends—at Springwood anyway,—were members of European royalty in exile. Crown Princess Martha of Norway and her children were Hyde Park favorites, Queen Wilhelmina of the

Netherlands and her daughter Juliana, Grand Duchess Charlotte of Luxembourg, Empress Zita of Austria and her daughters also were guests. The people's President used first names all around and seemed to find with royalty the same cheery rapport he had enjoyed with Vincent Astor and his economic royalists.

Yet Eleanor was often on his mind. Empress Zita visited Springwood at a time when the First Lady was in the Far East. "She must be very tired," Zita remarked politely. Roosevelt laughed. "No," he said, "but she will tire everyone else." When Eleanor was in England, Prime Minister Churchill hesitated to allow her to return home for fear the Germans would attack the plane. He communicated these fears to the President. SEND HER HOME ANYWAY, Roosevelt cabled.

One reason Roosevelt enjoyed Springwood was the good food served there. For, incredible as it may seem, the President of the United States seldom got meals he liked in the White House. Eleanor had brought Mrs. Henrietta Nesbitt from Hyde Park as White House housekeeper, but this wholesome lady's ideas of food clashed with Franklin's refined palate. Yet the softhearted President refused to discharge her, claiming it was not within his power. Eleanor, who never considered food important, valiantly supported Mrs. Nesbitt. However, Roosevelt was not the only one to complain of the uninspired White House fare. With wartime rationing, Mrs. Nesbitt's rigidity increased, and in retrospect her lack of concern for the President's appetite seems almost sadistic. Once he expressed a desire for canned asparagus tips. Mrs. Nesbitt replied tartly that such delicacies were unavailable in wartime. Whereupon Grace Tully angrily sent a messenger out to buy some.

"All that is within me cries to go back to my home on the Hudson River," said Franklin early in 1944. He was sixty-two years old, reaching the end of his third term. But once more a Republican victory seemed certain if another Democrat ran. Roosevelt had grown to admire Wendell Willkie, his opponent in 1940, but for Thomas E. Dewey he felt an acute distaste. The thought that Dewey might succeed him was more than the President could bear. He ran for a fourth term in a bitter campaign.

On election night Dewey conceded his defeat over the radio, but failed to send the traditional telegram to his victorious opponent. "I still think he's a son of a bitch," Roosevelt said, as he was wheeled to his Springwood bedroom.

Franklin Roosevelt's death has the same dreadful knell as his polio attack.

He was surrounded by people who knew he was failing. Anna Roosevelt Boettiger, James Roosevelt, Basil O'Connor, Grace Tully, William Hassett—all these and more had made unhappy mental note of his declining powers. Yet none actually thought the Boss could die. Nor was Roosevelt a man who could be ordered to rest, for no less than his mother he possessed a whim of steel. Still he was aware of his weariness and undertook the fourth term on the understanding that there would be more frequent visits to Hyde Park and Warm Springs. Nonetheless, he was sick. James Roosevelt, serving as an intelligence officer in the Marines, twice saw his father taken ill. The first time came in the summer of 1944 when the Commander-in-Chief reviewed the 5th Marine Division on the West Coast. James and his father were alone in the presidential railroad car just before the ceremony. Suddenly the President was hit by sharp pains. Slipping from his berth to the floor of the car, he lay for ten minutes wracked by agony. Then he felt well enough to diagnose his own attack as indigestion for which he used the old-fashioned term "collywobbles."

The White House physician was Rear Admiral Ross T. McIntire, a former nose and throat specialist. He and Roosevelt were close personal friends, which may have been a drawback in a doctor-patient relationship. McIntire was also worried about the President's health, though by some later opinions not enough. Early in 1944 Roosevelt had undergone a strenuous physical checkup by a team of doctors at Bethesda Naval Hospital. Danger signals showed even then. One doctor thought Roosevelt should rest for a year, while another wished to put him to bed for three months. Yet opinions differ among teams of doctors and still others thought he was in good shape for a man his age.

Two outside doctors, one a heart specialist, were called in. They advised the President to rest as much as possible. Dr. McIntire drew up a regime of lightened work and, to commence it, Roosevelt passed a month at Bernard Baruch's plantation in North Carolina. After this he returned to Washington and a supposedly relaxed work schedule. But the President of a country at war on two battle fronts is in no position to relax.

No strong pressures had been applied to prevent Roosevelt from running for a fourth term. Eleanor and Dr. McIntire, the only people who might have succeeded, apparently did not try. One reason may have been Roosevelt's continuing cheerfulness despite signs of strain. With this went his amazing recuperative powers. As always, he thrived on travel and returned from Hyde Park or Warm Springs apparently rejuvenated. He disliked air travel because it offered no view of the country. By the same token, he loved railroads and planned his own trips, for he knew the country's railroad network from boyhood travels with his father.

The 1944 campaign especially revived him. His Dutch was up over Dewey and this acted like adrenalin to his sagging vitality. His day of campaigning in New York City turned out to be windy and wet, but he insisted on going through with it, seated in the open back seat of his car. Three million people turned out to see him, and that night he buoyantly gave one of his best political speeches.

On Inauguration Day, January 20, 1945, came the second attack witnessed by James Roosevelt. To this fourth inaugural Roosevelt had summoned—did he have a premonition of death?—his army of children and grandchildren. Because it was wartime, the ceremonies were held on the south portico of the White House. It was a raw-cold day, yet the President refused to wear an overcoat. At the end, he took James's arm and started for the reception in the state dining room. En route they paused in the Lincoln Study where Roosevelt was seized by another attack. This time James thought it was a chill and rushed to get a hooker of whiskey in a tumbler. It was more liquor than James had ever seen his father drink at once, but F.D.R gulped it down like spring water. "Regardless of what the doctors said, I knew his days were numbered," James wrote later.

Ahead of the ailing President was the ten-day trip to Yalta, which has been called the greatest strain of all his years in the Presidency. This time travel failed to revive him. On the voyage home he sat in the sun, but his now-translucent skin failed to tan. "The Boss looks ill, color bad; but he is cheerful in spirit, always good-natured, with none of the ill-temper that sick folks are entitled to display," Hassett noted. Nevertheless, F.D.R. did have a period of unaccustomed testiness, for which he afterward apologized by calling himself a "grouchy old man."

For the first time, he addressed a joint session of Congress from his wheelchair, and it seemed to some that death was on his countenance even then. Merriman Smith recalls that on this occasion the rich voice was thin and strained, the delivery listless. He misread sentences and his head fell as he struggled along. His hearing was failing, and at a show business gala a few nights later the President cupped an ear but could not hear the words spoken onstage. Noting this, the entertainers cut the evening short. Dr. McIntire issued a bulletin calling his health "tiptop," but sharp-eyed Washingtonians noted that Secret Service men had been assigned to Vice-President Truman.

On the agenda was a trip on April 25 to the opening of the United Nations in San Francisco. Before it, Roosevelt decided to take a vacation at Warm Springs. One of his last meals in the White House was a fortieth wedding anniversary luncheon on March 17. Then he entrained for Georgia. Dr. McIntire remained in Washington, but sent Commander Howard Bruenn, a Navy heart specialist, in his place. Eleanor, too, stayed in Washington. The President's vitality was good in the mornings at Warm

Springs, but by afternoon he was worn, weary, and exhausted. Over recent months he had lost thirty-six pounds, and showed it. At times his fine voice was inaudible.

On March 29, Hassett said to Dr. Bruenn, "He is slipping away from us, and no earthly power can keep him here. . . . I am convinced that there is no help for him." To this the doctor replied that the President's life could still be saved if "measures were adopted to rescue him from certain mental strains and emotional influences." Dr. Bruenn outlined these measures to Hassett, who has since stated cryptically that they were impossible to meet.

On the morning of April 12, 1945, the President awoke with a slight headache. He worked on his mail with Hassett, then sought solace in his stamps. Over the telephone to Washington, he approved the design of a new United Nations issue. His portrait was being painted by a lady artist, and in honor of this he had put on a Harvard crimson tie. Shortly before lunch he summoned the artist. "We've got about fifteen minutes," the President told her. While she sketched, he immersed himself in government reports. His cousin Laura Delano also sat in the room.

Suddenly the President groaned and slapped his left hand to his temple as if swatting a fly. He pressed hard and rubbed the spot. "I have a terrific headache," he said. Then he fell backward in the chair. Secret Service men carried him to the bedroom, where his labored breathing could be heard throughout the Little White House. The stricken man was undressed and clothed in pajamas. He lay unconscious in a cold sweat, ashen-faced, while Dr. Bruenn tried artificial respiration and other emergency measures.

He lived for three agonizing hours and then died at 3:35 without regaining consciousness. The cause of death was a massive cerebral hemorrhage.

With the death of the President, Eleanor became the foremost member of the Roosevelt clan. She carried on in the best family tradition to become—in Harry Truman's words—the First Lady of the World. It was Eleanor's belief that, during Franklin's lifetime, she had functioned mainly as a listener. To her husband she had also acted as a spur. "In a way my conscience bothered him," she had said.

As his widow she ceased to be a listener. Eleanor had always been more liberal and idealistic than Franklin, and in her far-flung activities as First Lady of the Land there was sometimes a suggestion of the amateur. But as First Lady of the World she was a thoroughgoing professional. Her Oyster Bay cousin Nicholas, not always sympathetic to Franklin's family, thinks Eleanor's final tempering came with her work as delegate to the United Nations. The U.N. must have thought so, too, for when her Declaration of Human Rights was passed, delegates rose to their feet and cheered her.

To the end Eleanor steadfastly remained herself, performing prodigies of integrated activity with each new day. With everything else, she wrote, in the seventeen years of her widowhood, fifteen books, together with innumerable magazine articles and her daily newspaper column, "My Day." She could never understand why people were impressed by her. Always touching in "My Day" was the genuine surprise she felt when taxi drivers expressed themselves honored at driving her and refused to accept a fare.

Eleanor Roosevelt died in 1962, of a rare tuberculosis of the bone-marrow. She was seventy-eight. Franklin and Eleanor lie beside each other at Hyde Park in the Rose Garden—surrounded by neat greensward and high hemlock hedge—between the Springwood house and the Franklin D. Roosevelt Library.

Edith Carow Roosevelt died in 1948, aged eighty-seven. She lived out her life at Sagamore Hill and rests beside Theodore in the Cove Neck graveyard. All Theodore's sons served with distinction in World War II. Archie, a colonel, lived through the conflict. Kermit died on active duty in Alaska in 1943. Brigadier General Theodore Roosevelt, Jr., a much-beloved commander of men, was the first high-ranking American officer to set foot on French soil in the D-Day invasion of 1944. A short time after, he was felled by a fatal heart attack.

Since Theodore first attained his great fame as a Rough Rider, there have been few years when a Roosevelt was not prominent or pre-eminent on the American political scene. But with the death of Eleanor, this Roosevelt Era of more than sixty years appeared ended.

Yet Roosevelts have continued well known, if no longer prominent or pre-eminent. Of the lively offspring of ebullient Theodore, Alice, Archie, and Ethel Roosevelt Derby are living survivors of the wonderful days at Oyster Bay—that Happy Land of Woods and Waters! As ever, Alice is the most conspicuous of Theodore's children. Energetic, vocal, acidulous, politically partisan, she celebrated her eightieth birthday in 1964. "I'm just a kindly, amiable old thing," she told reporters. Then she gave a Roosevelt grin and added, "If anyone takes that seriously, hah! My specialty is detached malevolence." After some years in the Washington political shadow, Alice was frequently seen in the company of the John F. Kennedys, who found her personality invigorating. Indeed, if Eleanor Roosevelt became the First Lady of the World, Alice Roosevelt Longworth—by dint of Oyster Bay vigor and family longevity—can be called the First Lady of Washington.

Of the children of Franklin and Eleanor, Anna has for the last ten years been the wife of Dr. James A. Halsted. James Roosevelt is a conspicuous and fittingly liberal congressman from California. Though he spends part of his time on the familiar terrain of Washington, James seems happiest in the far-from-the-Hudson regions of the West Coast. Elliott Roosevelt, ever the family rebel, prefers Texas and Florida. Franklin Jr., who retired from politics after an ambitious try for office in New York State, was appointed Under Secretary of Commerce by President Kennedy. John Aspinwall, the youngest son, has remained closest to Hyde Park.

He is a New York businessman, like his ancestors. In a curious cutback, he has also reverted to the Roosevelts of old by becoming a registered Republican.

These five Roosevelt children live far from one another and have chosen varying careers. Yet they speedily joined in opposing the impressively modern monument planned as a memorial to Franklin Delano Roosevelt in Washington. If their father were alive to make his own choice—they declared—he would undoubtedly prefer a simple grove of his beloved trees.

Today both Sagamore Hill and Springwood are National Historical Sites, part of the National Park Service, under supervision of the United States Department of the Interior. They are, of course, open to the public. Far more than the millions of words written about the titans of the family, these handsome residences reflect the personalities of the two Roosevelts who last lived in them.

BIBLIOGRAPHY

The author is indebted to the staffs of the Franklin D. Roosevelt Library; the New York Genealogical and Biographical Society; the New-York Historical Society; and the New York Society Library. Also to Professor Edwin Arthur Hill of the College of the City of New York, for advice; and to William Poole and Mrs. Ad Schulberg, for advice and encouragement.

For genealogical data on the Roosevelt, Delano, and Aspinwall families, the following general sources were used: *New York Genealogical and Biographical Record; Colonial Families of America; Colonial Families of the United States; Dictionary of American Biography; American Ancestry; American Genealogy.*

In listing individual books, special mention must be made of *The Amazing Roosevelt Family, 1613-1942,* by Karl Schriftgiesser, a pioneering volume in tracing the family history. To a lesser degree *The Roosevelt Family in America,* by Bellamy Partridge, was helpful.

Books consulted:

ABBOTT, LAWRENCE F. *Impressions of Theodore Roosevelt.* New York: Doubleday, Page & Co., 1919.

ALLEN, FREDERICK LEWIS. *Since Yesterday.* New York: Harper & Brothers, 1940.

ANDREWS, WILLIAM LORING. *New Amsterdam-New Orange-New York.* New York: Dodd, Mead & Company, 1897.

BARRETT, WALTER (J. A. Scoville). *The Old Merchants of New York.* 5 vols. New York: Carleton Publishers, 1863.

BEALE, HOWARD K. *Theodore Roosevelt and the Rise of America.* Baltimore: Johns Hopkins Press, 1956.

BEER, THOMAS. *The Mauve Decade.* New York: Alfred A. Knopf, Inc., 1926.

BURNS, JAMES MACGREGOR. *Roosevelt: The Lion and the Fox.* New York: Harcourt Brace and Company, 1956.

COBB, WILLIAM T. *The Strenuous Life: The Oyster Bay Roosevelts in Business and Finance.* New York: William Rudge's Sons, 1946.

COLLINS, FREDERICK L. *Money Town.* New York: G. P. Putnam's Sons, 1946.

DANIELS, JONATHAN. *The End of Innocence.* Philadelphia, New York: J. B. Lippincott Company, 1954.

DAY, DONALD (ed.). *Franklin D. Roosevelt's Own Story.* Boston: Little, Brown and Company, 1951.

DELANO, DANIEL W. JR. *Franklin Roosevelt and the Delano Influence.* Pittsburgh: James W. Nudi Publications, 1946.

EARLE, ALICE M. *Colonial Days in Old New York.* New York: Charles Scribner's Sons, 1896.

FAY, BERNARD. *Roosevelt and His America.* Boston: Little, Brown and Company, 1933.

FEDERAL WRITERS PROJECT. *New York Panorama.* New York: Random House, 1933.

GILMAN, BRADLEY. *Theodore Roosevelt, The Happy Warrior.* Boston: Little, Brown and Company, 1921.

GUNTHER, JOHN. *Roosevelt in Retrospect: A Profile in History.* New York: Harper & Brothers, 1950.

HAGEDORN, HERMANN. *The Roosevelt Family of Sagamore Hill.* New York: Macmillan Company, 1954.

HAMM, MARGHARITA. *Famous Families of New York.* New York: G. P. Putnam's Sons, 1902.

HARRITY, RICHARD, and RALPH G. MARTIN. *Eleanor Roosevelt.* New York: Duell, Sloan and Pearce, 1958.

HASSETT, WILLIAM D. *Off the Record with F.D.R.* New Brunswick: Rutgers University Press, 1958.

HEMSTREET, CHARLES. *When Old New York Was Young.* New York: Charles Scribner's Sons, 1910.

HOFSTADTER, RICHARD. *The American Political Tradition.* New York: Alfred A. Knopf, Inc., 1948.

JOHNSON, ALVIN P. *Franklin D. Roosevelt's Colonial Ancestors.* Boston: Lothrop, Lee and Stoddard, 1937.

JOHNSON, GERALD. *American Heroes and Hero Worship*. New York: Harper & Brothers, 1943.

————. *The Lunatic Fringe*. Philadelphia, New York: J. B. Lippincott Company, 1957.

————. *Roosevelt: Dictator or Democrat?* New York: Harper & Brothers, 1941.

KERFOOT, J. B. *Broadway*. Boston: Houghton Mifflin Company, 1911.

KESSLER, HENRY H., and EUGENE RACHLIS. *Peter Stuyvesant and His New York*. New York: Random House, 1959.

King's Handbook of New York City. Boston: Moses King, 1892.

KLEEMAN, RITA HALLE. *Gracious Lady: Sara Delano Roosevelt*. New York: D. Appleton-Century Inc., 1935.

LINDLEY, ERNEST K. *Franklin D. Roosevelt*. Indianapolis: The Bobbs Merrill Company, 1931.

————. *Half Way with Roosevelt*. New York: The Viking Press, 1936.

LONGWORTH, ALICE ROOSEVELT. *Crowded Hours*. New York: Charles Scribner's Sons.

LORANT, STEFAN. *The Life and Times of Theodore Roosevelt*. New York: Doubleday and Company, 1959.

LORD, WALTER. *The Good Years*. New York: Harper & Brothers, 1960.

MacCRACKEN, HENRY NOBLE. *Blithe Dutchess*. New York: Hastings House, 1958.

————. *Old Dutchess Forever*. New York: Hastings House, 1956.

PARTRIDGE, BELLAMY. *The Roosevelt Family in America*. New York: Hillman-Curl, Inc., 1936.

PERKINS, FRANCES. *The Roosevelt I Knew*. New York: The Viking Press, 1946.

PICKARD, (Mrs.) M. FORTESCUE. *The Roosevelts and America*. London: H. Joseph, Ltd., 1941.

PRINGLE, HENRY F. *Theodore Roosevelt: A Biography*. New York: Harcourt, Brace and Company, 1931.

PUTNAM, CARLETON. *Theodore Roosevelt: A Biography*. New York: Charles Scribner's Sons, 1958.

ROBINSON, CORINNE ROOSEVELT. *My Brother, Theodore Roosevelt*. New York: Charles Scribner's Sons, 1921.

ROOSEVELT, ELEANOR. *This I Remember*. New York: Harper & Brothers, 1949.

————. *This Is My Story*. New York: Harper & Brothers, 1937.

ROOSEVELT, HALL. *Odyssey of an American Family*. New York: Harper & Brothers, 1939.

ROOSEVELT, JAMES, and SIDNEY SHALETT. *Affectionately, FDR*. New York: Harcourt, Brace and Company, 1959.

ROOSEVELT, NICHOLAS. *A Front Row Seat*. Norman: The University of Oklahoma Press, 1953.

ROOSEVELT, SARA DELANO (with Isabelle Leighton and Gabrielle Forbush). *My Boy Franklin*. New York: Crown Publishers, 1933.

ROOSEVELT, THEODORE. *Autobiography*. New York: Charles Scribner's Sons, 1958.

ROSENMAN, SAMUEL I. *Working With Roosevelt*. New York: Harper & Brothers, 1952.

SCHRIFTGIESSER, KARL. *The Amazing Roosevelt Family, 1613-1942*. New York: Wilfred Funk, Inc., 1942.

SMITH, MERRIMAN. *Thank You, Mr. President*. New York: Harper & Brothers, 1946.

STEEHOLM, CLARA and HARDY. *The House at Hyde Park*. New York: The Viking Press, 1950.

STEFFENS, LINCOLN. *Autobiography*. New York: Harcourt, Brace and Company, 1931.

STILL, BAYRD (ed.). *Mirror for Gotham*. New York: University Press, 1956.

SULLIVAN, MARK. *Our Times, 1900-1925*. New York: Charles Scribner's Sons, 1926.

TODD, CHARLES BURR. *The Story of the City of New York*. New York: G. P. Putnam's Sons, 1888.

TULLY, GRACE. *FDR, My Boss*. New York: Charles Scribner's Sons, 1949.

VAN RENSELAER, MAY KING. *The Goede Vrouw of Mana-ha-ta, 1609-1760*. New York: Charles Scribner's Sons, 1898.

WECTER, DIXON. *The Hero In America*. New York: Charles Scribner's Sons, 1941.

WERTENBACKER, THOMAS JEFFERSON. *Father Knickerbocker Rebels*. New York: Charles Scribner's Sons, 1948.

WHITE, WILLIAM ALLEN. *Masks in a Pageant*. New York: Macmillan Company, 1928.

WHITTLESEY, CHARLES B. *The Roosevelt Genealogy, 1649-1902*. Hartford: C. B. Whittlesey, 1902.

WILSON, JAMES GRANT. *Memorial History of the City of New York*. New York: New York History Company, 1892.

WISTER, OWEN. *Roosevelt, the Story of a Friendship.* New York: Macmillan Company, 1930.

WOOD, FREDERICK S. *Roosevelt as We Knew Him.* Philadelphia: John C. Winston, 1927.

Life, September 9, 1940. Article on the Roosevelt Family, by Joseph Alsop and Robert Kintner.

Family Papers in the files of the Franklin D. Roosevelt Library. These include Isaac Roosevelt's will and Franklin Roosevelt's family genealogy.

INDEX

ABOUT THE AUTHOR

Allen Churchill is a native New Yorker and the author of seven books, including *Park Row, The Improper Bohemians,* and *The Year the World Went Mad*. He also published articles in many magazines.

Prior to 1946, when he began to devote himself to his own writing, Mr. Churchill was an editor with G. P. Putnam's Sons, and with *Town and Country* and *Yank*. He makes his home in New York City.

Claes Martenszen van
(landed New Amsterdam

Nicholas
(fur trapper,

Johannes, John (
(founded Oyster Bay branch)

Jacobus (1724-?)
(began hardware business)

James (1759-1840)　　　　　Nicholas (1767-1854)
(continued hardware　　　　(family inventor)
business)

Cornelius Van Schaack (1794-1871)　　James J. (1795-1875)
(turned hardware into　　　　　　(socialite, politician)
investment banking)

S. Weir (1823-1870)　　James A. (1825-1898)　　　Robert B.,
(lawyer)　　　(president of Roosevelt (conservationist
and Son)

Anna (1855-1931) Theodore (1858-1919) Corinne

Alice (1884-) Theodore (1887-1944) Kermit (1889-1943) Ethel

Anna (1906-) James (1907-)